SNAKES OF
THE WORLD

SNAKES OF THE WORLD

THEIR WAYS AND MEANS OF LIVING

By Hampton Wildman Parker

DOVER PUBLICATIONS, INC., NEW YORK

Copyright © 1963 by W. H. Parker.
All rights reserved under Pan American and International Copyright Conventions.

This Dover edition, first published in 1977, is an unabridged republication of the work originally published in 1963 under the title *Snakes*. It is reprinted by special arrangement with the original publisher, Robert Hale Limited, 63 Old Brompton Road, London SW 7, England, and this edition is for sale in the United States only.

International Standard Book Number: 0-486-23479-7
Library of Congress Catalog Card Number: 76-53977

Manufactured in the United States of America
Dover Publications, Inc.
180 Varick Street
New York, N.Y. 10014

CONTENTS

ILLUSTRATIONS

Photographic Plates

Figures in the Text

PREFACE

A new book about snakes may not be essential but may nevertheless be useful if only to re-state some of the facts in relation to the
many misconceptions, exaggerations and old wives' tales that sur-
round these unusual and unpopular creatures. The objects of this
book are to describe not merely what snakes have to do to exist in
a hostile world but how these activities are carried out, their needs,
their adaptations, their capabilities and their limitations. To ac-
complish such a task within the limits of so slight a volume clearly
verges on the impossible, but there is no pretence that this is a
comprehensive treatise, nor even a handbook. It is a brief summary
of some of the presently accepted facts and of the interpretations
that can be placed upon them. The latter may, of course, be controversial, especially some of those proffered here for the first time,
but only speculations and theories can bring dull facts alive.
Emotions may be more exciting (and snakes probably evoke a wider
range of feelings than any other animals) but when they are un-
reasoning they bedevil true understanding; if this book contributes
anything at all towards a better understanding of animals that are
so remarkable in so many ways it will have served its purpose.

To express gratitude "to all those whose labours have lightened
my own" is very necessary but quite inadequate. Since this is not
a text-book or a work of reference, indications of the sources of
information have been omitted, but some of them have been used
on such a scale that it would be more than merely ungracious not
to acknowledge the debt. Above all I wish to record my very great
indebtedness to the works of Laurence Klauber and, moreover, to
thank him for much personal kindness over many years. His mag-
nificent two volume account of *Rattlesnakes: their Habits, Life
Histories and Influence on Mankind* is the outstanding work of this
century for all students of snakes and the frequency with which
rattlesnakes are mentioned in the chapters that follow testifies to the
extent to which I have profited from his vast knowledge. In the
same way I have freely used the writings of all those authors whose
more recent and popular books are cited in the Bibliography and
whose friendship I hope I have not forfeited by doing so! More
direct help has been given to me by many others, but especially
by Miss A. G. C. Grandison, whose criticisms have been invaluable,

and by those who have so generously allowed me to use selections from their collections of photographs: Mr. C. M. Bogert of the American Museum of Natural History: Dr. L. D. Brongersma of the Rijksmuseum van Natuurlijke Historie, Leiden: Mr. G. Kinns of the British Museum (Natural History): Prof. Robert Mertens of the Senckenbergische Naturforschende Gesellschaft, Frankfurt: Mr. Hans Rosenberg of Hamburg: and Mr. W. H. Woodin of the Arizona-Sonora Desert Museum. To all of them and to Miss R. S. Garrett, for her interest as well as her skill with a typewriter, my sincere thanks.

Acknowledgements are also due to the following institutions and individuals who have courteously permitted the reproduction of plates and figures from other books and periodicals: the Zoological Society of London; Prof. Carl Gans and the New York Zoological Society; *Ecology*; Mr. Walker van Riper, Mr. Wilhelm Hoppe and Mr. R. Stubenvell.

London, 1963   H. W. Parker

I

Origins and Evolution

"There are three things which are too wonderful for me, yea, four which I know not: The way of an eagle in the air; the way of a serpent upon a rock; the way of a ship in the midst of the sea and the way of a man with a maid" (Proverbs xxx, 18-19).

Much has been learnt of most of these things in the intervening centuries, fortunately without entirely destroying their wonder and fascination. The way of the serpent, alone, lags far behind all the others in its appeal and the mere mention of snakes in any conversation is almost certain to produce grimaces of distaste or disgust. The violence of this emotion is indicative of the great impact snakes have on mankind and, so far as the emotion is one of fear, it is readily understandable; for the venomous nature of many snakes is universally known, at least by hearsay, and has lost nothing in the telling. But, since very early times—and engravings of snakes occur on worked antlers of palaeolithic age (Magdalenian, 8-15,000 B.C.)—mankind has endowed snakes in his imagination with a good many other attributes less easy to understand. They have, or have had, a prominent place in the religious beliefs of most primitive peoples and serpent worship may well be the greatest of all animal cults. To the early Hebrews ". . . the serpent was more subtil than any beast of the field. . ." (Genesis iii) and was the personification of evil. Even in our own days a "snake in the grass" is symbolical of something or someone devious, underhand and fundamentally wicked: Roget's Thesaurus includes the phrase amongst the words apt for the description of the ideas "evil-doer," "deceiver," "badness," "pitfall" and "knave." In truth, of course, snakes have not the intelligence to be deliberately subtle and to endow them with guile as an attribute is the result of that very common fallibility, anthropomorphism, the interpretation of animal behaviour in terms of human motives, feelings and emotions. There can be little doubt that it is their silent, unobtrusive ways, their unwinking stare, their uncanny powers of locomotion without any, to us essential, limbs and their startling appearances in unexpected and apparently impossible places that combine to produce the illusion of stealthy cunning.

The absence, or apparent absence, of limbs is the most obvious characteristic of snakes and few people would fail to recognize a typical snake on sight, largely on this account. There are, however, numbers of other limbless creatures which are often confused with snakes, most of them being lizards. Degeneration of limbs or fins, to the point of their complete loss, has occurred in all the groups of lower vertebrates, fishes, amphibians, and reptiles, and so it is clear that limblessness is not necessarily a criterion of kinship. Amongst the reptiles, the class to which snakes belong, there are no forms which lack limbs living at the present day, except the snakes themselves and some lizards. But, in this latter group one can observe every stage in the disappearance of these organs, from a mere reduction in relative size, through loss of the fingers and toes one by one, to the complete suppression of either the fore-limbs, or the hind-limbs, or both. Moreover there is good evidence that these degenerative changes have taken place not once only in the course of evolution but many times, in no fewer than nine different groups of closely related forms (zoological "families"); the "Slow-worms" and "Glass-snakes" are familiar members of one such family and their vernacular names indicate how little they resemble normal lizards.

It is clear that no animal could just lose its limbs and survive, unless the loss was accompanied by other, compensatory, changes in its organization. It is, therefore, not at all surprising that snakes and legless lizards share a large number of features that have arisen directly or indirectly from the loss of limbs. They also have, however, a great number of other similarities that have no connection with this and, in fact, it is a difficult matter to find a single characteristic, or small group of characters, that would, by themselves, distinguish any snake from every lizard. The points of similarity between the two groups are so numerous that they can only be interpreted as the outcome of a common heritage and so, since it is almost impossible to draw a clear-cut line of demarcation between the two, they are grouped together by most zoologists in a single "order," the Squamata, which also contains some related but extinct forms. Corresponding groups living at the present time are the Tortoises and Turtles (order Chelonia), the Crocodiles and Alligators (order Crocodilia) and the unique Tuatara of New Zealand (order Rhynchocephalia); these, together with some extinct orders such as the Dinosaurs, Ichthyosaurs, Cotylosaurs and Pterodactyls constitute the Reptilia one of the larger and more important "classes" and the one which gave rise to the birds and the mammals, including mankind.

Whilst it is reasonably certain that the snakes are the culmination of a line of limbless specialization, a side shoot from the main lizard stem, it is not at all certain what their ancestors were, nor when the branch began to diverge from the main stem. Various possibilities can be inferred from a comparison of the points of resemblance between living forms; for instance it has been suggested that the rare Bornean lizard *Lanthanotus*, a relative of the Monitor Lizards, has so many similarities with the snakes that it may perhaps be the unique survivor of the stock from which they evolved. All such theories, however, must necessarily be controversial and certainty, or near certainty, could only be achieved if it were possible to trace both lizards and snakes backwards in time, by means of fossils, to the point at which no difference at all could be detected between the two. Unfortunately this is virtually impossible since, not only is there no very clear gap between the two even at the present time, but the fossil record is not at all satisfactory. The fossils, even when comparatively complete, consist only of the remains of the bony skeleton (except in a very few instances where scales are also preserved) and reveal little or nothing else of the creatures that gave rise to them; the vast majority of them are, moreover, very incomplete or even fragmentary. The most that can be deduced from this meagre material is that the lizards probably arose sometime during the Triassic period of the earth's history, about 190 to 160 million years ago. By the times of the next succeeding geological period, the Jurassic (160 to 135 million years ago) there was a multitude of lizard-like forms in existence but nothing with snake-like characteristics has so far been found. However, early in the next period, the Cretaceous, which began about 135 million years ago, some forms existed (*Pachyophis* and *Mesophis*) which were distinctly snake-like in many ways although they differed considerably from any snakes known today.

Under what environmental conditions snakes evolved must be a matter of speculation since the fossil record is so incomplete and controversial. Some authorities believe *Pachyophis* and *Mesophis* to have been sea-snakes, but others maintain that they could equally well have been terrestrial animals. Other theories have been propounded, all hinging basically on the matter of locomotion without limbs, it being very clear that no limbless group of animals could have come into existence, and flourished as the snakes have done, except under conditions where the lack of limbs was, at the very least no handicap or, more likely, where it gave them an advantage. Three possibilities have been suggested: in water, underground or on surfaces clothed with dense herbage. In water, many fishes and amphibians swim effectively by means of side to side undulations of the body, making no use of fins or limbs; crocodiles and alligators, too, swim in the same way with their limbs folded against their sides and only brought into action for crawling over the bottom or on land. Burrowing into very loose soil or through dense herbage can also be accomplished by swimming movements of the body and without the use of limbs; witness, for example, the well known Medicinal Skink of the Sahara and the European Slow Worm. The former, though possessing short limbs, burrows through soft sand by swimming movements which have earned it the name of *"poisson de sable"* and the limbless Slow Worm glides through the herbage of shady banks in essentially the same way. Limbs folded against the body offer little impediment to forward movement in these environments, but if the direction is reversed they will tend to dig into the soil or entangle with the vegetation and become a hindrance.

None of the three possibilities can be eliminated entirely, but the aquatic habitat commands the least support despite the possible marine nature of *Pachyophis* and *Mesophis*. One would expect that some, at least, of the snakes that have continued to live in the original conditions in which the group originated would have retained more ancestral characteristics than those others which, having migrated into different environments, have become further modified to meet the changed conditions. No aquatic snakes show any preponderance of "primitive" characters. In fact the reverse is the case, but the groups which possess the greatest number of indisputably primitive characters are the pythons and the Sunbeam Snake. The former are mainly inhabitants of the dense and often swampy tropical jungles of the Old World and the Sunbeam Snake (a single species only) lives in the loose earth of rice fields and gardens in Burma and the Malayan region.

Areas of dense vegetation offer obvious advantages to any predatory animal that is capable of swift and silent penetration of the dense cover it affords to a host of other animals that seek its concealment and protection, and which form a vast and varied potential food supply. As we have seen the absence of limbs coupled with a "swimming" gait are well suited to such an environment and this type of locomotion brings an additional advantage in its train. The longer the body is, within limits, the more effective the swimming movements become in producing a forward (or backward) thrust. Simple arithmetic shows that if a cylinder is reduced to half its diameter it must be increased to four times its previous length to have the same cubic capacity; reduced to one third or one fourth in diameter it needs to be nine or sixteen times as long, and so on. So, reduction in diameter to permit easy passage through dense vegetation or loose soil requires a very great compensatory increase in length and this meets the requirements for locomotion admirably. But the evolutionary path of attenuation, which the snakes have taken, calls for some reorganization of the internal organs.

The functions of the alimentary canal of any animal require large areas of digestive and absorbent surfaces. Since a long, narrow tube has a greater internal surface area than a shorter wider one, short-bodied animals, such as ourselves, have to accommodate a relatively long tube in a short, wide, body-cavity by folding and coiling it. The much longer cavity of a snake, however, obviates the necessity for such an arrangement which, since it must impede the flow of the contents of the canal, cannot be ideal. The snake's alimentary tract is an almost straight tube; the stomach, instead of being a curved sac lying transversely, is merely a simple enlargement of the fore-gut and the only coiling is in the region of the small intestine. For the other internal organs, however, the snake's tubular body cavity is less satisfactory. There is no wide thorax to accommodate the heart and lungs, nor is there room in the abdominal region for a large bi-lobed liver nor for globular kidneys and genital glands to lie alongside one another in pairs. The situation has been countered either by the suppression of one member of a pair and elongation of the other in compensation, or by staggering the paired arrangement or by a combination of both.

The heart is scarcely affected except that it is displaced backwards to a position about one third of the distance from the head to the vent, where it lies just in front of the stomach and liver. This last-mentioned organ is very much elongated with the left lobe shorter and the right sometimes prolonged into a thin "tail"; usually it ends slightly behind the middle of the body. The gall bladder, instead of being embedded in the liver has been moved backwards and lies a short distance behind it. The organs most affected by the stream-lining of the body are the lungs and in the majority of snakes the left is very much reduced in size or is completely absent; only in the boas, pythons and sunbeam snakes is there a functional left lung and even there it is distinctly smaller than the right. Compensation for this loss is achieved partly by a backward extension of the right lung and partly by the development of an additional respiratory surface along the wind-pipe—the so-called tracheal lung. The wind-pipe in vertebrates is normally reinforced by a series of closely spaced cartilaginous rings which prevent it from collapsing under pressure as, for instance, when food is being swallowed. In reptiles the rings are not quite complete along the upper (mid-dorsal) line of the tube and in the majority of typical snakes the membrane along this strip between the ends of the incomplete rings is expanded so that it forms, as it were, another tube overlying the trachea and connected with it by a slit running its whole length. This upper tube has a lining not like that of the trachea, but exactly similar to that of the lung, of which it is, functionally, a forward extension. The hinder extension of the true lung lacks this respiratory lining and is a simple, thin walled air sac. The whole lung system, with its tracheal extension in front and reservoir behind, frequently extends over more than three quarters of the body.

The largest of the other paired organs in the body-cavity are the kidneys and the genital glands (testes or ovaries) and both are not only elongated but those of the right hand side tend to be larger than those of the left, and to lie in front of them. The extent of the elongation may be gauged from the fact that whereas in a normal lizard only a single artery is required to supply each kidney, in snakes there may be as many as ten or even more. Finally the only other large organ normally occurring in the abdominal cavity, the urinary bladder, is completely absent, its loss without compensation being tolerable

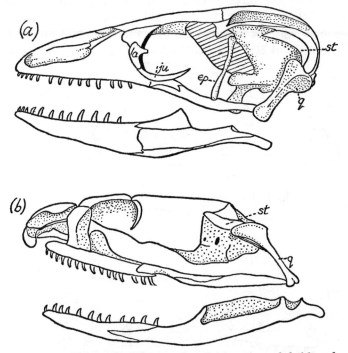

Figure 1. Skulls of a Monitor lizard (a) and a colubrid snake (b). The cross-hatching indicates exposed parts of the brain. The bones marked 1a. (lachrymal), ju. (jugal) and ep. (epipterygoid) are not found in any snake. Q. is the quadrate bone, on which the lower jaw hinges, and St. the supratemporal that connects it to the cranium. (*After* Bellairs & Underwood)

because in reptiles nitrogenous waste is excreted mainly in the form of uric acid, a chalky solid that is nearly insoluble in water.

The head, and especially the skull, of a snake shows a great many modifications compared with that of a typical lizard though there are few points in which they differ absolutely. Even a cursory glance at figures one and two will show that whereas surface dwelling snakes and lizards (Figure 1) differ markedly in their general appearance there is less disparity between a burrowing snake and a limbless burrowing lizard (Figure 2). Since both the latter are equally as attenuated as typical snakes it is unlikely that such differences as exist between them are directly connected with their stream-lining. Many of the differences between snakes' and lizards' skulls are associated with the fact that the bones forming and supporting a snake's snout and upper jaw are much less firmly connected

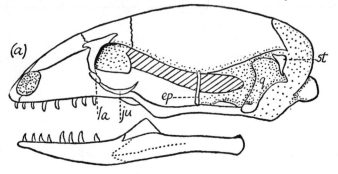

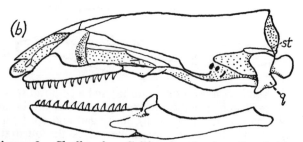

Figure 2. Skulls of a Californian Legless lizard (a) and a Pipe-snake (b). Both are burrowing forms. Cross-hatching and bones as in fig. 1. (*After* Bellairs & Underwood)

to the rest of the skull and so have a certain degree of mobility that is denied to the lizard. This mobility, which is associated with the method of feeding (in which connexion more will be said about it) has been achieved to a large extent by the loss of certain bones which, in lizards, act as struts between the upper jaw and cranium and help to make the whole skull a relatively rigid structure; the bones lost in all snakes' skulls are indicated in the figures. A secondary, but important, consequence of these losses has resulted in one of the very few characteristics that distinguish snakes from lizards without exception. In lizards the combined rigidity of the snout, upper jaws, and cranium results in a basket work which provides adequate protection for the sides of the forward part of the brain which are not invested by bones or cartilage; these areas are shown in the figures. In snakes, however, there is no such rigid basket work and the corresponding parts of the brain would be relatively exposed; protection has been provided by a downward growth on each side of the bones that form the roof of the cranium, so that the whole of the brain is enclosed in a complete bony capsule.

In all reptiles the brain is very small in comparison with the higher vertebrates. Writing of crocodiles, Richard Owen the great anatomist described the brain case as "miserably small" and says that it "may be filled by a man's thumb in a skull of three feet in length." In a typical, four-limbed lizard such as a Green Lizard the weight of the brain is only about one eighth of that of a Great Tit of comparable body weight. Loss of limbs may be expected to bring about some reduction in the size of the brain since those parts of it concerned with the control and co-ordination of the limbs are no longer needed. Furthermore the increased amount of the spinal cord in an attenuated animal will cater for many of the nervous reflexes, particularly those at the hinder end of the animal. As flippantly recorded of that enormously elongated dinosaur *Diplodocus*:

> "The creature had two sets of brains—
> One in his head (the usual place),
> The other at his spinal base.
> Thus he could reason *a priori*
> As well as *a posteriori*.

No problem bothered him a bit;
He made both head and tail of it.
So wise was he, so wise and solemn,
Each thought just filled a spinal column.
If one brain found the pressure strong
It passed a few ideas along
If something slipped his forward mind
'Twas rescued by the one behind."
                    etc., etc.

Some idea of relative brain sizes can be gained from the not very happily named "index of cephalization," a figure calculated from the quantity of brain in relation to body size. Thus, for instance:

Fishes   0.0045 (Eel)—0.0255 (Pike)
Amphibians   0.0062 (Crested Newt)—0.0179 (Tree Frog)
Reptiles   0.0071 (Slow-worm)—0.0191 (Green Lizard)
Birds   0.045—0.30 (Parrot)
Mammals   0.027 (Water Vole)—2.80 (Man)

Within the class of Reptiles some random samples are:

Slow-worm	0.0071—0.0082
Black and White Cobra	0.0098
Adder	0.0102
Monitor Lizard	0.0165
Green Lizard	0.0191

These comparable figures indicate clearly that elongation, at least in the lower vertebrates, is associated with a smaller brain. Amongst reptiles, the snakes and snake-like lizards such as the Slow-worm, do not differ greatly but have a brain only from about 40 per cent to 60 per cent the size of that of a typical lizard.

However, this reduction in weight and volume, large as it may be, will not result in any very great reduction in diameter to help in stream-lining since the greatest diameter of the brain arises from the size of the optic lobes which, being concerned with vision, are not reduced in size in any except some burrowing forms. But the brain is not the principal factor that determines the diameter of the reptilian head since the greatest diameter of the skull may, in a typical lizard for instance, be three or more times greater than the maximum diameter of the brain. The difference is due to the spread of the upper jaws, i.e. to the width of the mouth. The greatest diameter of a lizard's head is behind the eyes, in the region of the ears and it may, therefore, be significant that in snakes, where the upper jaws are not rigidly strutted out from the cranium, there are no ears. There are no ear-drums, tympanic cavities or eustachian passages; in fact all those parts of the auditory apparatus concerned with the reception of atmospheric vibrations are absent and all that remains is the bony rod (the columella) which normally transmits these vibrations to the inner ear that lies embedded in the side wall of the cranium. Some confirmation of the idea that this loss of an important sense organ is connected with a narrowing and stream-lining of the head is to be found in the fact that a similar condition is found in at least three different, and not at all closely inter-related, groups of snake-like, burrowing lizards.

II

Locomotion

In the previous chapter it was stated as an axiom that an animal could not "Just lose its limbs and survive" unless the loss was accompanied by compensatory changes. The prime function of the limbs is undoubtedly locomotion and their employment for other purposes such as digging, holding and fighting, vitally important though it may be, is a secondary development. So it seems certain that any evolutionary process which reduced an animal's limbs to the point where they became useless for locomotion would result in the creature's extinction unless it already had either the ability to lead a completely sedentary life or to move effectively and efficiently by some other means. There are many invertebrate animals that lead sedentary lives (e.g. sea-anemones, corals, barnacles, sea-squirts) and either have no limbs at all or use them solely for purposes other than locomotion, but very few vertebrates. Almost the only ones that come readily to mind are the parasitic males of certain fishes which, once they have attached themselves to a female, lose their fins and many other organs as well. But these are rather irrelevant exceptions and, as already mentioned, there are many vertebrates, whether limbless or not, that are able to move effectively by side to side undulations of the body. This actual or potential ability must have been possessed by the ancestors of snakes before limb-reduction began and it is still the principal mode of progression for all their descendants.

It is easy to see that an eel, or a slow-worm, or a snake makes a series of wriggling movements of its body and tail when it is in motion, but it is not at all obvious how or why these wriggles propel the creature. The mechanics of the process are, in fact, quite complex and not easy to explain. Starting from the very obvious, the animal must exert a force that is greater than the frictional resistance opposing its motion. Secondly this force must be applied to an external object; it is useless for the animal to push its head against its own body or squeeze itself into a ball. Thirdly there must be friction somewhere between the animal and the outside world to offer resistance to the force it is exerting. This last point can be appreciated from what happens when a snake is placed on a sheet of polished glass, or ice. As the animal tries to escape it executes its usual writhing movements, generally with progressively increasing violence, but is unable to make any appreciable progress despite the fact that there is very little frictional resistance opposing it. There is, of course, nothing to provide any resistance to the forces it is trying to exert; it can get no purchase. If, however, the glass plate is dotted with scattered, firmly fixed pegs, the undulations of the body will come into contact with them sooner or later and then the animal quickly glides off the plate; the pegs have provided the necessary purchases. Comparison of successive frames of a ciné film of this event shows that the snake's wriggles are a series of "waves" thrown out on opposite sides alternately. They begin at the anterior end and, if one looks at the snake without reference to the background, each wave appears to travel backwards along its whole length. But if one studies the position of the waves in relation to the background it will be seen that they remain stationary and the snake flows past them. This is shown in Figure 3, a diagrammatic sketch of successive stages in the motion of a Grass-snake across a grid drawn on a peg-studded background; the waves are pressing against points of resistance which, being fixed, do not allow of any change in shape. But this still does not explain the movement of the snake past the fixed points.

The writhings of a snake are produced by the alternate contraction and relaxation of a series of muscles attached to the vertebrae, there being one set of muscles on each side. Contraction on one side with relaxation on the other bends the body and waves of contraction followed by relaxation pass from head to tail in opposite phase on the two sides. If there is no impediment to their passage the loops formed by this muscular action pass along the body with no effect, as when the snake is on a sheet of glass. But if there are any projections on the ground these will interfere with the backward movement of the

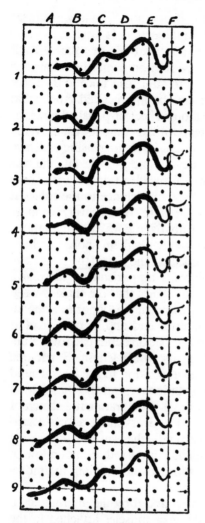

Figure 3. Stages in the movement of a Grass-snake. Time interval between successive stages one fourth of a second. Grid lines A—F three inches apart. (*After* Gray)

loops and a pressure will be generated at each point of contact; and, if this pressure is greater than the sliding friction of the snake, forward movement results. The action is exactly similar to what happens with a skater who can propel himself on one skate only. The skate travels a sinuous course and a series of thrusts is given diagonally sideways and backwards, first to right, then to left as the foot turns to right and left on either side of the straight track. The skate is, of course, making a continuous groove in the ice and the diagonal thrusts are directed against the sides of the groove which provide the resistance and give the purchase the skater requires to propel himself. The points at which the thrusts have been applied are revealed by chips of ice thrown out by the skate. A snake may be likened to an articulated chain of skates following a similar winding course, each skate pushing sideways and backwards before it reaches the apex of each outward curve. Naturally a snake will not cut a groove in ice, but on grass or sand its own weight makes such a groove and the same principle applies. This may be seen from Plate 1 which shows the track of a snake on loose sand; successive thrusts have piled the sand into crescentic ridges on the outer, rear sections of each loop. On unyielding surfaces where the weight of the body makes no groove the snake deliberately selects a course to bring fixed objects, stones, humps, tufts of grass or twigs, into the correct relations with its body-loops to provide resistance where it is needed. A snake in motion will be seen to have its head raised slightly off the ground and questing to right and left as it moves along. The pattern of curves will therefore vary according to the substratum, being more regular on uniform surfaces, as in Plate 1(a), but irregular and asymmetrical on rougher ground. It also varies considerably from snake to snake, long slender species not unnaturally throwing more loops than shorter and stouter species and thereby acquiring the advantage of more thrust points. And again, the pattern varies according to the circumstances of the moment. During a slow prowl there are more and shallower loops than when movement is more urgent and it is safe to say that the greater the degree of excitement the fewer and deeper the loops become, so much so that they may be quite ineffective; a badly frightened snake will often thrash around so frenziedly that it gets nowhere.

This wild, ineffective thrashing arises through "slip". Lateral resistance points that are sufficiently rigid to withstand the gentler pressures when the animal is not in any hurry give way when full power is applied and a large part of the energy of the muscular contractions merely serves to increase the curvature of the loops instead of driving the animal forwards. Slip is always a bugbear both to animals and engineers. In animals using limbs, and vehicles using wheels, slip most usually occurs when the frictional resistance between the limb or wheel and the substratum is less than the force being applied. But in snakes the less the friction between the animal and the ground at these points the better it is, since motion depends on one surface sliding over the other. Here what is needed is resistance to the displacement of the objects against which the pressure is being exerted, i.e. to friction at a place one degree removed from the actual point of contact. Ideally a snake requires a surface with a series of smooth, unyielding projections, a circumstance seldom likely to be encountered in the natural course of events. When an approximation to such conditions is artificially provided a snake can exert a remarkably high tractive effort. For example a Grass-snake moving freely exerts a force equal to about a third of its own weight, and if restrained from movement it can sustain a pull of four or five times its own weight. This compares more than favourably with man-made machines. A steam locomotive moving at slow to moderate speeds under good track conditions cannot exert a draw-bar pull of more than about one fifth of its own weight and in diesel and electric locomotives this ratio only exceptionally rises to more than one quarter. In these instances, too, the weight factor favours the locomotives since they do not have to carry, as must the snakes, all the apparatus needed for the production of their fuel and to make good the ravages of wear, tear and accidental damage!

It might be expected that a snake, which can exert such a proportionally high propulsive force, would be able to move at a considerable speed, and there are many observers' "estimates" of speeds exceeding 30 miles per hour. Several different snakes in different parts of the world have at various times been reported to be able to outpace a galloping horse, but the few careful observations that have been made make anything of the kind seem extremely improbable. Although snakes are undoubtedly extremely quick in their motions, as for instance when striking at their prey, their rate of movement over the ground is never great because, despite their muscular power, the frictional resistance of a long body sliding along its whole length is disproportionately high in comparison with the resistance encountered by a running animal or a wheeled vehicle. Moreover they can seldom or never encounter the environmental conditions which would enable them to use their power to the best advantage. Most of the "estimates" of snakes' speeds are subjective and were made without any opportunity of measuring distances or times: and the observations are bedevilled by the fact that an excited snake will seldom maintain a steady course for long, but will feint, dodge, stop and restart with bewildering rapidity. This behaviour makes accurate measurements of the speed of wild specimens exceedingly difficult and the actions of individuals that have been kept in captivity can be equally misleading. For instance, in a "Rattlesnake Derby," held in America in 1939, the winner's time over a thirty foot course was 12 minutes 12 seconds, equivalent to a mean speed of about two thirds of a mile a day; and rattlesnakes are amongst those reputed to be as swift as a galloping horse! Nevertheless some fairly reliable and consistent measurements have been made and, as might be expected, there are variations between species; long slender species are swifter than stout ones. Relatively heavy-bodied forms such as rattlesnakes and side-winders were found to be capable of two miles per hour or perhaps even three for a short burst. The Grass-snake, of average build, may reach four miles an hour and the very slender Coachwhip Snake, certainly one of the fastest moving snakes of North America, was timed at 3.6 miles per hour, though adjudged capable, under exceptional conditions of maybe 5.4 m.p.h. over a short distance. Even when allowance is made for the 25-35 per cent greater distance a snake must travel between two points because of its meandering course, there is nothing to suggest that even the Coachwhip Snake can exceed more than about seven miles an hour; nor are there any grounds for believing that other species are likely to be appreciably better performers.

Given appropriate environmental conditions, all snakes as well as limbless lizards and amphibians, can move by horizontal undulations in the way just described; it is their basic method and the one most commonly used. But for certain special purposes, or under different conditions other methods are employed and three types can be distinguished. Some of these involve a side-to-side looping of the body but are fundamentally different in that the loops do not exert a backward thrust to make the animal slide forwards. Snakes that burrow, or have to move through confined spaces do so by "concertina" movement. A surface dwelling species such as a Grass-snake can pass through a narrow, smooth-walled cleft, or a rat hole, or a drain pipe, where normal undulatory movement would be impossible, in the following way. Horizontal loops are formed, as before, starting at the anterior end, and these loops are pressed outwards against the walls of the passage so that they get a frictional grip. The rest of the body and tail are then drawn up into similar loops, the waves of contraction to form the loops passing progressively backwards. As successive loops secure a grip the ones in front relax and the body is straightened out. Then the whole process starts again from the head end so that the anterior part of the body is being continuously pushed forwards against the frictional resistance of loops farther back whilst the hinder end is being simultaneously drawn forwards to the anchored loops in front of it. The whole cycle of events is continuous so that, as in the case of undulatory motion on the surface, each loop travels from one end of the snake to the other but does not move relative to the substratum. This method is very effective for passage through an existing channel or burrow that is appreciably wider than the snake's body, but the thrust that can be exerted is limited by the extent of the frictional grip that can be secured. It is doubtful whether sufficient thrust could be produced in this way alone to enable a passage to be forced through the earth, which is what burrowing snakes have to do, although the overlapping arrangement of the scales on the flanks is suitable for preventing backward slip against a forward push; the free edges of the scales are directed backwards and will tend to dig into the sides of burrow. Many truly burrowing snakes have developed an additional device to provide a non-slip fulcrum against which pressure can be exerted. The tail is short, thick and muscular and either terminates in one or more spines or is flattened and equipped with specially roughened scales. No one has actually seen how the creatures use these devices, but it has been observed that the tails of specimens caught when the soil is damp are often caked in mud. It seems probable that the snake anchors itself in its burrow at the head end and then draws the whole of its body up into a complete series of small loops. Then the spines or roughened surfaces of the tail are either dug into, or firmly pressed against, the sides of the burrow and the whole body forcibly straightened out. There will not be the continuous flowing gait of typical "concertina movement" but a succession of jabs each of which carries the full force of the whole body behind it. This method of locomotion has been called "thrust creeping."

Yet another type of looping gait is practised by some snakes, mostly vipers, that frequent the loose, shifting sands of deserts. The normal undulatory method is not very effective on this kind of surface which offers little resistance to the driving forces and there must inevitably be much slip. The surface is, however, much more resistant, relatively, to a downward pressure than to a sideways thrust and the snakes take advantage of this in the very peculiar gait known as "side-winding." In this method of locomotion the body is lifted clear of the ground and the snake moves crab-wise. The motion is so extraordinary that the ancients who observed it in some Saharan vipers such as the Horned Asp attributed it to a defective spine and the legend grew up that this was the outcome of being accidentally trodden on by Helen during her elopement with Paris. The sequence of events is best seen from a diagram, Figure 4, that shows successive stages. Here the J-shaped outlines indicate where the snake has rested (continuous lines), is resting (solid black), or is going to rest (dotted lines), parts of its body on the ground. In stage one, top left, the snake has bent its anterior end into a double loop, lifted these round towards its left rear and allowed the neck to come to rest on the ground again in a new position. During the remaining stages more and more of the body and finally the tail is lifted over to this second position whilst at the same time another loop forms in front and this lifts the head and neck over to yet a third position. And so on. Although the snake travels in the direction in which its head is facing, it is "looking over its shoulder," in this case its left "shoulder," and the body appears to travel tail first in this direction. Plate 1(b) shows the actual tracks made by a side-winding snake, the hook of the J in each imprint being made by the head and the cross-bar by the tail. Ungainly as this method of locomotion may sound, the whole sequence of movements proceeds gracefully and the animal moves smoothly and fluidly, achieving a speed quite comparable with that reached by the more usual serpentine undulations. Side-winding is the normal

—*Direction of Travel*— ▷

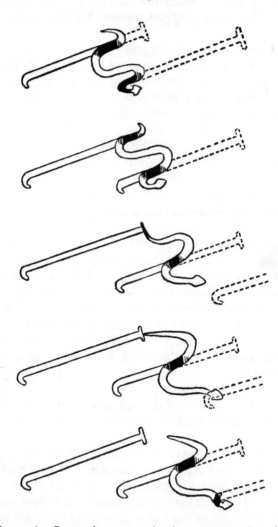

Figure 4. Successive stages in the progress of a side-winding snake. The J-shaped outlines are where the animal comes into contact with the ground. Solid black indicates actual contact at that moment; continuous lines show areas of past contact; dotted lines indicate future contact. (*After* Mosauer)

method of locomotion in a few desert-dwelling forms in different parts of the world; for instance a small North American rattlesnake, called the Sidewinder, the Asp, Horned Asp and Saw-scaled Viper of the Sahara and Arabian deserts, and a few small species of puff-adder in south-western Africa. These forms have perfected the method, but a great many others, whether desert dwellers or not, including the common European Grass-snake and the American garter-snakes which normally move by the more usual side-to-side undulations, will sometimes attempt to side-wind, especially if they are alarmed when on a smooth surface. They show varying degrees of competence, or lack of it, but most of them fail to lift the body clear of the ground and none has the rhythmic flow of those that use the method habitually.

All the foregoing methods depend basically on the action of muscles which flex the vertebral column. A great many snakes can, however, move without any bending of the body, by the so-called "rectilinear creeping." This method is unique amongst vertebrate animals which otherwise all rely exclusively upon parts of the skeleton acting as jointed levers. "Straight-line" creeping results from the motion and ratchet-like action of the scales under the belly and on the lower flanks and can only be achieved when the skin in these regions is not firmly attached to the other body-tissues, but is able to slide freely over them for short distances. Snakes that possess this looseness of the skin are mostly heavy bodied forms like puff-adders, rattlesnakes, boas and pythons; most other snakes have the skin firmly attached to the underlying muscles and are incapable of this type of movement. At one time it was thought that the belly scales were carried backwards and forwards by the ribs which were moving like the legs of a millipede, but this has quite recently been shown to be incorrect. Instead, it now appears that the scales of the flanks and lower surface are moved by two sets of muscles attached to the ribs, which do not move. One muscle lifts a belly scale very slightly and draws it forwards a short distance; then this muscle relaxes and the other comes into play, contracts, and draws the scale back again to its original position. The flank scales are operated similarly. The two muscles act as a team, in the same sequence, and waves of joint action pass along the body, from the neck to the base of the tail, one after another at fairly close intervals. Owing to the fact that the scales overlap one another and that there is a slight lifting action, when a scale is pulled forwards it slides over the ground and becomes "bunched up" with the one in front of it. But when the other muscle tries to draw it back again there is no lifting action and its rear edge, which is directed backwards and downwards, acts like the pawl of a ratchet and digs into the ground. The pull of the muscle against this resistance hitches the snake forward. So, each ventral scute in turn provides a forward hitch, those in front dragging the rest of the body and those behind pushing it; as there may be up to 400 ventral scutes a snake creeping along in this way is not likely to lack footholds. The rate of progress is, however, necessarily slow since each forward hitch cannot be more than a fraction of an inch even in a very large boa or python, and any snake in a hurry tries to use the undulatory gait; sometimes the two methods are used simultaneously when prowling.

In the preceding paragraphs only movement on the ground, or under it, has been mentioned, but the same basic methods are used by the many species of climbing and swimming snakes, with very few additional specializations. Among aquatic forms there is every gradation between species that take to the water occasionally and those that never leave it voluntarily and cannot survive for long if accidentally stranded. All of them progress by the undulatory method, whether swimming or crawling over the bottom, though in the latter case they may also resort to concertina movement in restricted spaces between rocks and boulders. In swimming the undulations do not encounter the firm resistance that they do on land, but they nevertheless meet some resistance from the water and in overcoming it they displace the water backwards. Backward displacement of water is the fundamental principle in all forms of swimming and most types of marine propulsion, whether it be by jets (as in squids) paddles, paired fins, tails, oars or screws. The greater the mass of water so displaced and the greater its velocity, the greater is the resulting forward thrust. A cylindrical rod is clearly not well shaped for moving water; a pole makes a very indifferent oar. So, just as eels have a long, continuous median fin down the back and beneath the tail, the more aquatic snakes have some side to side flattening of the body, particularly to-

1(a) The track of a snake progressing over soft sand by undulatory movement. On the outer, rear side of each loop a heap of sand is thrown up, showing where a forward thrust was exerted. (*Photo*. Walter Mosauer; *courtesy* "Ecology")

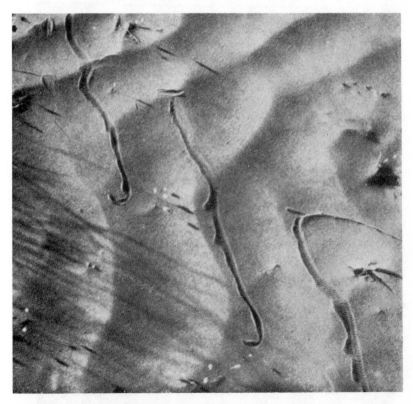

1(b) The track of a sidewinding snake. The direction of travel was from the bottom right to the top left and the hooked end of each imprint was made by the head and neck. (*Photo*. Walter Mosauer; *courtesy* "Ecology")

2 Head of a Grass-snake. The long forked tongue is collecting microscopic particles from the air to aid the sense of smell. (*Photo.* G. Kinns)

wards the tail, and this reaches its maximum development in the wholly aquatic sea-snakes (Chapter IX) where the tail is a broad, flat blade.

For climbing among the twigs and branches of bushes and trees the same combination of undulation and concertina movement, supplemented by creeping, serves without any additional modifications for the vast majority of the numerous different species that live in this environment. The major problem there is the passage from branch to branch and a very long tail to act as a counterpoise whilst the anterior end crosses a gap is obviously an advantage. Most of the arboreal members of the colubrid family (Chapter VIII Plate 13(a)) and the cobra group (Chapter IX), like the mambas, tend to great length, with inordinately long tails, but the heavier bodied boas, pythons and vipers often have another device which serves the same purpose; they have short, prehensile tails similar to, though less highly developed than, those of chameleons. Leaping from branch to branch would appear to be a most unlikely achievement for a snake, but one or two species have acquired the knack of doing this without any structural modification. The best-known of them is the Golden Tree-snake, or Flying Snake (Plate 14), of the Indo-Chinese region, a handsomely coloured but otherwise fairly typical tree-snake, elongate and slender, with a tail nearly half as long as the head and body. It is an extraordinarily accomplished climber able to ascend almost vertical walls or tree trunks by taking advantage of every slightest irregularity, and can spring across gaps of three or four feet, sometimes nearly vertically. This is done very simply by coiling on one branch and then straightening out with explosive speed. Its more remarkable accomplishment, however, is its ability to glide through the air from bough to bough or to the ground. There is no special gliding membrane such as Flying Lizards, Flying Squirrels and similar gliding animals possess, but the maximum of surface area is produced by holding the body straight and rigid and spreading the ribs outwards to their limit. At the same time the middle of the belly is drawn in slightly so that a long, slightly concave lower surface is formed. This offers enough resistance to the air to convert a vertical fall into an oblique descent at an appreciably reduced speed. The angle of descent is steep, and there is very little probability that the creature can take advantage of upward air currents to indulge in soaring flight. Nor can it, apparently, exercise much control over the direction of travel once it is launched into the air; but it can drop from considerable heights, and land safely which, in view of its adventurous and acrobatic climbing habits, must be no little advantage.

All the methods of locomotion employed by snakes, except the rectilinear creep, have the same basic structural requirements. The body must not only be long, but very flexible and this means that increased length must be achieved by increasing the number of vertebrae and not, as in a giraffe's neck (where there are only seven vertebrae as in most other mammals including man) by increasing their length. The muscles that flex the body from side to side, being the source of the propulsive forces, must be proportionally powerful, and, since they pull on the back bone, the articulations between the vertebrae must be designed to withstand the strains imposed without being dislocated. The body musculature is, in fact, highly elaborated, its most important feature being the great elongation of the individual muscle segments and the linking of these segments into chains which may bridge more than thirty vertebrae. Of these latter there are varying numbers, according to species, with totals from about 180 to 400. They articulate, as in most creatures, by a ball and socket joint with interlocking projections to prevent them rotating on one another and so wringing the spinal cord. In most reptiles there is a short bony prong on each side of the ball which engages with a similar prong on each side of the socket of the adjacent vertebra. Each forwardly directed prong has a flat horizontal facet facing upwards and the backwardly directed prongs have similar facets facing downwards; oppositely facing surfaces are in contact and slide over each other when the back bone bends from side to side (Figure 5(a)). In snakes, and most of the snake-like lizards the prongs are stouter and the number of articular facets is doubled in the manner shown in Figure 5(b). This arrangement strengthens the joint against rotational stresses and limits the extent of vertical bending to about 13 deg. downwards and 12-18 deg. upwards; but it does not restrict side to side movement and adjoining vertebrae can usually bend about 25 deg. in either direction.

Another requirement in connection with undulatory motion

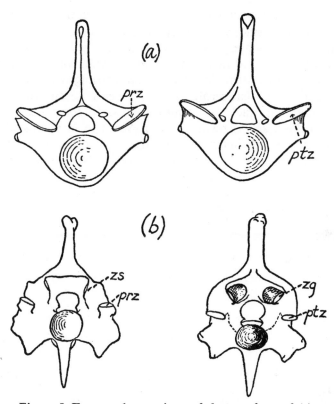

Figure 5. Front and rear views of the vertebrae of (a) a typical lizard and (b) a snake. Additional articular facets in the snake's vertebra are indicated by Zg. and Zs.

has already been mentioned; the skin must be as frictionless as possible. At the same time it must be tough enough not to be easily abraded and it must be very flexible. A smooth, elastic skin lubricated by abundant mucus is the answer that other groups of animals have found for these requirements, and the unobservant or prejudiced often refer to snakes as cold, slimy things. Cold they may be, but slimy they are not; and could not be to be able to survive without desiccation in many of the arid environments they have mastered. Instead, their ancestral inheritance of a covering of dry but highly polished, overlapping scales meets all their requirements. More will be said in a later chapter about the skin and scales in relation to their protective functions, but one exclusively ophidian modification must be mentioned now since it is concerned with locomotion and with rectilinear creeping especially. The scales of the lower surfaces are greatly increased in width so that the whole of the belly is covered by a long strip of very wide scales arranged in a straight longitudinal line that recalls in both appearance and function the "caterpillar track" of some vehicles. In some boas and pythons this track is relatively narrower than in most snakes but it is absent only in burrowing and aquatic forms.

III

Senses and Perceptions

However well mechanically adapted an animal may be, its success in life depends primarily on behaviour that takes advantage of favourable circumstances and avoids those that are unfavourable. Its behaviour may be instinctive, a series of completely automatic and unthinking responses, or intelligent, but in either case the starting point is perception of what is going on in the world around it. It is customary to speak of the five senses, sight, hearing, smell, taste and touch as our methods of perception, but there are others. Some of these, like our temperature sense, are concerned with the perception of conditions in the outside world, but others deal rather with internal circumstances. These latter, for example those which tell us whether we are hungry, thirsty or sleepy, naturally have a profound effect on our reactions and some of them may also supplement the knowledge of the external world that we obtain from other sources. Thus, we have a sense of balance which is partly visual, but in which two other senses also play a part. Associated with our ears are our semicircular canals (labyrinths) which inform us of any tilting or rotatory movements, backwards, forwards or sideways, to which we are being subjected but which, alone, cannot distinguish accurately the angle of tilt. They react to movement (acceleration) and, in fact, are not very sensitive to slow movement; in a darkened room a man seated in an arm chair can be tilted several degrees without his being aware of it, provided that it is done very slowly and smoothly. When, however, the angle of tilt reaches a certain limit, gravity begins to alter appreciably the strain on the various muscles that are maintaining the position of the body and limbs and the alteration is felt. The muscles perceive the change and pass the information to the brain; they are receptor sense organs (technically "proprioceptors").

It is clear that snakes possess all the senses that we have, but they also have some additional sense organs. It is also very probable that even when the sense organs are the same, the sensations they record are different, at least in degree. To ascertain exactly what sensation an animal perceives when any particular organ is stimulated is virtually impossible. Even two human beings do not always receive the same impression from the same stimulus, witness the effects of colour-blindness, and with other animals the position is much more complex because they cannot communicate their sensations. Almost the only direct evidence that can be obtained is by measuring the electrical effects in the nerves that connect the sense organs with the brain; if the electrical currents do not alter when the organ is subjected to a certain stimulus it can be assumed that the organ does not react to that stimulus, and vice-versa. But it does not necessarily follow that an electrical reaction indicates that the animal will perceive anything since there are unknown thresholds of intensity that must be exceeded before any sensation results. So in most instances we have to observe the animal's reactions and make inferences by analogy with our own feelings and sensations, and this procedure is beset with difficulties and pitfalls. One of the principal difficulties arises from the fact that reactions to a stimulus are often modified by the uncontrollable and unknown factors of memories of past experiences and by the physiological and psychological conditions; thus a man who lives beside a railway is not awakened by every train that passes, but an anxious mother will hear her baby's cry through a hubbub that would drown it for any other ear.

Nevertheless it is still possible by critical examination of an animal's reactions, coupled with an assessment of the physical and mechanical capabilities and limitations of its sense-organs, to reach some fairly definite conclusions and to estimate the relative importance of each sense. In man sight is almost certainly the most important single sense, but in snakes this is true in only a very limited number of forms. In a great many burrowing types the eyes are so minute and so degenerate in structure that they may well be capable of little more than distinguishing daylight from darkness, which, of course, is all that the animals need; in their subterranean haunts vision would be no advantage and even if they possessed it they would have to rely entirely upon their other senses. Is is, however, of considerable scientific interest that even in forms that live above ground and in which eyes are not only functional but of prime importance as sense organs, they are structurally very different from those of the snakes' nearest relatives, the lizards; and the differences are of a nature to suggest that in snakes the eyes have been re-developed to their present state from the degenerate condition characteristic of a burrowing creature. It is a cardinal principle that, once a structure has been lost during the course of evolution it is never regained, but if the need for it should recur some other structure becomes appropriately modified to take over its functions; the eyes of snakes lack several of the component parts that occur in lizards but the functions of the missing parts are performed by other structures, sometimes in essentially different ways. The most obvious difference is that whereas lizards, like birds and a great many mammals, have three moveable eyelids—upper, lower and nictitating membrane—snakes appear to have no eyelids at all, the delicate cornea being protected by a fixed, circular, transparent scale that is continuous with the scaly covering of the rest of the body and is shed and renewed with it. From an anatomical standpoint this transparent scale (the "spectacle") is really the lower eyelid which has become transparent and fused along its upper edge to a completely vestigial upper eyelid. This condition is foreshadowed in a few lizards where the lower lid has a transparent window in the middle and is kept continuously in the closed position. The ophidian condition has obvious advantages for a creeping, semiburrowing creature in that the cornea is continuously protected and, should the protective covering receive an injury it is renewable; the only major disadvantage is that when the skin is undergoing the periodic changes that precede sloughing it becomes opaque for a day or two and then the snake is almost or quite blind. The most fundamental differences, however, between the eyes of snakes and those of lizards and the other higher vertebrates are concerned with the focusing arrangements and with visual acuity. In lizards' eyes, as in our own, the lens is a rather flattened biconvex structure and the images of near or distant objects are focused onto the retina by a ring of muscles which change its curvature and so alter its focal length. But in snakes the lens is almost spherical and its curvature remains unaltered since the appropriate muscles for changing it are absent; focusing is achieved by a different set of muscles which move the lens bodily, as in a camera, either away from, or closer to, the retina. Observations of the behaviour of snakes indicate that the range of accommodation they can achieve in this way is limited and that their distant vision is poor.

Our own eyes and those of most other terrestrial vertebrates have, in addition to the focusing arrangements, a small central area of the retina, known as the fovea, which is structurally somewhat different from the surrounding areas and gives much clearer definition. If one looks straight ahead only the central area of the whole field of vision is seen clearly and objects elsewhere in the periphery, though visible lack clarity. Any movements in these other regions attract immediate attention and, unless there is preoccupation with something in the central area, one automatically changes the direction of the head or eyes to bring the image of the moving object onto the fovea where it can be seen in greater detail; one looks directly at any object of interest. Except in a very few arboreal species, snakes have no fovea and so their whole retinal picture is presumably similar to that in our peripheral field of vision; it will be sensitive to movement but lacking in clarity and no advantage will result from looking directly at any particular object. This conclusion is supported by the fact that the muscles which rotate the eye-ball are less complex than in other creatures, and by the ways in which snakes behave. The eyes, though situated on the sides of the head are directed slightly forwards and are capable of a limited amount of independent horizontal and vertical rotation. These movements can be induced by tilting a snake's head, when it will endeavour to maintain the optical axis of each eye as nearly horizontal as possible. This, parenthetically, indicates a good sense of balance, but snakes seldom attempt to follow moving objects with their eyes. When hunting they react to movement by pursuit, but the prey is usually followed only so long as it remains in motion; if it stops or "freezes" they seem to lose contact at once and then attempt to regain it by using one or more of their other senses.

Another device for improving visual acuity which is common in lizards and other animals is a system of colour filters which, like those used in photography, reduce the glare resulting from an excess of light at the blue end of the spectrum. In lizards these colour filters have the form of yellow oil droplets in those cells of the retina (the cones) that are concerned with daylight vision, but in diurnal snakes, which also have retinal cones (though some of them are of a unique type not found in other animals), there are no oil droplets and, instead, the whole of the lens is coloured yellow, an arrangement which, of course, serves the same purpose. Other features of the eye show no differences from the lacertilian pattern and so call for little comment. There is a normally contractile iris and the pupil may be round or may contract to a narrow vertical or horizontal ellipse in nocturnal and twilight species all of which have typical rod-like cells in the retina for night vision. Whether snakes have colour vision is uncertain; there is nothing in the structure of the eye to preclude the possibility but it has been found experimentally that dyeing the prey in bizarre colours makes no difference to its acceptability.

Thus it seems that, whilst burrowing snakes may be nearly blind, the majority of surface-dwelling forms also have poor sight for detail, especially at a distance, but are very sensitive to movement over a field that is particularly wide because vision is mainly monocular and the eyes are directed laterally. The only known exceptions to these generalizations are certain tree-snakes, the oriental whip-snakes (*Ahaetulla* and *Dryophiops*) and the African twig-snakes (*Thelotornis*). These have a very long horizontal pupil, extending across nearly the whole width of the eye-opening, and since the sides of the snout are hollowed out to produce two grooves, light from objects directly in front of the snout can enter through the anterior corner of the slit-like pupil and form images on the posterior part of the retina where there is a fovea. This structural arrangement should give these species more acute vision than is usual and it may also be binocular and stereoscopic for objects directly in front of the end of the snout. Their behaviour indicates that this is the case, for they follow the movements of objects they are investigating by turning their heads to look at them and *Ahaetulla* and *Thelotornis* are amongst the few snakes that are able to pick out and recognize their prey even if it is motionless.

There is no indication that snakes have any means of perceiving radiations in the ultra-violet range of the spectrum, but they are sensitive to infra-red (heat) rays, the receptors being widely diffused over the whole skin. This dispersal over a wide area endows the animal with a general sensitivity which may have some directional sense arising from shadow effects; radiations from a warm source on, say, the animal's right hand side will stimulate the skin on that side, but the skin of the left side will be shaded and receive no stimulus. One group of vipers, the pit-vipers (Chapter IX) which includes the rattlesnakes, has, however, a stereoscopic heat-receptor organ which enables the animals to detect not only the existence, but also the direction and distance away, of objects hotter or colder than themselves. These paired organs are situated on the sides of the head between the eye and the nostril (Plate 10(a)) and each consists of a roughly spherical cavity divided by a diaphragm into two unequal chambers. The larger of the two is the more superficial and is wide open to the exterior with an aperture considerably larger than the nostril. The smaller chamber lies behind the larger one and is more deeply embedded in the head; it, too, communicates with the exterior, but only by a narrow duct with a minute pore-like opening just in front of the eye. There is a valve, controlled by muscles, which opens or closes the duct and by this means the atmospheric pressure on the inner side of the diaphragm, which has a very generous and complex nerve supply, can be controlled as the temperature changes. At various times these "pit-organs" have been credited with diverse functions; they have been described as ears, organs of smell or touch, glands, pressure gauges and even as organs of an unspecified "sixth" sense. In recent years, however, it has been established experimentally that the nerves of the diaphragm give no electrical responses to sounds, odours, vibrations, light or touch, but they do respond and with great sensitivity to infra-red rays impinging on the diaphragm. Any object even slightly warmer than the general temperature at the pit produced a response provided that it was in such a position that the radiation from it could fall directly upon the diaphragm. The field covered by each pit extends over an arc of about 100 deg. in the horizontal plane and since it extends to about 10 deg. on the opposite side of the centre line, there is binocular "vision" of warm objects immediately in front of the animal. The response naturally varies in intensity with distance from the warm object (the amount of heat reaching the pit will vary inversely as the square of the distance) but the warmth of a human hand was detected nearly a foot away and temperature differences of as little as a third of a degree Fahrenheit at the membrane produced a reaction. Such a mechanism is clearly useful in pinpointing warm-blooded prey at close range in the dark, more especially in the cool of the night when the difference in temperature between the prey and its surroundings is greater, and tests with rattlesnakes show conclusively that they are able to locate and strike with great accuracy at warm, moving objects without the benefit of any other sense organs. Pits with a similar function, but much less elaborate structure, are also found in the scales bordering the lips of many boas and pythons though there is little precise information concerning their efficacy; and there is no information at all about the functions of certain deep, sac-like cavities associated with the nostrils of some of the Old World vipers, such as the puff adders, which have been suspected of being heat receptors.

Although it is an ancient belief that some snakes, at least, are deaf, it is equally widely believed, even today, that many are not merely capable of hearing but are appreciative of music. The Psalmist wrote "They are like the deaf adder that stoppeth her ear; which hearkeneth not to the voice of charmers, charming never so wisely . . ." and Jeremiah (viii, 17) wrote "For, behold, I will send serpents, basilisks [or adders], among you, which will not be charmed; . . .". Controversy still rages on the matter and this is almost certainly due to the extreme difficulty of isolating an experimental animal from all sources of stimulation other than the one under investigation. As an example take the experience of the most distinguished student of rattlesnakes, Laurence Klauber. In his monumental work on these creatures he writes (Vol. I, p.362): "I made a series of experiments on a large red diamond rattler (*C.r. ruber*) that would rattle upon the slightest disturbance. . . . The snake taught me how necessary, yet difficult, it was to eliminate the possibility of sense impressions reaching it by unsuspected avenues, before one could really judge whether it was susceptible to the direct air waves that we call sound. When I clapped sticks together, with my hands beyond its range of vision, it reacted, but I found it was watching the swinging of my feet beneath the table, for I was sitting on a high stool without a footrest; and when a screen was interposed it caught my movements reflected in a nearby window. It was so extraordinarily sensitive to ground vibrations that footfalls fifteen feet away on a cement floor alarmed it, and this whether it rested on sand or on a blanket. Placed in a closed fibreboard box, and suspended by a rubber band from the centre of a stick that in turn rested on a pillow at each end —a precaution against vibration reaching it through the suspension—it reacted quite readily to sounds of clapped sticks or a radio; but clearly these were transmitted through the box acting as a sounding board, despite the deadening quality of fibreboard. Placed in a muslin sack with the same support it failed to react, but I found it was because this bundling of its body seemed to cow it. Finally, I placed it in a Chinese basket formed of woven bamboo withes, using the rubber band and pillow method of suspension. Again it showed normal sensitivity by rattling at the slightest movement seen through the weave of the basket or to the dropping of a few grains of sand on it from above. But the basket evidently failed to respond to airborne sounds, and the rattler in turn did not react to clapped sticks or a very loud radio but a few feet away, provided the radio was never turned completely off; if it was, the rattler sometimes sensed the heating of the tubes when it was turned on. I eventually tried alternating the radio between silence and full power at a distance of only six inches from the snake's basket, and with the noise at times so loud as to be quite distressing to a person ten feet away. Once or twice the snake reacted—to low notes it seemed to me—but only hesitatingly and briefly; yet with this fearful clatter continuing, it would rattle violently if I came in sight, or touched the supporting crossbar, showing that it was still on the *qui vive*. I finally reached the conclusion expressed by others: that rattlesnakes are deaf to air-borne vibrations unless these vibrate the solid material on which the snake rests or which a part of its body may be touching. To any vibrations so conducted the creature shows extraordinary sensitivity." To this account it might, perhaps, be added that a snake, with its lung full of air, may itself be resonant to sound waves of an appropriate frequency and sense its own vibrations, just as one can often "feel" a loud, low-pitched musical note in the pit of one's stomach.

Observations on other snakes show that the conclusions are generally applicable and not peculiar to rattlesnakes and adders. It is often argued that the behaviour of cobras that "dance" to the piping of snake-charmers must surely indicate their ability to hear their masters' music. But the explanation seems to be that these snakes, accustomed to being kept in the semidarkness of their baskets, rear up in alarm when the lid is taken off at the commencement of a performance. Half blinded by the sudden flood of daylight their attention is caught by the nearest moving object, the swaying piper, and they then sway from side to side in time to his movements. A well-known journalist visiting a "school for snake-charmers" in India found that a radio set held over a tame cobra in its basket elicited no response at all; but when the set was very gently lowered until it touched the basket the reaction was immediate and violent. The air-borne sound waves covering a frequency range at least as great as that perceived by the human ear, from 16 to 20,000 cycles per second, had no effect on the snake, but immediately the cabinet of the set, vibrating at its relatively low resonant frequency of, perhaps, 200 cycles, touched the basket a stimulus was transmitted to the animal. This inability to perceive air-borne vibrations but sensitivity to contact vibration is what one might expect from the structure of a snake's hearing apparatus. In most terrestrial animals, including man, an essential part of the ear is a diaphragm stretched across a cavity which responds to sound waves by vibrating in sympathy with them; each pressure pulse of the sound waves displaces the diaphragm. These very delicate movements of the diaphragm are transmitted by a bony rod, or series of bones, to the inner ear where they activate certain sensory nerve endings that pass messages to the brain via the auditory nerve. Snakes have no ear drum and all the cavities and passages associated with it are lost; so there is nothing to convert the pressure pulses of the sound waves into movements to be transmitted to the inner ear. There is, however, still the bony rod that normally transmits these movements, but its outer end, instead of abutting against a tympanum, is in contact with the bone on which the lower jaw hinges. With such a system the animal cannot be regarded as completely "deaf" since the brain can receive messages through the auditory nerve if any movements are transmitted to the inner ear by the bony rod. This will clearly pick up and transmit vibratory movements of the earth, or whatever it may be, on which the creature's lower jaw is resting and also movements arising from sound waves that are sufficiently violent to, literally, rattle the bones of its skull. The snake's auditory apparatus is useless as a distant warning device by means of sound waves, but it is effective enough in detecting local earth tremors. This fact is reflected in the traditional methods of many primitive peoples for scaring snakes away; when walking abroad at night they thump the ground with a stick, or wear creaking sandals, or walk with an exaggerated shuffling of the feet.

Associated with the ears are the labyrinths which, as already mentioned, work in conjunction with the eyes and muscles to give the sense of balance. These organs operate by the inertia of fluid contained in three intercommunicating semicircular canals each of which lies in a different plane. When the head is moved in any direction the liquid in one or more of the canals tends to get "left behind," setting up currents whose direction and intensity signal to the brain the direction and speed of the movement. The ability of snakes to balance themselves on a twig, or a fence rail, by disposing the body in a series of symmetrical loops on either side of it is well known but the following incident shows their extraordinary power of balancing. A common Grass-snake was picked up out of the water of an estuarine creek and deposited in a small dinghy that was then tied up astern of an anchored yacht, at the end of a painter about ten feet long. There was a slight ripple on the water which kept the dinghy continually bobbing about and snubbing at the painter which was alternately slack and jerking taut. After investigating the inside of the dinghy the snake crawled up on to its gunwale and thence up the jerking, half-inch diameter, painter for a distance of more than six feet. At that point it was alarmed by an inadvertent movement of the observer and immediately turned right round and went back the way it had come. No mean "slack wire" act, performed without benefit of balancing pole or parasol!

The sense of touch is equally as acute as the sense of balance and, as in ourselves is generally disseminated. In many terrestrial and arboreal snakes, however, but not in completely aquatic or burrowing forms, there are some localized sensory spots which some observers think may be special organs of touch though they may equally well be heat receptors. These organs are non-committally referred to as the "apical pits," for they appear as minute circular concavities, just visible to the naked eye, at the tips of all the scales on the back and flanks; sometimes there is a single pit on each scale, sometimes a pair and, more rarely, up to four or five. Each "pit" consists of a circular local thinning of the horny covering of the scale and the epidermal cells beneath it are liberally supplied with bundles of nerve fibres. Whatever may be their function they would not seem to be of very great importance since they may be present or absent even in closely related forms of similar habits. Of considerable importance, however, are some specialized tactile papillae that occur in many colubrid snakes such as the Grass-snakes, Smooth-snake, garter snakes and racers. These papillae, though similar in external appearance, are of two kinds, one of which occurs on the lips and under the chin and the other in the region of the vent. They are used in courtship, when the male rubs his chin over the female's body, and seem to stimulate this activity as well as enabling the animals to orientate themselves correctly towards each other when they are in intimate contact.

The remaining external sense organs come under the heading of chemo-receptors—they sample particles of matter chemically. Human beings have two such senses, smell and taste, and these are present in snakes also, though the latter is probably of little consequence since the tongue, being considerably modified for other purposes, lacks any taste-buds. The nasal passages, however, are dilated into well developed nasal cavities lined by olfactory epithelium that is connected to the brain by a pair of specialized olfactory nerves, and it is a fair presumption that the sense of smell is at least as good as, if not better than, our own. Whether it is as sensitive and discriminating as that of mammals that hunt by scent is doubtful because snakes obviously place more reliance on another organ which has more or less the same functions. This paired organ, known as Jacobson's organ, is a very minor structure of unknown function in other vertebrates, but in snakes and a few lizards it has become the paramount chemo-receptor. Each of the organs is a deeply pigmented saccular structure lying embedded in the anterior part of the palate close to the nasal cavity and communicating with the mouth by a short duct which opens on the palate. They operate in conjunction with the tongue which is very long, with a deeply bifurcated tip and which is highly protrusible (Plate 2), its anterior part telescoping backwards into a sheath-like base. The repeated rapid protrusion of the tongue and the flickering of its twin tips is one of the most characteristic features of snakes and the action is an essential part of the operation of Jacobson's organs. The vibrating tips of the tongue pick up minute air-borne particles which either adhere to, or are dissolved in, the film of moisture on them and then, when the tongue is drawn back into the mouth, they are thrust into the two openings of Jacobson's organs so that the materials they have collected are transferred to the sensory epithelium that lines these structures. The nerve connexion between this epithelium and the brain is a part, though quite a separate and distinct part, of the olfactory nerve, and this suggests that the stimuli conveyed are probably very much akin to those transmitted from the olfactory epithelium of the nasal cavities. In other words snakes have what appears to be an accessory organ of smell, and the almost continuous use of the tongue indicates the reliance that is placed on this sense. Whenever a resting snake is disturbed the first and immediate reaction is protrusion of the tongue, and if attention is drawn to an object by any other sense it is always further investigated by Jacobson's organs. Just as a dog will almost always use its nose to supplement its visual impressions or to regain contact with an object that has disappeared from view, so does a snake use its tongue.

To sum up, snakes have relatively indifferent distant sense receptors; the eyes are ill-adapted and badly situated for detailed distant vision, though sensitive to movement over a wide field, and the ears are incapable of perceiving sound waves though receptive of ground vibrations. For the perception of close range or contact stimuli, however, they are exceptionally well endowed and their whole sensory armature is thus eminently suitable for life in a circumscribed world of near horizons.

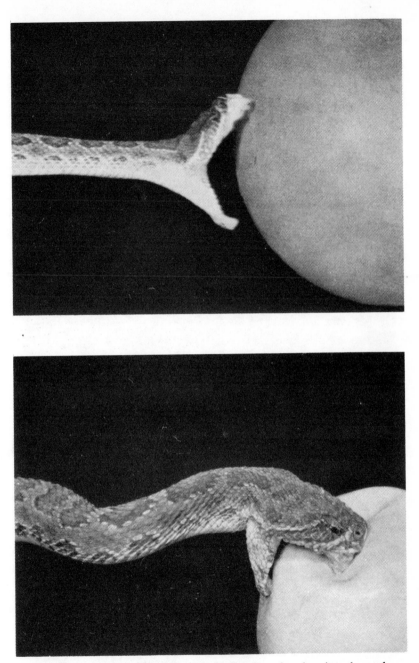

3 Stages in the strike of a Prairie Rattlesnake showing the stabbing action before the mouth closes in a true bite. (*Photos*. Walker Van Riper)

4 African Egg-eating Snake swallowing a hen's egg. (*Courtesy* Prof. Carl Gans and the New York Zoo. Soc.)

IV

The Physical Environment

In these days any discussion of human survival and well-being centres almost automatically on international politics, nuclear physics, diseases, malnutrition and the like; but important as these hazards may be in the artificial world mankind has created they are almost insignificant compared with the dangers that a man, like any other animal, must successfully meet or evade in his daily life. The living organism, be it a man or an amoeba, is a highly complex and intricately integrated assemblage of delicate tissues than can only exist and continue to function within a very narrow range of physical conditions. Unless the tissues get these conditions they die or fail to function, and the organism perishes. Only in a very few places, such as the depths of the oceans, is there any constancy in the physical environment; temperature, light and humidity fluctuate widely by day and by night, from season to season and from place to place; air, soil and water are equally, though less noticeably, variable in their chemical composition. So, to survive, each individual animal must maintain within itself a set of physical and chemical conditions that is not only constant but different in most particulars from those existing in the world around it; only transiently will any one external factor be even approximately suitable for the delicate internal tissues; two or more concurrently, seldom or never.

The external covering must obviously play a vital part in isolating the two environments from each other; not only must it protect against mechanical damage, abrasions and so forth, but it must also be resistant to desiccation, a good thermal insulator and impervious to injurious radiations such as ultraviolet light. The snakes' methods of locomotion, with much sliding friction, make for a great deal of wear, but the need for

49

flexibility precludes the development of a thick, resistant armour such as many other reptiles possess. Their skin, like that of other vertebrates, consists of three principal layers of which the innermost is the thickest and composed mainly of fibres; this layer, the raw material of leather, is soft, elastic and permeable and in it are embedded the pigment cells which produce the colours and pattern. Externally there is a layer of dead, horny material, keratin, which is tough, resistant and almost impervious to water and which is constantly being produced by the middle zone. Reptilian keratin is chemically similar to mammalian hair, nails and claws, but has a lower sulphur content and is tougher and harder, with little or no elasticity. Flexibility and distensibility are provided by a complex series of pleats that divide the surface of the skin up into the scales. The surface of each scale is an unfolded portion of the epidermis and its horny layer is about one thousandth of an inch thick in a medium sized snake. Between the scales the epidermis is continuous and folded inwards under their edges as simple pleats in some places or as box-pleats in others, and is only about half as thick. Where there is a row of transversely enlarged plates across the belly the pleats between them are simple, but on the back and sides where the scales are arranged quincuncially (i.e. like the spots on the fives and tens of playing cards), to form straight rows longitudinally but diagonal rows transversely, the pleating is correspondingly complex, and this no doubt is the reason why the number and arrangement of the scales is quite constant from birth to death in individual snakes and shows little variation from one specimen to another within each species.

Wear and tear are made good by the production of more keratin by the living cells below the epidermis, but whereas in man and other mammals the rate of production is geared to the rate at which the surface is being worn away or subjected to chafe, so that there is continuous and almost imperceptible replacement, in lizards and snakes replacement occurs at periodic intervals when the whole of the epidermis is shed to disclose a completely new layer that has been formed beneath it; in lizards the old skin flakes away in fragments but snakes shed theirs in one piece. This process of sloughing is preceded by physiological changes which result in loosening the old epidermis from the underlying new layer. When this is taking place the skin acquires an opaque, milky appearance that is particularly noticeable over the eyes and which is due to a layer of exudate between the two "skins." At this stage the animal is partially blind, a condition that lasts from a few days to a week or more, and during this time it seeks concealment. The eye then clears and four or five days later the whole of the outer skin is sloughed. The moulting usually begins with much yawning and the snake may be seen rubbing the tip of its snout and its lips on the ground or against some convenient object. Eventually the old skin becomes detached along the lips and the continued rubbing turns it inside out and pushes it backwards over the head. Rippling contractions of the body muscles loosen the skin still further and the snake then crawls out of it, turning it completely inside out in doing so. A normal healthy snake will complete its moult in a matter of minutes, or hours at most, depending upon weather conditions and the availability of suitable objects to rub against, but in captivity the process may take several days and, rarely, assistance may have to be given.

Young snakes undergo their first moult very shortly after they are born or hatched, or even, so it is said in the case of the Adder, before birth. The frequency of subsequent moults varies widely with conditions and the snake's age. In the uniform conditions of captivity they may slough every month or thereabouts, but in the wild state there is less regularity. The Adder, and probably many others too, shed their skins in spring soon after awakening from hibernation, but during the rest of the summer and autumn the frequency depends on age and feeding conditions since, in young snakes it is associated more with growth than with wear. In their first year of life there may be as many as seven or more moults, individuals with abundant food growing more rapidly and sloughing more often; but with increasing age the number diminishes. Individuals and species vary and no hard and fast generalizations are possible; mature individuals of some species, such as a Colorado Desert Sidewinder, have been found to slough only six times in six years, but a five-year-old Mexican West-Coast Rattlesnake moulted six times in one year.

The shed skin of a snake is as delicate and translucent as

tissue paper and has only the slightest suspicion of the snake's colour pattern since, as noted above, the pigment cells lie mainly in the deeper layer of the dermis which is not shed. With the loss of the outermost layer, which by the time it is sloughed is usually discoloured to a pale, dirty brown shade, the natural coloration is more clearly revealed and a newly sloughed specimen is always more brightly coloured and distinctly marked than before. The role of coloration lies mainly in the field of concealment and protection (Chapter VI) but it is also important in relation to the physical environment. Snakes are not known to change colour with variations in the intensity of light, or the colour of the background. as many lizards do, but their pigments form a screen to protect the internal organs against the injurious effects of short wave-length light rays. Many of the deep-burrowing blind snakes, which seldom or never appear on the surface and consequently have no need of such protection, tend to have pale pinkish brown colours due to sparse pigmentation and the only known cave-dwelling snake, found in the Batu Caves near Kuala Lumpur, where it preys on bats, is sometimes called the White Snake. This is something of a misnomer since it is not a distinct species but a very pallid race of the Oriental Striped Racer, a grey or brownish snake with a handsome pattern consisting of an open black network on the fore part of the body and two broad, jet black stripes, one on either flank, posteriorly.

Although the direct effects of light, or the lack of it, are not strikingly evident in the lives of snakes, the effects of temperature are much more profound and widespread, affecting almost every phase of their existence. It is common knowledge that reptiles are "cold-blooded"; this does not mean that they remain constantly at a temperature lower than that of their surroundings but that they have no insulating layer of hair, feathers or subcutaneous fat to conserve heat, or sweat glands or their equivalent to reduce their temperature if it rises unduly. It is nevertheless obvious that, in spite of the lack of these controlling devices, they must so regulate their lives that they avoid or counteract very high and very low temperatures since their tissues are subject to limitations not very different from those of other animals. The upper temperature limit is the more narrowly critical of the two since it has been found that snakes which will tolerate temperatures perhaps as high as 98° F almost indefinitely will die, if exposed to the hot sun or kept in overheated cages, when their body-temperature rises to much more than about 105° F. That is not to say that a snake cannot withstand a higher external temperature for a short period since time is required to raise the body temperature to the lethal level and, moreover, although there are no sweat glands there is some evaporation of moisture from the skin and the internal surfaces of the throat and lungs; so long as this evaporation is maintained it will check or retard any rise in the temperature of the tissues and a snake can actually reduce its temperature by panting. Without doubt there are differences between individual snakes, even of the same species, in the length of time they can withstand supra-lethal external temperatures, mainly because of differences in their weight and volume; smaller specimens will heat up to the danger point more rapidly than larger ones. Between species there are differences in the relative proportions of their lungs and in the permeability of their skins, so that the extent to which they can control their temperature by evaporation will also vary and their heat tolerances will differ accordingly. In addition there are slight, but important, differences in the basic temperature tolerances of the tissues of different species; for instance the Sidewinder, a desert species, has a lethal limit of 108·5° F nearly three degrees higher than that of its fairly close relative the Southern Pacific Rattlesnake which inhabits all types of cultivated land, brush and scrub country from sea-level to 6,000 feet, but avoids the deserts.

The lower temperature limit for survival is less critical, in a sense, because although no snake is known to be able to withstand complete freezing of its tissues, which would occur a few degrees below 32° F, there is a slowing down of all physical activity even at temperatures considerably higher than this and different species differ widely in the duration of the enforced inactivity they can withstand. For example, in one experiment a number of rattlesnakes of six different species were kept at a temperature of 39° F, well above the freezing point, for about ten days; all the specimens of four of the species survived, but those of the other two species, which were lowland forms and normally subject to less rigorous winters, succumbed. In another instance snakes of a different species were kept in a state of complete torpor in an ice-house for three and a half years and all survived. It is, however, clear that although these animals survived under the conditions of the experiments, their chances of doing so under natural conditions would have been negligible unless they had first found a place of safe refuge from enemies and other hazards.

Like all other cold-blooded animals, snakes have to face these two critical problems of avoiding over-heating and over-cooling since there is scarcely a single place on the earth's surface where the temperature remains constantly within the range of 50°—105° F, their approximate lower and upper danger points. It is a common fallacy that a snake's temperature must be very nearly the same as that of the air. In fact, their temperature, except in unheated indoor cages, is almost always very different from that of the air because it is the result of the combined effects of many other factors. These include the heat produced by their own activity; conduction from the ground; radiation from the sun and surrounding objects; their colour and size which determine the amount of radiation absorbed or reflected; and humidity and wind velocity which influence the rate of moisture evaporation. Of these factors conduction and radiation are probably by far the most important, but all of them play their part in determining a snake's reactions which are directed towards maintaining its own temperature at an optimum within the vital limits. At low air temperatures they seek out dry sun-warmed spots where they will obtain a maximum of both conducted heat from the ground and direct solar radiation; but at high temperatures, approaching the lethal level, their reactions are completely reversed and they search for cool, damp and shady places. In these reactions they are extremely selective and can achieve a very remarkable degree of body-temperature constancy. A Sidewinder, for example, has been found to be able to maintain its temperature within the very narrow range of 87°—89° F by alternately exposing itself to the sun or concealing parts of its body in a cavity. And again, many species that live in deserts where the surface temperature varies from below freezing point by night to perhaps 180° F by day, habitually burrow into the soil just far enough to reach a layer of the correct temperature where they remain except for forays in early morning and late evening when the surface temperature is tolerable.

Lizards are able to exercise a considerable amount of temperature control by colour-change; dark colours, being more absorbent of infra-red radiation, lead to a more rapid rise in temperature on exposure to the sun and light colours have the reverse effect. Very few snakes have any marked powers of colour-change but a few of them vary their colour slightly, becoming darker at lower temperatures, and this will undoubtedly enable them to achieve the temperature necessary for full activity more quickly in the mornings after the chill of the night. But, although few species show any powers of individual colour-change, different species and races often exhibit distinct colour adaptations to differing temperature environments. When, for instance, a species has a considerable altitudinal range, from valleys and plains to high mountains, it is often found that the individuals living at the higher levels, where air temperatures are appreciably lower, are much darker in colour; so much so that these highland populations have often been thought to belong to different species. Conversely, species of the tropical deserts tend towards very light colours which, since they reflect the heat rays, will delay a rise in body temperatures on exposure to the sun and so lengthen the periods they can safely spend in its glare. Size, too, is linked with environmental temperatures, since the ratio of superficial area to weight diminishes as size increases (if there is no change in shape or proportions) and the rate of exchange of heat with the environment, whether by conduction or radiation, is closely linked with the total area. So it is to be expected that wherever the environment permits snakes to be fully active for only a brief period during the middle of the day smaller size will be an advantage; not only is the mass to be warmed smaller, but there is a proportionally greater area for heat exchange and they will warm up more quickly in the sun's rays. The species and races of high mountains are consequently not only darker, as already mentioned, but smaller than their lowland relatives; and no very large species occur anywhere in the higher latitudes of the temperate zones. The very large species, such as some of the boas and pythons, can only exist in the tropics because of this time factor in warming up; in colder climates their daily periods of activity would be too short for them to be able to secure sufficient food to carry them over the long periods of forced inactivity. This factor also affects habits as well as controlling geographical distribution. Those first afield in the morning, or on emergence in the spring, will be the smaller individuals, generally the young ones or, if there is a size-difference between the sexes, the smaller sex; males of the common Adder, for example, are active in spring some weeks before the females which are nearly 10 per cent longer and of stouter build.

Winter sleep, or hibernation, is not uncommon even in the "warm-blooded" mammals which are able to maintain their temperature at an optimum and constant level independent of any external source of heat. In their case the need for it is probably more concerned with the necessity for conserving their resources during periods when their normal food is scarce or unobtainable than with the prevailing temperature, but this factor nevertheless has to be reckoned with. When they become inactive their internal supply of heat diminishes and their body temperature then falls as their environment cools. This would be dangerous if it went too far, but they have a physiological warning device which awakens them before the danger point is reached, and the resumption of activity on wakening restores their temperature level. In reptiles, however, the maintenance of an adequate level is so very much dependent on external sources of heat that any such alarm system would be ineffective and their only hope of survival through prolonged periods of frost lies in the selection of a hibernating place where the temperature will not fall below freezing point, except perhaps very transiently. For terrestrial species this almost always means that they must go underground, and the depth to which they must go depends on a variety of factors, but mainly on the conductivity of the soil in relation to the minimum temperatures that will be reached. This at once sets limitations on the areas of the earth's surface that can be inhabited by snakes. None could survive in the arctic or antarctic polar regions where the subsoil is permanently frozen, and very few indeed can approach these limits because, even though refuges safe from frost are available, the summers are so short that the creatures would have to spend too much time in hibernation. In the same way there are limits on mountains, even in the tropics, above which daily "hibernation" would be obligatory. So it is a general rule that the farther north or south one goes from the tropics, or the higher one climbs in the mountains, the fewer are the kinds of snakes to be met. This generalization does not, however, apply to the numbers of individual snakes since population density is controlled by quite different factors such as the availability of food supplies and the prevalence of enemies; one very experienced and internationally known herpetologist has recorded seeing more snakes, mostly Adders, in a single day on heathlands in southern England than during many months' residence in tropical Africa. In northern Europe the Adder crosses the Arctic Circle in Scandinavia and Finland, reaching 68 deg. N. latitude, and the same species reaches nearly 10,000 feet in the Swiss Alps. No snakes range as far north in Asia, but the Himalayan Pit-viper, which favours altitudes of 7—10,000 feet, has been found at the foot of the Dharmsala Glacier at 16,000 feet. On the North American continent a single species, the Common Garter Snake, extends northwards into Labrador and the Yukon, where it reaches 67° North, whilst a close relative, *Thamnophis scalaris* ranges up to 13,000 feet in the mountains of Mexico; in this region the record seems to be held, as in the Himalayas, by a pit-viper (the Mexican Dusky Rattlesnake) which reaches 14,500 feet. In the southern hemisphere no snakes reach Antarctica or any of the sub-polar islands, and the most southerly snake is yet another pit-viper, *Bothrops ammodytoides,* which extends to about 50° South in the province of Santa Cruz, Argentina.

Hibernation in reptiles is not a period of sleep but a state of torpor directly induced by a low temperature. As soon as the animals are unable to keep their temperature up to a certain level they begin to search out suitable quarters in which to take refuge. In the case of the Adder this movement occurs when the maximum shade temperature falls to about 48°—50° F and hibernation ends on the first sunny days after the maximum temperature has reached 46·4° F, although a recurrence of colder weather may drive the animals back again. The duration of the period of hibernation will thus vary with geography and topography and from year to year; the recorded maxima and minima are 275 days in the north and 105 days in southern Europe, with an average of 150 days in Denmark and about a fortnight less in Britain. Probably no other snake has a longer hibernation period than the Adder, the most northerly snake of all, but except in the tropical lowlands all snakes hibernate for longer or shorter periods. To do so successfully burrowing types naturally extend their burrows deeper, but others are to a large extent dependent upon naturally occurring clefts and crannies or upon burrows constructed by other creatures. It is uncertain how they determine in advance (and their torpor precludes the possibility of a second attempt once the temperature has dropped near the danger point) which situation will give the necessary protection. They cannot learn by trial and error, since one error would be fatal, nor is it likely that they learn from the experience of others, directly, since they are for the most part solitary creatures and do not live in family parties. The fact that the same "den" is often tenanted year after year by a number of individuals, and not the same ones, suggests the likelihood that with their highly developed sense of smell they can locate sites that have been previously tenanted and have proved their worth. The required depth of the retreat depends not only on climate and soil conductivity, but on other factors such as aspect, size of aperture, prevailing winds and the nature and amount of the vegetational cover. In Britain a depth of eight inches to a foot in peaty soil suffices for the Adder, but in Denmark, with a more severe winter, the same species is found at varying depths from ten inches to four feet, the shallower burrows being below a cover of heather. In North America some species of rattlesnakes habitually use the burrows of prairie-dogs which may be ten or twelve feet deep, but similar snakes using fissures in rock go down to eight or fifteen feet. Dens are frequently to be found on south-facing slopes, often as if this aspect had been deliberately selected in preference to a nearby north slope which has similar holes or burrows. It is, however, unlikely that this is intelligent selection, but is more likely the outcome of using the south slope, the warmest one, for basking during the days before hibernation begins. The frequency with which dens have more than a single inhabitant indicates that there may be an aggregation instinct as winter approaches, since it is not always due to a scarcity of suitable places. This is indicated by the fact that when known sites are disturbed over a period of years they are abandoned and new ones are brought into use. An observer in British Columbia who was attempting to control the numbers of the dangerous Northern Pacific Rattlesnake raided the dens in his neighbourhood for twenty-four years—and incidentally accounted for close on three thousand in that time. In the first four years only two dens were located and these contained 188 snakes; the larger of the two never had less than fourteen inhabitants and the largest number in any of the winters was fifty-five. During the whole of the remaining twenty years, however, only two snakes were found in the smaller den and thirty-nine in the larger, with none at all in many years. As the numbers in these two dens declined other, new ones were found and each of these in turn showed a similar progressive decline whilst yet other new sites were found which were always more fruitful. The numbers using the same den may be even higher than in this particular instance. As many as forty Adders, accompanied by ten toads and a large number of lizards have been found together in England, and "several hundred" have been found elsewhere in Europe, whilst from South Dakota, it has been reported of rattlesnakes "I think about 250 is the average number hibernating together, though I know of several times this number using the same dens." Such gregarious behaviour has one obvious advantage; a number of snakes massed together present a smaller surface proportionally than they would separately and this must result in greater conservation of the very small amount of heat that is generated in their tissues.

The snakes in a single hibernaculum are usually, but by no means always, of the same species, and other animals too, are often found with them. The presence of lizards and toads with Adders has already been mentioned but in the United States combinations of up to nine different kinds of snakes have been found together, along with, at different times, frogs, toads, lizards, tortoises, bees, skunks, ground-squirrels, raccoons, rabbits, prairie-dogs, mice, other small mammals and the Burrowing Owl (*Speotyto*). The association together of the cold-blooded creatures is fairly obviously the chance result of their convergence upon a single suitable site, but it has been claimed that the co-habitation of snakes with warm-blooded mammals and owls is a mutually beneficial arrangement where the snakes profit from the warmth of the other creatures and give them, in return, some measure of protection against marauding carnivores. This belief, once widely held and still persistent, will not withstand careful scrutiny for although the associations do exist occasionally it is much more usual to find that the entry of snakes into a burrow is soon, if not immediately, followed by a wholesale evacuation of the warm-blooded creatures that were previously in possession.

As well as altering the length of the hibernating and active seasons changes in latitude also affect the daily cycle owing to changes in the proportions of night and day. The two combine to produce marked effects on habits and on growth, the reproductive cycle and even longevity. Many species, and again the Adder provides a good example, are crepuscular in their habits at lower latitudes; with a long, warm summer they tend to be most active in the dusk and early night. But in higher latitudes with their active season reduced, perhaps to a third, life becomes more urgent and to secure enough food to build up reserves for the long winter, to mate and to reproduce, they have to take advantage of every warm hour throughout the day. Even with this increased tempo of summer living, however, they cannot always keep abreast of time. Their rates of growth and development are inevitably slowed down so that, amongst other things, sexual maturity is delayed and the reproductive period extends into two seasons instead of one with the result that young are produced only every other year instead of annually. In compensation, however, their potential life-span is probably increased, though whether this has any practical result for the species as a whole may be doubted because of the increased hazards of the longer severe winter.

It is often said that in warm climates snakes and other reptiles undergo a period of "aestivation" during the hotter part of the summer and that this summer rest is comparable with hibernation. The two phenomena are, however, essentially different in their nature. Hibernation is a state of torpor induced by a low temperature and it becomes progressively more intense as the temperature falls; there is a wide gap between their activity temperature and the lethal level. At the other end of the temperature scale, however, there is an abrupt transition from temperatures that can be tolerated (for longer or shorter periods) to those that produce rigor of the muscles and death;

there is no half-way house of compulsory physiological torpor. So, at high temperatures the animals have to take refuge underground or in cooler, shady places where they remain physiologically active but are too confined to be able to go about their normal business. For the inhabitants of the true sub-tropical or temperate-zone deserts short periods of stagnation of this nature are of almost daily occurrence but in other tropical countries, where there are often well-marked wet and dry seasons, aestivation of longer duration is associated with the latter, and it may not be wholly a temperature effect. Apart from their cooling effect in hot weather, rainfall and increased humidity have their own effects which arise from the need of all animals for water. In this respect snakes are physiologically better able than most animals to get along with the minimum amount to drink though they all need to do so on occasion. Mammals have to replace the large amounts of water lost in perspiration and in getting rid of their waste products in solution in their urine; but a snake loses relatively little by evaporation and there is no urine, waste nitrogenous material being excreted in a semi-solid form as uric acid. Species living under different conditions have different water requirements, e.g. desert species lose less water by evaporation through their skin than do those living in more humid places, but the water requirements of an average snake are surprisingly low. It has been calculated that the *annual* liquid intake of, for instance, a Northern Pacific Rattlesnake, is no more than about its own body weight, whereas under similar climatic conditions a human being would need, proportionally a similar amount, or more, every month. Snakes drink from any available source such as ponds and streams or dew drops, usually by sucking up the liquid, though a few observers have claimed, rather improbably, that they also use their tongues to lap. During hibernation or aestivation the amount of water needed is less than at other times, because of the reduced activity, and the animal's needs are supplied by what is known as "metabolic water," i.e. water produced by the animal in its own tissues from its food reserves. Every hundred grammes of reserve fat used up produces more than its own weight of water by oxidation, and other reserve foods, such as proteins and carbohydrates, produce water in the same way though in lesser amounts. All snakes accumulate considerable food reserves in a pair of special "fat-bodies" which, lying alongside the testes or ovaries, occupy a large part of the hinder part of the body cavity. These reserves are consumed during the winter and are a vital part of the adaptations that make hibernation possible. During the active parts of the annual cycle, however, whilst reserves are being replenished, the animals must drink and it is very noticeable how rain increases their activity. In countries with alternating wet and dry seasons the onset of the monsoon or the rainy season brings out the terrestrial snakes in numbers and even in countries such as England where there is no such periodicity, rain following a dry spell in July will cause an apparent increase in the numbers of snakes, especially Grass-snakes.

As well as being a physiological necessity, water in bulk affects snakes as it does all other air-breathing creatures; it is a restricting factor circumscribing the areas in which they can live. For the majority it presents a hazard since, although all snakes can swim, those not specially adapted for aquatic life are indifferent performers. Sudden floods take a heavy toll, especially among burrowing species that may be trapped in their burrows and on the great waterways, of South America in particular, it is a common occurrence for numbers of snakes of all kinds to be swept away on rafts of drifting vegetation to destinations where they will be unable to survive. A large number of species, however, have achieved an effective compromise between life in water and life in air. Their methods of locomotion in water have already been discussed, but their other major problem is that of respiration. Although a few newts and salamanders are able to obtain all the oxygen they need through their skin, no other terrestrial vertebrates have been able to dispense with their lungs when they have reverted to life in water. Instead, they have developed nostrils sited so that they may breathe in whilst they briefly visit the surface but which can be plugged to exclude water when submerged. The truly aquatic snakes have nostrils of this pattern and, with their very extensive lungs and their air sacs (see Chapter I) they can remain under water for lengthy periods. Parenthetically it may be noted that some desert snakes, such as the vipers *Pseudocerastes* and *Eristicophis* of Arabia and Baluchistan, also have valvular nostrils to exclude dust and sand. It is not known whether any aquatic snakes possess a mechanism such as seals have and which slows down the rate of heart-beat to reduce oxygen consumption during submergence, but this may occur in some sea-snakes which are amongst the most completely aquatic of all air-breathing animals. They are reported to be able to supplement their supplies of atmospheric oxygen by taking up dissolved oxygen from the water through the skin but they have another problem which does not confront their freshwater relatives; they cannot avoid taking in vastly more salt than their tissues can tolerate. A human being whose salt concentration in the blood must remain at about 0·75 per cent cannot drink sea water with an average content of about 3·5 per cent of salt and survive for very long. And nor could a seasnake unless it had the means of getting rid of the excess. The kidneys of mammals normally remove a certain amount of salt in solution, but the quantity the reptilian kidney can deal with is negligible because of the very small amount of liquid it excretes. Marine birds, which have exactly the same problem, have acquired special salt-glands that secrete a liquid which may contain 50—60 per cent more salt than the sea water in which they live, and the marine turtles have glands with a similar function. In their case the glands discharge by ducts opening in the posterior corner of the eye and their copious secretion produces the tears that are such a frequently noticed accompaniment of their egg-laying visits to the shore; even Lewis Carroll's Mock Turtle "looked at them with large eyes full of tears!" Sea-snakes shed no such tears since any lachrymal fluid drains from the space between the cornea and the spectacle into the nasal cavity via a large lachrymal duct; and it is still uncertain which of the numerous head glands is the one concerned with the elimination of salt. The probability seems to be that it is not one of the glands associated with the eye but, as in the marine iguana from the Galapagos Islands, one of the nasal glands. These lie beneath the skin on the sides of the snout, discharging by ducts into the nostrils, and if the iguana's blood stream is overloaded with salt, their secretion becomes very saline, containing nearly 60 per cent more salt than normal sea water.

V

Food and Feeding

In any large group of animals it is usual to find great diversity in the nature of the food and in the methods of securing it, but snakes are exceptional in that there are neither herbivores nor carrion eaters amongst them; they are all strictly carnivorous and even freshly killed animals are not accepted under the normal conditions of freedom. A very wide range of animals enters into their dietary, though individual species may have strictly limited preferences, but they are again unusual since they must swallow their victims whole; no snakes have cutting or grinding teeth to reduce the prey to smaller dimensions. This is the more remarkable since their elongate shape must be accompanied by a smaller and narrower mouth relative to the volume of their body and this would restrict them, other things remaining equal, to a diet of small animals that would have to be available in very great numbers to provide sufficient nutriment. This limitation has, however, been overcome by the development of a distensible mouth that can be stretched in almost all directions; not only is there a tremendous vertical gape but the two halves of the lower jaw can be pushed apart sideways and can act independently and alternately. The result is a mouth that, when fully stretched, will permit the entry of objects of much greater diameter than the snake's own head. Naturally, as mentioned in an earlier chapter, the skull has had to be much modified to make this mobility and distensibility possible and the salient points in these modifications can be seen by reference to Figures 1 and 2. In a typical lizard the bones that compose the upper jaw are firmly united with one another to form a rigid U-shaped structure which, in turn, is firmly attached to the other bones of the snout; the complete assembly of snout and upper jaws has, at most, a slight vertical hingeing movement on the hinder part of the skull. In a typical snake, however, the upper jaw bones, though arranged in the same U-shape, are only loosely attached to each other and to the rest of the snout, by elastic ligaments so that each can move a short distance in any direction independently of the other elements. Even the bones of the snout are not firmly fixed to one another and there are three transverse hinge-lines so that the end of the snout can be curled upwards. A lizard's lower jaw also forms a nearly rigid U that has only a vertical swinging movement on the hinges where it is attached to the hinder part of the cranium; but in a snake the arrangement is very different indeed. The front part of each half of the lower jaw, the bone on which the teeth are inserted (dentary), is not only slightly moveable on the hinder part, but is not attached to its fellow of the opposite side; instead the two halves of the jaw are connected by an extremely elastic ligament. As a result each half can swing downwards at the point where it is hinged to the cranium and can also rotate sideways and outwards, stretching the ligament that connects it with its fellow. As if this were not enough the hinge joints, instead of being actually on the rigid cranium, are on the ends of two struts (quadrate bones) that can swing outwards from the cranium and so increase the distance between the hinges themselves, sometimes by as much as fifty per cent. To permit all this movement the skin and other tissues naturally have to be extremely elastic, but it must not be assumed that all the movements are under direct, voluntary muscular control. A snake can open its mouth in a wide yawn, and can wrinkle its nose, and slide its upper jaw backwards and forwards or even rotate it so that the teeth point forwards instead of downwards, by direct muscular action; but it cannot separate the two halves of its lower jaw sideways to their full extent against the pull of the elastic ligament, except by forcing something into the mouth. Having no limbs with which to do this it is rather in the position of a one armed man trying to push his hand into a rubber glove; and the swallowing process is correspondingly complicated.

Basically the process depends on two factors, the teeth and a co-ordinated system of movements by the right and left halves of each jaw. The teeth vary in size and number in different forms but are always sharply pointed, curved and thorn-like

(Figures 1 and 2) with their tips directed backwards; there are normally six rows of them, four along the crests of the half-jaws and a parallel pair on the roof of the mouth. They are fused into shallow pits on the bones and, not being deeply rooted and socketed like those of mammals, they are comparatively easily broken off. To compensate for this, there is a system of regular and continuous replacement throughout life. By the side of each of the six rows there is a shallow trench, bordered by a fold of skin (the *vagina dentis*), and in it replacements for each functional tooth develop one after another. From time to time every other tooth of the functional series is shed and the most advanced of the replacement series moves up into its place and becomes fused to the jaw bones so that at least every alternate tooth in each series is always fully formed and ready for action. The frequency with which the regular changes are made is not known but is almost certainly variable with age and conditions, and from species to species; in captive rattlesnakes the intervals between fang replacements have been reported to be from three to twelve weeks. When, however, there is accidental damage replacement follows almost at once and a captive snake whose fangs were extracted regularly produced replacements equally regularly, sixteen times in sixteen weeks.

In the swallowing process the victim (which may or may not have been immobilized by one or other of the methods to be discussed later) is seized in the mouth at some point, usually the head, which is sufficiently narrow for the teeth of both upper and lower jaw, at least of one side, to be engaged. Then, whilst the teeth of one side, say the right, maintain a grip those of the left side are pushed forwards over the prey for a short distance; and so on. The hooked shape of the teeth permits them to slide forwards over the meal when the jaws are pushed forwards, but causes them to dig deeper when the thrust is reversed. So, there is a succession of ratchet-like actions by alternate sides of the head which slowly but inexorably draw the snake's mouth over its food. The whole procedure is very laborious, the more so the larger the meal, and the time taken varies accordingly from a minute or less to an hour or more; stories that it may take days or even weeks can be discounted. Nevertheless it is clear that, with its mouth and gullet stretched to capacity and blocked by the food, even for minutes, any snake would be in danger of suffocation unless it had some special provision for breathing whilst eating. This exists in the form of a protrusible glottis. The anterior end of the wind-pipe is furnished with special muscles by whose action it can be protruded out of the mouth, or withdrawn, and during a meal it is pushed forwards over the tongue until it lies between the separated halves of the lower jaw where it is clear of the food; the wind pipe itself is prevented from collapsing under pressure by a series of annular rings of cartilage that reinforce its walls.

The swallowing apparatus of all snakes conforms to this pattern, though the degree of mobility and distensibility of the mouth varies, being least developed in those which prey on soft-bodied invertebrates such as earthworms. These types also have little difficulty in subduing their victims which are just seized and swallowed without more ado. But, where the normal food consists of the larger, more active and stronger vertebrates, the victim must be killed or immobilized before swallowing can begin, or a bitter struggle would develop with the issue not always a foregone conclusion. The methods used for the subjugation of the prey are brute force, constriction, or venom, though popular belief often adds a fourth—hypnosis. The literature of travel, exploration and natural history, particularly in the seventeenth and eighteenth centuries, abounds in recorded instances of animals being "charmed" out of safe retreats to become the apparently willing victims of hungry snakes; and a belief in their hypnotic powers still persists where a morbid thrill is preferred to the mundane truth. Many of the stories undoubtedly have some factual basis. Sick or moribund animals, like a rabbit with myxomatosis or one that has been bitten and then released by a venomous snake, will offer no resistance to capture and be unable to flee; or like a rabbit watching the approach of a fox or a stoat it may be just inquisitive and unsuspecting; or perhaps a bird was fluttering around in its endeavour to distract attention from a near-by nest. There is certainly no worth-while evidence in favour of hypnosis and very little suggestion that any creatures except men and monkeys, and a few that prey on snakes, regard them with any but neutral feelings.

Most snakes show limited preferences in their selection of prey; thus, in a survey of the diet of adult snakes of some eighty-two species more than half (forty-four) were found to eat only animals of one particular class, e.g. birds, or frogs, or fish or insects; twenty-eight others were less selective, eating two classes; six spread their attentions over three classes and two each over four and five. One of them, the Indian Rat-snake ate frogs, lizards, snakes, birds and mammals. Size naturally enters into the question so that the same species often has a different dietary at different periods of its life. For instance, the common Grass-snake as an adult is mainly a frog-eater but the very young take worms and slugs and tadpoles; and though young Adders eat insects, spiders and worms, adults prefer lizards and small mammals. A great many non-venomous snakes are restricted in their choice to small or feeble creatures that can be swallowed without any preliminary subjugation, but a great many others will often throw one or two coils of their bodies around the victim to hold it whilst the swallowing process gets under way (Plate 5). This is a simple form of constriction that reaches its peak in the large boas and pythons (though by no means restricted to these groups) and which is subject to much popular misconception. It is one of the common fallacies that the large constricting snakes, indiscriminately referred to as "boa constrictors," crush their victims into a sausage-like mass and lick them all over to cover them with saliva for ease of swallowing. This fantastic belief has almost certainly arisen from the appearance of prey that has been regurgitated by a snake disturbed during, or just after, a meal. The victim has been crushed and mangled not only by the constricting coils but during the swallowing process, and is covered with mucus and digestive juices from the snake's stomach. Constriction kills not so much by crushing as by strangulation, the victim being unable to breathe because of the pressure on its ribs and, this, in the case of a large snake, can be very great indeed. Boas, pythons and anacondas can, and often do, kill and eat such muscular animals as pigs and deer and reports of these incidents can conjure up quite erroneous impressions of the size of the victims. The deer and wild pigs that can be swallowed even by the biggest snakes are not in the size-range of even the smaller domestic breeds; proportionally the largest meal ever observed by a very experienced game warden in Africa was a not quite fully grown Situtunga, weighing about 60 lb. that had been eaten by a thirteen-foot Rock Python and the same observer estimated that a thirty-foot python "would probably be able to swallow an antelope of not unusual bulk, weighing about 150 lb."

Effective as constriction certainly is for subduing prey, it cannot compare with the hypodermic injection of venom, which is practised not only by snakes but other creatures such as insects, spiders and some fishes. The full development of an efficient venom-apparatus requires the evolution of two things harmoniously; production of a substance that will either paralyse or kill and the means of delivering it. In snakes the venom is the product of the salivary glands. which normally produce digestive enzymes capable of breaking down complex organic compounds to simpler substances, and it is introduced into the victim's blood stream by the teeth. The first stage in the evolution of poisonous snakes probably arose when the saliva became a more potent digestive agent, powerful enough and sufficiently rapid in its action to cause almost immediate damage to the tissues of any animal that was bitten. This condition still exists in some of the "harmless" snakes of the family Colubridae (Chapter VIII) where the saliva is weakly toxic, but where there are no specially modified teeth to carry any considerable quantities of it into the victim's blood. As an example the Yellow-lipped Snake of the south-eastern United States may be mentioned. It is a frog-eater and when it captures one it does not immediately commence swallowing it, as most other snakes would do, but holds it in its mouth until the small quantity of saliva that has entered by the tooth-punctures takes effect and causes paralysis. From such a simple beginning it is only a short step to the condition of the fairly numerous "back-fanged" snakes that are all technically venomous but of which only a few are dangerous to human beings. In this group the last two to four or five teeth at the hinder end of the upper jaw are enlarged to a greater or lesser extent and each has a groove from its base to its tip. The ducts from the salivary glands, which lie on the sides of the head behind the eyes, open near the bases of the fangs and the grooves provide a channel along which the toxic saliva enters the fang punctures. This mechanism is not highly efficient and usually the snakes need to maintain a grip on their victims until the small quantity of venom injected has had time to take effect. Much greater efficiency exists in the cobras and their allies (Chapter IX) where the fangs, as well as being larger, are situated in a more advantageous position at the front of the mouth and are perforated by a canal instead of an open groove. The canal is, in fact, derived from an open groove, but this is so deep that its lips grow over to meet each other except at the base and tip of the tooth, where it remains open; the duct from the venom (salivary) gland is closely applied to the basal opening and muscular pressure on the gland forces poison through the canal and out at the tip of the fang. When these creatures strike at their prey, and this takes place with great speed (eight to ten feet per second), the mouth is opened nearly to 180 deg. and at the same time the end of the snout is curled upwards so that the fangs point slightly forwards instead of vertically downwards as they do when the mouth is closed. At the moment when the fangs touch the victim the mouth is closed driving the fangs in and simultaneously a jet of venom is forced through them. There is no need here for the grip to be maintained if the strike has gone truly home since the poison acts so rapidly that, normally, any animal small enough to be eaten will be overcome within minutes and the snake will be able to trail it by scent and devour it at leisure. This is not, however, an invariable rule for some of the true cobras are notorious for hanging on and "worrying" their victims, driving their fangs in again and again.

More elaborate still is the injection apparatus of the vipers (Chapter IX), where the fangs are not only perforated from base to tip by a completely enclosed duct, but are so long that they have to be folded back to allow the mouth to be closed. This is made possible by a great shortening of the maxillary bone which, instead of being as long as the mouth with anything up to fifty or more teeth as it may be in the non-venomous snakes, is shorter than it is deep and bears only a single functional fang (though two may be present for short periods when replacement is taking place). As may be seen from Figure 6 the maxilla can be rotated on a horizontal axis transverse to the head so that the fang lies parallel with, or vertical to, the palate. This movement, contrary to what is sometimes stated, is under voluntary muscular control and a yawning viper may sometimes be seen to erect first one fang and then the other, or both together. When about to strike the mouth is widely opened, the head thrown back and both fangs erected so that they point

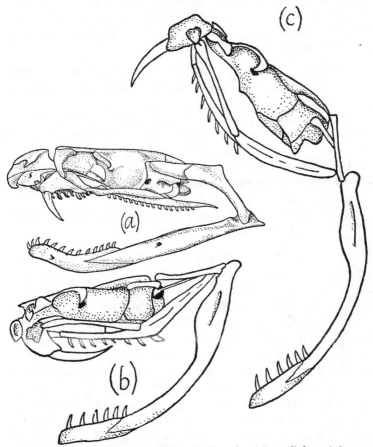

Figure 6. Side views of the skulls of: (a) a Cobra (*after* Bogert); (b) a rattlesnake with mouth nearly closed and fangs folded (*after* Klauber); (c) a rattlesnake ready to strike (*after* Klauber).

nearly straight forwards; the victim is stabbed with the fangs before the mouth closes in a bite, as may be seen from Plate 3.

Since the poison apparatus is primarily concerned with securing food, it is to be expected that the toxicity of the venom will be related to the kind of food eaten, and within limits this is so. The venom is not a single substance common to all poisonous snakes but a complex mixture in which the proportions of the different ingredients and their nature varies from species to species and even from individual to individual. The number of different chemical substances involved is quite large but they can be conveniently grouped into a few categories according to their effects. One such grouping is:

(1) Neurotoxins that act on the nervous system, especially the motor nerves; they cause cardiac and respiratory failure.

(2) Blood clotting agents which produce thrombosis.

(3) Anti-coagulants that reduce the clotting power of the blood and result in profuse bleeding.

(4) Substances that destroy the blood corpuscles, the linings of the blood vessels and other tissues (haemorrhagins, haemolysins, cytolisins, etc.)

(5) A substance that causes rapid spreading of the venom through the tissues (hyalurodinase).

Substances of the last two categories probably occur in the venoms of all poisonous snakes. Their injection into the prey not only kills or incapacitates it but also accelerates digestion; it has repeatedly been observed that the rate of digestion in captive snakes is much faster when they are fed on live animals that they kill for themselves than when they have been trained to accept dead food. In fact, snakes whose venom contains a preponderance of tissue destroying agents are practising a form of "external digestion" very much in the same way as do spiders and such insects as the larvae of glow-worms and water beetles (*Dytiscus*) that have perforated mandibles through which digestive juices are pumped into their victims to kill and predigest them. Few snakes, however, rely entirely on these tissue destroying agents whose action is rather slow to incapacitate, but the back-fanged snakes and the vipers tend on the whole, though with many exceptions, to have venom in which they preponderate. The vipers always have some of the more rapidly acting nerve poisons and in the cobra group substances of this type are the main constituents of the venom. In general, snakes of the same species have toxins of the same chemical composition but the proportion in which each is present, and the total concentration is subject to variation depending on age, and other factors. Thus, in young snakes the total concentration is often less than in adults and it may also be lower for some time after a meal on account of the time taken to secrete a fresh supply; when rattlesnakes are milked of their venom the yield of dry venom may be only 15 per cent of the original yield seven days later and even after fifty-four days the original strength may not have been regained. The range of individual variation within a local population can also be very high; on the basis of the least quantity required to kill test animals of a standard size Cottonmouths were found to vary by 15 per cent and adult Timber Rattlesnakes show differences as great as five to one in their venom-toxicity. With so much possible variation in animals from one geographical area it is naturally difficult to say precisely how much of the variation that exists between different geographical races is genuinely due to inherent differences in the different stocks. One experimenter who allowed himself to be bitten by Adders from various parts of Europe came to the conclusion that, using the nature and severity of his symptoms as a criterion, the Adder was not a single species at all, but ought more appropriately to be subdivided into two genera with not less than about twenty-one species and varieties galore! More precise experiments confirm that there are, indeed, marked differences in the venom of individuals from different areas (though not to the extent suggested) and this appears to be the general rule for all snakes with a wide geographical distribution; as another example, in three geographical races of the Prairie Rattlesnake, from the Great Plains, the Grand Canyon and the Great Basin of California, the toxicity of the venom to mice was in the ratio of 3·1 to 2·2 to 1.

Another factor that complicates the picture and makes it impossible to compile any graded list of snakes in order of virulence is that the same venom usually has different effects on different kinds of animals. Thus, rabbits are twice as susceptible to cobra venom as dogs, and twenty-five times more susceptible than the Asiatic Mongoose; it takes six times as much venom from a Diamond Rattlesnake to kill rats as it does to despatch rabbits or guinea-pigs; the minimum lethal dose of Australian Black-snake venom is ten to twenty times greater for cats than for monkeys of the same size; and so on. Differences such as these arise, of course, from differing degrees of immunity. The Asiatic Mongoose has a high degree of immunity, at least to cobra venom, the European hedgehog to viper poison, and certain skunks and opossums to the bites of the snakes on which they may feed. Sometimes immunity arises from naturally occurring anti-bodies in the blood-serum; for instance a single cubic centimetre of the serum of an Argentinian skunk will neutralize, in a test tube, quantities of Pit-viper venom that would kill several pigeons. In other instances, however, there may be natural immunity without anti-bodies; another skunk, which occurs high in the Andes where no vipers occur, is equally immune to their venoms, but its blood contains no anti-bodies. Immunity is obviously as complex a problem as the composition of venom.

Chemically, the different ingredients of venom are all proteins and the extent of the chemical differences between species may be judged from the estimated molecular weights of some of them; for example, the molecular weights of the active principles in three mainly neurotoxic poisons were found to be: South American Rattlesnake nearly 30,000; Australian Tiger Snake more than 20,000; some cobras, less than 5,000. With so much possible variability in both the composition of venom and in the susceptibility of different animals there is clearly a large number of possible permutations and combinations in some of which venom will be particularly deadly for one animal and almost innocuous for some other with every gradation in between. It is sometimes stated that the venom of a snake is "adapted" to its normal prey and there is often a very close linkage. To some extent this may arise from necessity and experience. A snake with a venom effective against, say, birds but less effective against some other equally abundant creature, such as lizards, would catch many more birds if it attacked both indiscriminately, and would fare even better if it learnt by experience. But this can scarcely be the whole story for it seems unlikely that sea-snakes took to the sea, with all the complications that involves, because their venom was especially toxic for fish but less so for terrestrial creatures; nor, again, is it likely that the Indo-Australian White-bellied Water-snake took to such an unusual diet as crabs merely because its venom was very lethal for these creatures and less so for fish and frogs.

There is naturally a close linkage between a snake's habitat and the nature of the preferred food; Grass-snakes which feed mainly on frogs frequent open woodlands, hedgerows and marshy places whereas Adders, that prey on lizards, field mice and voles, show a preference for open moorland, sandy heaths and dry hillsides; and so forth. In most instances the food is actively hunted by sight or smell though species with concealing colours often prefer merely to lie in wait, relying on their colour and posture to disguise them until a suitable victim wanders within range for a sudden strike. Only a few species appear to have any arrangement for attracting their food, but the presentation of a lure seems to be reasonably well authenticated in a few. For example, the Hump-nosed Viper of Ceylon and southern India has a general grey or brown colouring, with rows of darker spots, but its tail is yellow or reddish and is in striking contrast to the rest of the body, especially in young specimens where the colour is more vivid. Juveniles observed in captivity were found to lie coiled up when at rest with their tails concealed under the coils of the body; but when lizards were put into the cage the young snakes protruded and wriggled their tails. The lizards promptly investigated and snapped at these "worms" only to be themselves bitten. Similar behaviour has been recorded in the American Copperhead and other species with distinctively coloured tails may also use them in the same way. But another type of lure is used by the Fishing Snake, a species found in the pools and sluggish waters of Siam and neighbouring countries. On the tip of its snout are two blunt tentacles which, unlike the nasal horns that are found in some other snakes, are muscular and can be agitated to act as decoys for unwary fish.

Although such devices for attracting victims within easy reach are rare, specializations for actually capturing and dealing with particular types of food are more common. In the same way that there is a connexion between the venom and the preferred food, some snakes profit from a natural immunity to prey on other venomous snakes. Amongst the better known examples of this phenomenon are the King-snakes of North America which, though they are not themselves poisonous, are very resistant to the venom of pit-vipers; they are constricting snakes with a varied diet which includes such dangerous forms as rattlesnakes, copperheads and cottonmouths. The African File-snakes, too, presumably have some immunity (though this has not been checked experimentally) for they are constrictors like the king snakes and prey almost exclusively on the venomous Night Adder. The Hamadryad is another almost entirely snake-eating species; it is not a constrictor but a poisonous species with a highly neurotoxic venom and, contrary to what might be expected, seems to have relatively little immunity since, although it does take venomous snakes, including its own kindred, it prefers those that are non-poisonous. Other species also show varying degrees of fondness for snakes as food, but many of the recorded instances of one snake eating another as big as itself, or attempting to eat one even larger, arise from crowded conditions in captivity where a single cage houses several specimens, maybe of different species. Under these conditions it is inevitable that, from time to time when food is introduced into the cage, two snakes seize and being to swallow the same object from opposite ends. Once the swallowing reaction is under way it is not easily stopped so that when the two heads meet, the one with the larger gape is quite likely to engulf the head of the other and just go on swallowing. Many other abnormal events may occur under the conditions of captivity and articles of diet will be accepted that would never be taken by a wild snake. There is a widespread belief, fostered by the *Jungle Book* and other works of fiction, that milk is a highly prized natural food. In nearly every country in the world there is the belief that snakes in general, or one species in particular, habitually suck the teats of farm stock and seriously diminish the milk yield. In North America, for example, a near relative of the king-snakes has the accepted though completely misleading popular name of Milk Snake, but there is not a shred of evidence that this, or any other snake, indulges in such a malpractice. Even captive snakes usually refuse milk unless they are denied access to water, and it is in the highest degree unlikely that a milch cow, or any other mammal, would willingly suckle anything with a mouth as full of sharp, needle-like teeth as a snake. The origin of the legend probably lies in a lowering of the milk yield caused by nocturnal disturbances when snakes have been hunting rodents or seeking warmth and shelter in and around the byres.

Another popular belief is that all snakes are fond of eggs and will raid nests and hen-houses in search of them. There is more truth in this since, although the commotion in the fowl-house, with broken eggs resulting, is more often caused by a marauding snake looking for rats or perhaps even a chicken, there are species that do take eggs. Some of them, such as the Scarlet Snake of North America and *Oophilositum* in Africa concern themselves with the eggs of other snakes and lizards, which, having a parchment-like, and not a hard, shell can be swallowed with no more difficulty than any more usual article of food. Some others will also take birds' eggs, if these are small enough, but six species, five in Africa and one in India, have a special device for dealing with eggs, and live on them almost exclusively. In the region of the throat there is a row of twenty-nine to thirty-four tooth-like structures which are bony projections from the lower surface of some of the vertebrae. The first seventeen to eighteen of these prominences are long blade-like keels and this series is followed by a smaller group of four to eight which are broader and flatter, being merely oval, rounded humps. These are followed by a group of five to nine strong, peg-like projections which point downwards and forwards, and project into the throat through its dorsal wall. These structures are employed in breaking the egg-shell and the method of swallowing an egg and bringing them into play verges on the incredible. The egg is first investigated by the tongue (and if addled it will be ignored) and then, if it is a large one, the snake arches its head and neck over it as if measuring it for size; an adult African Egg-eater three feet in length and with an average diameter of about one inch will tackle an average-sized hen's egg with a diameter of about one and three-quarter inches. After a few preliminary yawns, as if limbering up, the widely opened mouth is pushed against one end of the egg which is prevented from sliding away by a loop of the hinder part of the body (Plate 4). Then the normal swallowing movements begin, alternate sides of the head being successively advanced until the egg is completely engulfed, a process which may take perhaps a quarter of an hour. The snake then arches its neck so that the egg in its throat is gripped between the blade-like vertebral "teeth" nearest the head and the peg-like teeth farther back, and, as pressure is applied, the latter puncture the shell. When this has been achieved the curvature of the neck is reversed so that the egg is pressed against the blunt, oval teeth in the middle of the series and the shell, weakened by the punctures, collapses and its contents are squeezed onwards into the stomach; some time afterwards the crushed shell is regurgitated. In the equatorial belt, where birds nest continuously the year through, the egg-eaters face no seasonal shortage, but some of them occur outside this zone, in northern Bengal, for example, and in the Union of South Africa. What alternative diet they have seems to be unknown though one of the African species has been recorded as feeding on the fruits of *Mormordica* and this constitutes one of the only two records of snakes deliberately eating vegetable matter; the other concerned an Indian python which was killed and found to have two mangoes in its stomach.

The rejection of crushed and unwanted shells is a unique phenomenon despite the fact that many snakes eat equally hard-shelled food such as insects, crustaceans and snails. In dealing with snails the thirst snakes (somewhat inappropriately named after a mythological serpent, Dipsas, whose bite was fabled to engender an overpowering and fatal thirst) avoid eating the shell and have developed a method of extracting the soft tissues. Their upper jaw is very short, sometimes with only four or five teeth, but the lower jaw is disproportionately long and very mobile, being capable of swinging forwards well in front of the end of the snout. Snails are seized by the head and, with the upper jaw teeth firmly fixed there, the lower jaw is forced into the opening of the shell, its teeth engaged in the soft tissues and then withdrawn with a slight rotary motion, dragging the snail with it (Plate 11(b)). Among the burrowing thread-snakes, too, there is at least one species that avoids overloading its digestive system with indigestible shell. Most of the thread-snakes frequent the habitations of termites and feed on some of the different castes of these creatures, notably the soft-bodied "workers"; the "soldiers" with their enormous armoured heads and powerful jaws are avoided. The only species whose feeding has been observed was found to seize its victim by the soft abdomen and suck out its contents, discarding the remainder.

Although there are advantages in specialization, even in

regard to food, there are clearly some drawbacks; notably when its abundance fluctuates widely and there are long periods when it is scarce or unobtainable. In such circumstances a snake must either rely on an alternative food supply or be prepared to fast. A snake's fat bodies which enable it to survive through many months of hibernation, can also tide it over other periods of food scarcity and some of the larger, stouter forms of the tropics, such as puff-adders, boas and pythons, which never need to hibernate, can survive without food and with surprisingly little loss of weight for periods of more than a year. Relatively few snakes are completely restricted to a single food-animal but in some instances their predator-prey relationship is so nicely balanced that changes affecting their prey may have considerable repercussions. For example, one of the snakes of California is a slug-eater and so restricted in its diet that at one time it was seldom or never seen except during a short season when the native Californian slugs were most active. When, however, some European slugs were introduced by accident and became established and abundant, the snake's habits altered and its seasons of appearance changed to coincide with the active periods of the new comer. The adage "Times change and we change in them" states a fact that applies not only to humanity.

VI

Defence

Although the Indian Mongoose, in the person of Rikki-Tikki-Tavi, has been immortalized as the arch-enemy of snakes, their foes include a vast number of other predatory creatures as well as their quota of parasites and diseases. Man is undoubtedly the greatest enemy of all, not only because of his incessant fear-engendered attacks but, even more, by reason of his continuous destruction or alteration of the environments in which they live. Among the predators, "cannibalistic" snakes like the file-snakes and the Hamadryad have already been mentioned and there are many others which, though less exclusively ophiophagous, prey on their kindred to some extent. The Mongoose is often credited with a special enmity towards venomous snakes, but this seems to be in the nature of a fable and the truth of the matter is indicated by the results that followed its introduction into some of the islands of the West Indies. This deliberate introduction was made late in the nineteenth century in an endeavour to control the numbers of rats and also of the Fer-de-lance which was causing many deaths among the workers in the sugar-cane plantations. But the experiment was far from being an unqualified success for, although there was some reduction in the Fer-de-lance population, the harmless local snakes were almost, or completely exterminated and worse was to follow. With no harmless snakes left, chickens were more attractive than Fer-de-lances, so that the original nuisance persisted and a new one was added! Many other predatory mammals, including such a diverse assortment as dogs, foxes, badgers, coyotes, opossums and skunks, will occasionally eat snakes, but probably the greatest enemy is the pig, a fact recorded long ago by Aristotle and Pliny and so generally appreciated that it is a common practice in many

5 Smooth-snake eating a lizard. (*Photo*. G. Kinns)

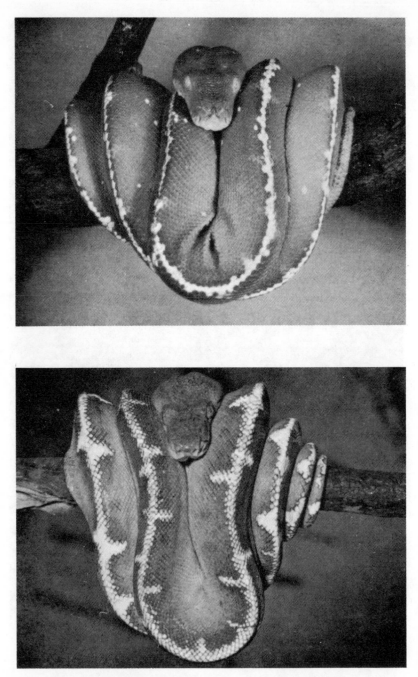

6 Two tree-snakes with almost identical concealing colouration. Upper figure a Papuan Tree-phython; lower, an Amazonian Tree-boa. (*Photos*. Wilhelm Hoppe and R. Stubenvoll)

parts of the world to turn pigs loose into snake-infested scrub before clearing it for agriculture. A number of birds, too, regularly include snakes in their diet. For example, at seventeen Golden Eagles' nests in California there were twenty-six Gopher Snakes (Plate 12), a King-snake and a rattlesnake amongst the recognizable items in the food-remains, and four per cent of the pellets of Horned Owls contained snake-bones or scales. Bateleur eagles, Red-tailed Buzzards and Harrier Eagles also regularly stoop on to snakes and carry them off, but the most persistent attackers of snakes are ground-dwelling types such as the Road Runners (a cuckoo, *Geococcyx*) of southern North America, Ground Hornbills and Secretary Birds in Africa, and the Cariamas and Chungas (relatives of the cranes) in South America. Some, if not all, of these birds lack any natural immunity to snake venom but they attack indiscriminately in much the same way as a mongoose, relying on speed and agility to avoid being bitten, though also using their outspread wings to act as shields, and killing their prey by pecking or stamping on them; the Hornbills frequently work in packs of as many as six or eight, forming a circle round the snake and dashing in on its flanks or rear. Other carnivorous birds, and other creatures, too, including crocodiles, alligators, lizards, fishes and even large frogs and toads, will sometimes snap up snakes, particularly young ones; but the most inexplicable records of snake destruction are a few scattered instances where antelopes and deer have been seen deliberately jumping on snakes and cutting them to pieces with their hooves.

Naturally, in a group of animals as diverse as the snakes, and with so many and varied enemies, there are numerous defensive reactions and devices. There is, however, one general pattern of behaviour. In the presence of a suspected enemy the first reaction is to try to escape observation; if this fails, the next resort is flight to some inaccessible retreat, but if this is not possible, or is circumvented, various kinds of intimidatory gestures and warning devices are brought into play; in the last resort the snake attacks. This pattern varies with the circumstances; some stages may be omitted or combined unpredictably whilst some notoriously irascible species may dispense with all the preliminaries and attack almost at once, though seldom or never without some provocation. The difficulty is

to know what constitutes provocation, a matter that is apt to
be debatable in other fields! Amongst the factors that increase
aggressiveness are hunger, the mating season and surprise, with
the last mentioned the commonest; when hunting for food or
for mates, activity and the aggressive instinct are both at their
peak, but it is when caught unawares that the normal chain of
reactions tends to become telescoped. Owing to their poor
sense of hearing snakes are very liable to be, quite literally,
caught napping and a similar situation arises during their
periods of temporary blindness just before sloughing begins.
By far the greatest number of snake-bite accidents results from
the unwitting disturbance of resting snakes and this hazard is
much increased with species that are well camouflaged and
whose natural instinct is to trust to this concealment as their
principal defence. As well as differences in aggressiveness between individuals of the same species according to the circumstances and conditions, there are also notable differences between species, even closely allied species; and the reports of
those who have been attacked may understandably be lacking
in objectivity. So it is impossible to forecast, even in outline,
how any encounter will develop. The Hamadryad, for example,
is usually credited with being amongst the most aggressive of
snakes, and there are many accounts of unprovoked attacks;
yet on one occasion fourteen men and seven dogs passed and
returned within two yards of a nest and no snake was seen
although the female, which guards the nest, could not have
been far away. The Black Mamba, too, has an evil reputation
for ferocity, and has been luridly described as the "Attila of
Snakes"; yet the author of this purple passage (who must surely
have been Irish) admits that their temper is uncertain and that
although they "invariably flee when disturbed by man they can
never be relied upon to do so," especially during the mating
season. Green Mambas are frequently credited with the dia-
bolical habit of lying in wait concealed on the branches of trees
bordering a path to strike at unsuspecting passers by; yet they
are, in fact, timid and relatively docile but as unpredictable as
any other wild creature. One very well-known student of snakes
once parked his car under some trees near Nairobi and on his
return found a small green snake on it. Being preoccupied at
the moment he gave it only a cursory glance and, thinking it

was a common harmless tree-snake, bundled it unceremoniously into his pocket; it was, as he later discovered to his horror, a young Green Mamba but it made no attempt to bite despite the rough treatment it had received. Almost all the larger venomous snakes have at least local reputations for aggressive behaviour, sometimes quite undeservedly as a result of confusion between species of very different dispositions. All rattlesnakes, for example, are popularly regarded as irascible, but whilst this is true enough of species like the Eastern Diamondback and the Western Diamond-back which, if provoked, will actually pursue an aggressor with a succession of lunges, others like the Red Diamond, are comparatively inoffensive and, unless roughly treated, can often be caught without their attempting to bite or even rattle a warning.

The proportion of the snakes of the world that have some form of procrypsis (i.e. resemblance to the background) is very high, but the frequency with which the resemblance results in accidents suggests that it is incorrect to regard it as primarily a "protective" device. There is every advantage to a predatory animal in being unobserved until its prey comes within striking distance, but it is distinctly hazardous to allow an enemy to approach closely with the hope, but no certainty, of remaining undetected. The commonest type of procrypsis is the result of colours that harmonize with those of the normal background, associated with patterns that disrupt the animal's outline or produce "counter shading," whereby those parts of the body that will be seen in shadow and appear dark, are lighter in colour whilst highlight areas are dark-coloured. Thus, many climbing forms that frequent leafy bushes have a general green tone with irregular lighter and darker spots and patches resembling the mottling of light and shadow, so that, as Kipling said of the leopard "You can lie out on a leafy branch and look like sunshine sifting through the leaves." Other arboreal types that live amongst the branches rather than the leaves have dull brown or grey colours that harmonize with the bark, and they frequently have patterns of darker and lighter stripes running the length of the body, or spots arranged in longitudinal rows. This type of marking accentuates length, making the snake seem even more slender, like some climbing vine or liana, and is frequently accompanied by a disruptive dark line along the sides of the head which breaks up the outline of the eye; in many species with especially large eyes the line is actually continuous across the iris. Among terrestrial forms, those that inhabit sandy or stony deserts are almost always pale grey or yellowish brown with darker and lighter spots and blotches that lack clear cut edges, like the Dwarf Viper shown on Plate 7; and those which live on red laterite soils with little vegetational cover are often pink or brick-red. For instance, one of the African Egg-eating Snakes, *Dasypeltis medici,* has this basic colour where it occurs on the laterite soils in the coastal regions of East Africa, but not elsewhere. In scrubby country dun colours are the rule and one of the common types of disruptive pattern consists of darker saddle-shaped markings, or a series of chevrons across the back. The common Puff-adder (Plate 8(a)) shows this to perfection and the species is notorious for the frequency with which it is accidentally trodden on; lying sunning itself at the edge of a path its dusty colour and disruptive pattern blend it so completely with the background that only a very alert eye is able to penetrate the disguise.

Another type of camouflage, in which there is no similarity to the background, is also found, but in relatively few instances. Here there is a purely disruptive geometrical pattern of contrasting colours which make it possible, to quote Kipling once again, to "lie right across the centre of a path and look like nothing in particular." The principle is, of course, the basis of much naval and military camouflage and is best exemplified in two forest-dwelling vipers, the Gaboon Viper (Plate 8(b)) and the River Jack. In the former there is a series of buff-coloured oblongs along the back, each enclosed in an ellipse of rich brown, the whole being again enclosed in a chain-like pattern of purple, edged with black or dark brown; on each flank there is a row of triangular blotches of purple-brown with darker edges; the background on which these markings lie is pale brown with a pink tinge and the small silvery eye stands at the apex of a dark brown triangle. Striking as this pattern is, that of the River Jack is even more colourful. The actual colours of a newly sloughed specimen are extraordinarily beautiful, giving "the effect . . . of a body of velvet softly blending a dark carmine and olive, with a pattern laid over. . . . Down the back is a row of large and nicked oblong markings of pale blue. Each of these has a lemon yellow line down the centre. The blue markings are enclosed in irregular black rhombs. On the lower sides is a series of dark crimson triangles narrowly bordered with blue. The top of the head is blue with a vivid black javelin-shaped mark pointing forward" (Ditmars).

Cryptic and camouflage colourings are often accompanied by structures which enhance their effects and by curious postures. The velvety appearance of the River Jack is far from unique and differences of "texture," from a soft bloom to hard, glistening enamel, arise from the structure of the surface of the scales. When these are smooth and highly polished a hard, glistening, almost metallic appearance, with strong highlights, results, but in a great many snakes each scale has a central longitudinal ridge, the keel. Although this may be primarily a structural stiffener it also has the effect of dispersing reflected light to produce a matt effect and this is sometimes further enhanced by almost microscopic striations of the scale's surface which disperse the light still more to produce a soft bloom. When keels are sufficiently large and prominent a general effect of roughness ensues and this is a common feature of many desert snakes; it matches the roughness of coarse sand. In this environment, too, many of the snakes have enlarged scales forming horn-like prominences either on the tip of the snout or above the eyes; these seem to have no function as weapons, but they break up the silhouette of the head and help to merge it into the background, especially amongst the thorny or spiky plants that are a characteristic feature of the vegetation of most arid regions. The Horned Asp of northern Africa, the Sidewinder of North America and the south-west African Horned Puff-adder are three desert vipers that have spine-like horns above the eyes. Horns on the end of the snout are less exclusively associated with arid conditions and are often associated with arboreal life, more especially with the attenuated liana type of procryptic colouring. Every gradation exists from merely an elongated and pointed snout to quite complex appendages such as those which characterize the bark-coloured species of the Madagascar genus *Langaha*. Here the appendage is nearly twice as long as the snout proper, and in the male sex it is triangular in section and sharply pointed; but in females it is flattened and, in one species curled up from side to side, like a withered leaf.

In other instances resemblance to the background is achieved by posture and behaviour. In the African Tree-vipers, for instance, and in another Madagascar tree-snake (*Mimophis*), the resting posture is most un-snake like, the head and fore part of the body being held at a sharp angle to the rest of the animal, producing the appearance of a broken twig. Others, again, merge themselves into the background quite literally, by partially burying themselves. In most instances this is achieved very simply by worming themselves into dense vegetation or into some cranny where they are partly concealed, but one or two desert forms, including the Dwarf Viper (Plate 7), the Asp and the Horned Asp, have a trick of shuffling themselves into loose soil by flattening their bodies and writhing from side to side until only the snout and eyes, and perhaps the tip of the tail, are left exposed.

All these methods of concealment, which depend upon resemblances to the inanimate background, naturally require complete immobility to be effective, and this is sometimes carried to extremes. The Fishing Snake, for example, has earned the Siamese vernacular name of "snake like a board" because it assumes a completely rigid and unbending posture that is maintained even when it is captured and handled; many of the tree-dwelling thirst snakes, too, if they are disturbed allow themselves to fall to the ground and remain there as motionless and inert as the twigs they resemble. A great many snakes will, however, adopt motionless attitudes in the face of danger that are not connected with concealment, but are part of their defence reactions. "Shamming dead," for instance, is a common reaction but, contrary to popular belief, this is not a calculated act of deception but seems to be some kind of fright reaction, like a man cowering in the presence of danger. One of the best known examples of shamming dead, and one which shows how very unintelligent the action can be, is the case of the Hog-nosed Snakes. These small North American snakes when disturbed indulge in an impressive threatening display, hissing violently, blowing themselves up and opening the mouth widely as if about to bite. But this is all bluff, for if the intruder fails to retreat no attempt is made to follow up the threats; instead the creature rolls over on to its back, gives a few convulsive wriggles and lies there with mouth agape as if dead. If however, it is turned over, right side up, it promptly rolls back and "dies" all over again. In the same category as shamming dead is the habit of many snakes of rolling themselves up into a tight ball with the head in the middle. In most instances, as for example in the Wood Snakes of the West Indies, some King-snakes and the Sand Boas, this defence reaction is normally elicited by the threat of danger, but in the nocturnal kraits it is induced by exposure to light. Sometimes the habit is accompanied by what has been called mimetic behaviour. The Rubber Boas, of western North America, for example, roll up into a ball when disturbed, but instead of remaining inert in this position, the tail is lifted up and waved around. This diverts the attacker's attention from the vitally important head which is in a protected position covered by one or more coils of the body. In other snakes the tail may be brightly coloured, which alone attracts attention, or may have markings similar to those of the head, even to the extent of having spots that superficially look like eyes. With this type of colour pattern there is an even chance that an enemy may attack at the wrong end, leaving the head free to deliver a surprise counter-attack, and one or two species go even further. For example, the Malayan Banded Coralsnake, which is a venomous species with the largest known poison glands, has a short, blunt tail that is bright red on the under side. This colour is exposed by carrying the tail erect and when a threat develops the upturned tail behaves exactly as one would expect the head to do, making darting movements, as if it were striking, to the almost certain confusion of the aggressor. The essential similarity of this head-mimicking behaviour to the luring of prey by the tail is very clear and there can be little doubt that the two are not separate and distinct phenomena. Just as striking and biting is primarily a means of catching food and only secondarily a defence reaction, so head-mimicry may well have developed originally as a feeding device. This would account for its occurrence in a number of unrelated forms and effectively dispose of the widely accepted, but improbable, theory that the harmless species which indulge in the practice are mimicking venomous species with the same habit; mimicry of a reaction that is itself mimetic! The classical example of head mimicry by a non-poisonous species is found in the Malayan Pipe-snake, which has a red tail and the same reactions as the highly venomous Malayan Banded Coral-snake; it is said to be a mimic of the latter and to gain, thereby, some degree of immunity from the attacks of enemies that had learnt by the misfortune of having previously attacked the venomous species.

Though scepticism may be justified in this instance there are numerous other cases where it is not, and these are mostly in the field of warning colours and not of behaviour. As in other groups of animals some venomous snakes have a "warning" livery which usually consists of bars of bright and strongly contrasting colours. Though few of the vipers have any such pattern it is widespread among the other venomous types; sometimes, as in the oriental kraits. the colours may be black and yellow, or white, but more frequently black, bright red and yellow are arranged in some regular pattern. Snakes with these colours are usually called "coral snakes" and this name is applied to a variety of venomous relatives of the cobras in Africa, southern Asia, Australia and the New World. In all these areas, except Australia, one or more species of harmless, or only slightly venomous, snakes have a very similar colouring, the resemblance in some instances being so close that the venomous and the harmless can scarcely be distinguished without very close examination. The best instances of mimicry of this kind are connected with the true coral snakes of North and South America, where such forms as the Scarlet King-snake, the Sonora Shovel-nosed Snake (Plate 9(b)) and the false coral-snakes have liveries of red, yellow and black markings almost identical with one or other of the venomous species.

Bright or contrasting colours and markings that can be suddenly displayed, or as suddenly concealed, are frequently associated with some of the other visual warnings that snakes may give. The commonest and least complicated of these displays is simple inflation which is often the preliminary to the almost universal audible warning of the hiss. A general inflation of the body may be assumed to have some deterrent effect upon an enemy simply as a result of the surprise produced by a sudden doubling of the snake's apparent size. In addition to this, its appearance may also be greatly changed because, in its inflated state the scales of the body become separated from each other, displaying the skin between them and this is frequently of a different colour (Plate 11(a)). In the Oriental Whipsnake, for instance, the general colour of the scales is a uniform green, or grey, or buff, but the skin between them is black and white in oblique bars so that when the snake puffs itself up this zebra pattern is suddenly displayed. In other instances the inflation may be localized in the neck region, and this may result in bizarre shapes. In forms such as the Guiana Chicken-snake the inflation is globular so that the creature looks as if it had just swallowed an egg, but in other instances the expanded neck is flattened from side to side. The tongue, also, may be used as part of the inflationary display. The Boomslang, an African tree-snake that preys to a large extent on chameleons and has a greenish cryptic colouring, inflates its neck to display a vivid pattern and at the same time protrudes its tongue and holds it vertically erect and motionless; and some rattlesnakes behave in a similar manner, holding the protruded tongue vertically erect for a time and then pointing it vertically downwards.

In the neck displays so far mentioned the mechanism is simple inflation of the tracheal lung (Chapter IV), but a totally different method is employed by the cobras for the production of their well-known hood. Here the horizontal flattening of the neck is brought about by ribs that are very long and moveable and which are spread outwards as the fore part of the body is raised off the ground. This distends the neck and, as in the previous instances, displays the markings that are normally concealed between the scales; in the Indian Cobra the well-known spectacle marking is on the back of the neck, though it can also be seen by transparency from the front, but in others, such as the Black-necked Cobra and the Ringhals, the markings, in the form of black and white cross-bars, are on the throat. Raising the fore part of the body erect is a common reaction, even among species that display no distensions or hoods, and it can be a very impressive display especially when the mouth is widely opened and the creature is hissing explosively. But occasionally the display is so stereotyped that the intimidatory effect is lost; the Australian Bandy-bandy just tries to stand on end, holding nearly half of its body stiffly vertical and the effect, to the human observer at least, is merely incongruous.

Nearly all snakes give audible warnings as well as visual warnings despite the fact that none of them has a true voice. The commonest sound is, of course, the hiss which, though seldom loud can be very penetrating and, at times, startling. The distended tracheal and pulmonary lungs probably act as resonators to amplify the sound produced as air escapes from the glottis, and some stout-bodied forms with large lungs can produce an unexpected volume of sound; the vigorous hiss of the Puff-adder, for example, has been described as "resembling more the noise that horses make when forcing air through their lips." Other species, like some of the North American Bull Snakes, have a special membrane just in front of the glottis and, when air is forced past it, it vibrates like a musical reed to produce a staccato effect. The most unexpected wind instrument in the snakes' orchestra is, however, played only, so far as we know at present, by two North American species, the Sonora Coral-snake (Plate 9(a)) and the Western Hook-nosed Snake. These snakes draw air into the cloaca and expel it rhythmically at intervals of about a second to produce a popping noise; the vibrations are in the frequency range of 1—7 kilocycles per second. Other audible warnings are produced by percussion. A few Old World snakes, including the saw-scaled vipers and asps of northern Africa and western Asia, and the African egg-eating snakes have a stridulating mechanism; a few rows of scales along the lower flanks are set obliquely and the large and stout keels on them are serrated. The snake inflates its lungs and puffs the body up so that these scales project, and then adjacent coils of the body are rubbed together by characteristic writhing movements so that the teeth on the comb-like keels scrape over one another with a grating, hissing noise that is audible for many yards. In its characteristic posture whilst giving this warning an egg-eater looks almost like a flat disc. The body is, in fact, thrown into a series of four or five side to side loops which increase in size from the head backwards, and the ends of the loops are brought forwards on either side of the head to form a series of concentric C-shaped figures, as shown in the accompanying diagram (Figure 7). Whilst in this position, side to side waves similar to those used in locomotion, originate in the neck region, first to right, then to left (open arrows). The snake "flows" into these waves as they are formed and increase in size, adjacent coils travelling in opposite directions as shown by the solid arrows. As a result there is constant movement with friction between adjacent loops and the rasping sound produced as the comb-like scales scratch over each other is loud and continuous. The performance is quite uncanny to watch, since adjacent parts of the body are continually moving in opposite directions and the effect is thoroughly confusing; a friend of mine who had seen it but did not know what was happening insisted (despite some ribald comments) that he had seen a snake "spinning like a tee-to-tum." After giving the warning the snake, if still excited, will strike with widely opened mouth, rising from its coils to do so.

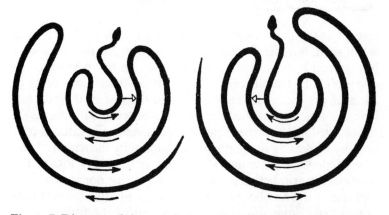

Figure 7. Diagram of the warning reaction of an African Egg-eating Snake. The open arrows indicate the formation of body-coils to right and left and the solid arrows show the direction of movement of the body as the coils increase in size during their passage towards the tail. (*After* Gans and Richmond)

The only other percussion instrument is the tail. In a great many snakes excitement is accompanied by rapid vibration of the tip of the tail and if the animal is on a suitable substratum, such as dry leaves or twigs, a rustling sound is produced. Sometimes, as in the case of the Bushmaster and the North American Pine and Bull Snakes, it is such a regular occurrence that the action seems to be deliberate and the noise that is produced is not unlike that made by the special tail structure of rattlesnakes. This "rattle" is a very complex organ, but fundamentally it consists of a series of loosely interlocked shells each of which was originally the scale covering the extreme tip of the tail. In most other snakes this terminal scale is a simple hollow cone that is shed with the rest of the skin at each successive moult. In the rattlesnakes, however, the scale is not only larger, but is very much thicker and has one or two annular constrictions which give it the two, or three, lobed shape shown in Figure 8.

Figure 8. Diagrammatic section through a rattlesnake's rattle showing four interlocking segments. (*After* Klauber)

Except at the first sloughing immediately after birth, the scale is not shed, but merely becomes loosened on the new scale that has formed beneath it. During its formation this new scale has one more lobe than its predecessor, the additional part being in front of the old scale, between it and the rest of the tail; but before the next skin shedding occurs the terminal lobe, inside the old scale, is absorbed and lost. As a result the rattle is continually increasing in length at each moult, by the length of one lobe of the new scale and at no time is there any loss of the interlocking grip between successive segments; nor is there any increase in the number of lobes per segment after the first (terminal) two. From this simplified account of the formation of the rattle one might infer that it goes on increasing in length, indefinitely, at the rate of one lobe per moult, and this was at one time thought to be so. In fact, however, the oldest segments at the tip of the rattle wear out and drop off from time to time without any regularity, so that the number of segments is very variable even in animals of the same age. In wild specimens the number seldom exceeds twelve to fourteen, however old they may be, though in the less turbulent conditions of captivity as many as twenty-nine have been recorded. When the tail is vibrated the loosely interlocked horny segments make a characteristic rattling noise whose volume depends partly upon the species of snake but also upon the number of segments and the rate at which they are being shaken. The rate of vibration is very distinctly dependent upon the temperature, and, in the case of the Prairie Rattlesnake, it was found that the rate increased from twenty-one cycles per second at 50° F to nearly 99 at 104° F, the increase being almost arithmetically regular at a little less than 1·5 cycles per degree.

In addition to visual and auditory signals most snakes possess one or more chemical deterrents. Inside the base of the tail there is a pair of sac-like glands communicating with the vent and their secretion is often distinctly foul smelling. Usually the secretion is not discharged until the snake is actually touched, and whoever has kept Grass-snakes will know the vile stench that newly caught specimens can emit if they are roughly handled. Many other species have skin glands in other positions and, although most of these are believed to be concerned with species recognition or courtship, their secretion may be unpleasant either in smell or taste. Some Asiatic grass-snakes, for instance, and their relatives the keel-backs, have two rows of glands on the back of the neck whose secretion is a skin irritant. Although its main purpose is almost certainly not defensive, any predator that seized one of these snakes in its mouth might well change its mind. The most curious defence reaction, however, if indeed it is a defensive device, is the "auto-haemorrhage" of some of the West Indian wood-snakes. The behaviour of the Cuban species has been described by an observer thus: "When taken the snake coils into a ball with its head in the middle and offers no physical resistance. A very offensive anal secretion is produced, however, and immediately thereafter auto-haemorrhage begins. The blood is allowed to flow slowly from the mouth with so sign of its being ejected under pressure, and is usually sufficient to form about four large drops. During the bleeding the eyes turn from a dark inconspicuous shade to a colour most aptly described as 'ruby-red.' The blood itself is very nearly odourless, certainly far less offensive to human nostrils than the anal secretion. Unfortunately it did not occur to the writer to taste it for possible defensive flavours" (Darlington 1927). Subsequent observers have found that the blood flows from vessels on the palate and that it has no toxic effects on lizards or frogs; whether it makes the snake distasteful to a predator remains to be ascertained.

Although these chemical defences may be metaphorically offensive, the majority of snakes go over to the literal offensive sooner or later if they are sufficiently provoked. The pattern of their behaviour then is essentially similar to that employed in securing their prey. There is often, however, an apparent re- luctance to endangering their teeth, so that in the initial stages of an attack, when the creatures are more frightened than angry, they may lunge as if intending to bite, but without ac- tually doing so. Whilst making these feints it is not unusual for them to uncoil themselves, almost imperceptibly, so that they can suddenly draw back and dash off swiftly to one side in an endeavour to escape. If such manœuvres are unsuccessful they then strike in earnest and often with greater force than would be employed in catching food; the lunge of a large angry python can have the force of a sledge-hammer blow. Constricting snakes will also try to grip their assailants in their coils and how effective this can be was demonstrated in staged encounters arranged for some of the more deplorable horror films. When a twenty-eight-foot python was pitted against a leopard the fight lasted thirty-two seconds, and as this was regarded as insufficient "entertainment," a second encounter was arranged which lasted twenty-six seconds; in both fights the leopards were killed. The danger of large constricting snakes to human beings has been well publicized since time immemorial and, although there are many grossly exaggerated stories, a boa or python exceeding about fifteen feet in length could probably kill a man if once it succeeded in getting some coils around him. Should anyone be so unfortunate or foolhardy as to get to close quarters with an enraged python it is essential to avoid getting enmeshed and the best informed advice indicates that it is easier to unloop the coils from the tail end.

The venomous snakes have, of course, the most dangerous weapons, but whereas a constricting snake that has got a grip has its adversary powerless to do it much harm, a venomous one may itself be badly mauled or killed by its victim before the venom has taken effect. A few animals such as the Archer Fishes and some spiders avoid coming to grips with their prey until it has been partly immobilized, by shooting it down with a jet of water or a spray, and the curious caterpillar-like creature *Peripatus* squirts a white latex at its enemies to entangle them in a maze of sticky threads. A few cobras have adopted a similar device, not to secure food but as a measure of self defence; they "spit" venom at the eyes of an aggressor. In contact with unbroken skin the venom is innocuous, but if it comes in contact with the sensitive conjunctiva and cornea, immediate and intense pain is caused, with temporary blindness and much subsequent inflammation, perhaps resulting in serious permanent injury; so that, if their aim has been good these spitting cobras are almost certainly safe from further molestation. The term "spitting" though commonly used, is incorrect since the venom is not ejected by the action of the lips and tongue and the action is similar to that of a pneumatic spray-gun. The snakes rear up in the usual cobra fashion and deliberately aim at their enemy's eyes, tilting the head back if necessary. Then a blast of air is expelled from the lungs whilst simultaneously venom is squeezed through the twin fangs. The air-stream carries the liquid forwards as a shower of fine droplets with sufficient force to spatter audibly on objects as much as eight feet away in the case of species like the South African Ringhals and the Black-necked Cobra, in both of which spitting is the normal mode of defensive attack. In these two forms the orifices of the venom ducts at the tips of the fangs are directed forwards rather than downwards as they are in most of the other cobras. But these others, although their normal behaviour is striking and biting, may also spit on occasion. It is interesting that the Indian Cobra has the habit only in one or two parts of its considerable geographical range, as if it were a behaviour-pattern that is only just being acquired.

VII

Reproduction and Development

One of the more ancient and popular beliefs about snakes is that they not only associate in pairs habitually but that they are touchingly devoted to one another. According to Pliny asps always roam in couples and either of them will find its way through any barrier to avenge an injury to its mate; and it was generally believed that adders, and other snakes too, could identify the culprit even in a large crowd. This is, of course, the merest fantasy, but the myth doubtless had its origins in the behaviour of snakes at the mating season when one or more males will trail a mature female wherever she may go. Most snakes form only temporary partnerships and only in a few instances, amongst them the Hamadryad, is there even seasonal monogamy.

In the temperate regions where hibernation is general, the reproductive glands (ovaries and testes) mature during the winter months, nourished by the food reserves in the fat bodies, and the mating season usually begins almost immediately after the spring emergence; in Britain all three of the native snakes pair during the period between the beginning of April, approximately, and the middle of May. There is, naturally, a considerable amount of variation from year to year and from place to place, whilst it is not uncommon to find a recrudescense of mating activity in the autumn. Adders, for example, may often be observed pairing in the period from June to October, though there is some doubt whether these matings are ever fertile because by that time of the year the male gonads are almost inactive. Autumn pairing, however, seems to be the rule in some other temperate zone snakes, whilst in the tropics some species may be sexually active at any time of the year.

The first step towards mating is the obvious though not neces-

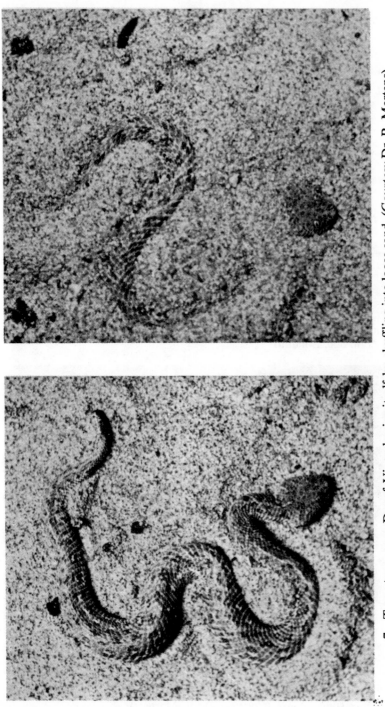

7 Two stages as a Dwarf Viper buries itself by shuffling into loose sand. (*Courtesy* Dr. R. Mertens)

8(a)   A Puff-adder; the pattern breaks up the outline and makes it difficult to detect the snake on a natural background. (*Photo.* Zool. Soc. London)

8(b)   The Gaboon Viper has a geometrical camouflage pattern of contrasting colours. (*Courtesy* Dr. R. Mertens)

sarily simple one of the meeting and mutual recognition of the sexes. In most of the higher vertebrates the dominant senses of sight and hearing play the major role in this activity, smell and touch being of less importance except in solitary and nomadic forms. With snakes, however, the position is reversed, and smell, their most acute sense, is the one of primary importance. Females are, for the most part, passive during the search for mates and the ensuing courtship, but during and immediately before their period of oestrus they produce odours that attract the males. In many forms the secretion of the glands inside the base of the tail is seasonally attractive, as may be judged from the experience of an ingenious rattlesnake hunter who has reported "I would take a female snake and get the musk out of her in mating time. This I put on my boots, then would walk around the heavy weeds in the afternoon, and go back the next morning and find that the rattlesnakes had trailed me, sometimes for quite a way. Then I took their trails and got as many as twenty-five or thirty in a morning. One morning I got thirty-five by ten o'clock." In other snakes, however, and especially among the Grass-snakes and their relatives, the secretion of these glands seems to have no such attraction, but to have a mainly defensive function. The attractive odour is produced by the skin and forms a trail wherever the female goes; it excites the males to follow it, completely ignoring any artificially laid cross-trails of anal gland secretion, and stimulates them to begin their courtship.

In comparison with the extensive knowledge that exists about the courtship of birds and mammals, relatively little is known about that of snakes. It is, however, clear that there is no common pattern of behaviour except that physical mating is always preceded by a stereotyped courtship that differs from species to species; unless the female is stimulated by the courtship appropriate to her species no coition ensues. When more information is available it may prove possible to classify the different types of behaviour and see how they have arisen from one another, but at the moment it would be premature and profitless to attempt to do this. Instead, some of the more interesting patterns, such as that of the Aesculapian Snake, may be mentioned. In this instance the female, somewhat unusually, takes an active part. When a pair has met and identity been established by their questing tongues, they dash wildly after each other, regardless of all obstacles, the male persistently manœuvring to try to get alongside the female. When, after much jockeying, he succeeds in doing so he coils around her, but even then the intertwined pair continue in a series of headlong rushes. Eventually, however, they rear up, almost vertically, and their anterior parts form a lyre-shaped figure, with heads facing one another and their hinder ends coiled round each other on the ground. This "dancing" may continue for an hour or more before copulation takes place and it has much of the aspect of a fight; in the Indian Cobra, where similar behaviour occurs, their heads, raised a foot or eighteen inches from the ground, have been aptly described as "sparring at each other like two young cockerels." As a matter of irrelevance but some interest, the Caduceus, symbol of Hermes, messenger of the gods, and one of the most ancient insignia known, derives from this characteristic mating posture of the Aesculapian Snake. And the same snake twined about a staff was also the symbol of the god of medicine and is now the emblem of the medical profession; the red and white striped barbers' pole, a relic of their ancient trade of blood-letting, is usually said to symbolize a bleeding and bandaged limb, but its spiral design suggests a possible derivation from the same device.

Behaviour and postures similar to those of the Aesculapian Snake have been observed in many others from all the continents, including adders, rattlesnakes, American copperheads, asps, Indian rat-snakes and Australian black-snakes. It was assumed that in all these instances courtship was involved, but during the last half century it has come to light that the participants in these dances are apparently always males. The performance is a remarkable and rather inexplicable form of stylized "combat dance" in which there is no real fighting and in which physical injuries are seldom inflicted although one of the combatants eventually gives up. Male rivalry at the breeding season, with much raw fighting, is common enough in other animals, especially where breeding territories are established and defended against intruders. But few, if any, snakes seem to have any such territorial sense and there is no indication that their combat dances are aroused by sexual rivalry; more often than not they take place in the absence of the opposite sex and in the many instances where several males have been seen trailing or courting a single female the rivals take no more notice of one another than they do of inanimate obstructions. It has been suggested that the dances may be displays of aggression which take place when, through some failure of the normal methods of sex recognition, one male attempts to court another; but it seems significant that the normal defence reactions are not employed. Rattlesnakes do not give any warning rattle before engaging in the dance, nor do the participants hiss, nor do they bite. One snake usually seems to be the challenger and approaches the other, rearing up as it does so. If the challenge is accepted, the other does likewise and they meet with the under surfaces of their necks pressing against each other. With this mutual support they rise higher and higher, heads facing each other and swaying unsteadily. They intertwine with slow writhing movements, as if wrestling, and eventually one thrusts forwards with sufficient force to throw the other off balance and the two collapse heavily, with the weaker underneath. Recovering, the struggle is repeated again and again until one withdraws and glides away, sometimes pursued by the victor. That the "dances" are associated with the sexual cycle appears certain since they seldom occur outside the mating season, and it may be that they are a pattern of behaviour inherited in degenerate form from ancestors which, like many present-day lizards, established restricted breeding territories and fought to maintain them inviolate.

In the majority of snakes true courtship behaviour follows a very different pattern. In some instances, as in the Black Racer and the Adder, when a number of snakes are together in one place there may be some excited dashing about by individuals of both sexes, but more usually the females take no apparent interest in other snakes near them. Males move around restlessly until they encounter a scent trail which they then follow with flickering tongues until they come up with the female. Still investigating with the tongue, the male then rubs the underside of his chin along the female's back, working slowly forwards towards the nape of her neck; his chin constantly moves from side to side across her back, or he may nod his head up and down nudging her as he does so. These actions bring into play the sensory papillae which are situated

on the chin and lips (Chapter III) of many snakes and although
it is not known how these organs function it seems essential
that they shall be stimulated by contact with the female; if they
are not, as, for example when they have been covered experimentally with adhesive tape, courtship is broken off. When
they do receive the necessary stimulus the male continues to
move forwards until his chin reaches his partner's neck. Then
a loop of the hinder part of his body is thrown across her back
and their tails are intertwined. This posture brings their cloacas
together, but copulation does not follow at once. In most of the
typical snakes (colubrids, elapids and vipers) the embrace continues whilst a series of waves, rapidly following each other as
ripples, run forwards along the full length of the male's body
from tail to head; and there may be some gentle nibbling of
the female's neck. These rippling movements are not produced
by boas and pythons but, instead, the claw-like vestiges of the
male's hind limbs scratch or stroke the scaly sides of his mate.
Throughout these amorous advances the female usually remains almost inert, and if she is not in oestrus she remains so
and the courtship ceases. But if she is physiologically ready, a
longer or shorter period of courtship by the male results in
coitus.

The male copulatory organs of snakes, like those of lizards,
are paired. Each has the form of an empty sac that can
be turned inside out or vice versa. The mouth of each
sac is continuous with the lining membrane of the cloaca
and when not in use the organs are withdrawn, outside in, inside the base of the underside of the tail, one on each side.
When coitus takes place the female opens her cloaca and one
or other of the male's organs is everted into it, being turned
right side out in the process. In many snakes the tip of the penis
is bifurcate, so that when it is extruded it is Y-shaped, and in
all of them it is covered with a complex pattern of soft longitudinal and transverse folds in the form of ridges and flounces
which, in combination, may resemble a honey-comb. In addition there is a deep longitudinal groove from the base to the
apex (or apices) for the conduction of the seminal fluid, and
frequently there is a formidable armature of horny spines
longer at the base than towards the tip. The pattern of ridges,
flounces, and spines, and the extent of the bifurcation are con-

stant in each species, but what the functional significance of this may be is unknown. The spines, however, ensure that once union has been established it cannot be broken until its purpose has been achieved, for the penis cannot be withdrawn without causing severe lacerations except by inverting it again so that the spines are individually disengaged as it is turned outside in. Fertilization of the eggs normally takes place shortly after mating, but sometimes the sperm may be stored for a longer period so that several successive broods of young or batches of fertile eggs may result from a single copulation. Thus a Night Adder kept in captivity without a mate laid four fertile clutches at approximately monthly intervals, the number of fertile eggs in each of them progressively diminishing; an American Cat-eyed Snake produced a fertile clutch of eggs after six years of isolation and an Indigo Snake after four years.

Snakes' eggs contain a large amount of yolk material (but relatively little white) and except in a few instances this provides all the food that is necessary for the growth and development of the embryos to the point at which they are able to fend for themselves and can be launched into the world. The laying down of such large reserves of nutritive material naturally takes some time and in the more equable parts of the temperate zone, where there is a three to four month period of hibernation, the eggs take a year to mature in the ovaries; they grow from the spring of one year to that of the next and are shed into the oviducts for fertilization a week or more after mating has taken place. In more rigorous climates, however, where there is a longer period of hibernation, the amount of food that can be garnered in one short summer allows insufficient margin for the maturation of the eggs and two years are required so that reproduction takes place only every other year. The Adder, for example, reproduces annually in central Europe as far north as Britain, Denmark and southern Scandinavia, but in the northern half of Sweden and in Finland reproduction is bi-ennial. Similarly in North America some rattlesnakes reproduce annually, especially in the southern states, but others, such as the Prairie, the Northern Pacific and the Great Basin rattlers, are bi-ennial. At the other extreme, in the damp tropics where there is neither hibernation nor aestivation it is likely that there may be more than one brood in a year, witness the instance of the Night Adder, just mentioned, which produced clutches of eggs at monthly intervals. Once the eggs have entered the oviducts and been fertilized, embryonic development begins, but they may not be laid at this stage. If they are going to be laid, and this may not take place for some time—two months in the case of the Grass-snake— they are provided with a tough, parchment-like shell for protection; but in a great many snakes, including most of the vipers and boas, they are not laid at all but remain in the oviducts until development is complete. These two methods of reproduction, technically known as oviparity and ovo-viviparity, are not associated immutably with particular groups of snakes; thus, for instance, the Grass-snake and many of its relatives in Europe and Asia lay eggs, but other species of the same genus (*Natrix*) in America and elsewhere produce fully developed young. And so on, with no means of telling, except by experience, which method any particular species may practice. Both methods have one feature in common; sufficient food for the development of the young is contained in the eggs, and even when these are destined to be carried in the oviducts until they hatch the only additional materials normally supplied by the mother are water and oxygen. These substances can pass by diffusion from the mother to the developing young through the egg-shell, but in a few instances their transfer is aided by the development of a very simple type of placenta, the structure through which a mammal transmits all the nutritive materials required by the foetus. The reptilian placenta is of a much simpler, and presumably less efficient, type than the mammalian and has been found in a few snakes of different groups, including some Garter Snakes, the Australian Copperhead, some sea-snakes and the Adder. In these instances there may be transference of small amounts of nutritive material as well as water and oxygen, and it is clear that a thick egg-shell is not needed for protection in ovo-viviparous forms and would impede the passage of these vitally important substances to the developing young; it is never more than a very thin, delicate and easily ruptured sheath.

The number of eggs laid by snakes varies from species to species, and even within the same species according to the size of the mother. A young Grass-snake may only lay eight or ten eggs, but the average clutch size is from thirty to forty and the maximum recorded is fifty-three; and in one of the most prolific snakes, the oriental Chequered Keel-back, clutches vary from eight to eighty-eight. Eggs are elliptical in shape, with bluntly rounded and symmetrical ends, and when freshly laid are usually creamy white in colour, the shell being damp and glistening. The moist film, which soon dries to leave a matt surface, is tacky and the eggs forming a clutch are often stuck together to form a solid mass. More rarely, when several females use the same nesting site, all the clutches adhere and as many as 250 Grass-snakes' eggs have been found together; on another occasion forty bundles each containing an average of thirty eggs were found in a hole in an old wall, producing a "plague" of about 1,200 young snakes. It is impossible to visualize the chances of such events occurring if snakes deposited their eggs at random and there is no doubt that nesting sites are selected; where there is a dearth of suitable places several females share the few that exist. The desirable conditions are rather narrowly circumscribed, especially in regard to temperature and humidity. The former affects the rate of development and mortality in much the same way as it affects the activity and mortality of the adults, and so, for rapid development, a consistently high temperature below the lethal level is required. A Grass-snake's eggs kept between 70° and 80° F hatch in about six weeks, but in the conditions prevailing in an average English summer eight weeks or more usually elapse between laying and hatching. Humidity requirements are equally exacting for, throughout the period of incubation but especially during the early stages, the eggs need much moisture which, perforce, has to come from their surroundings; a Grass-snake's eggs may increase in weight through water absorption by as much as 22 per cent during the first three days. Too damp conditions with inadequate ventilation will, however, encourage the growth of moulds which kill the eggs, and most people who try to incubate snakes' eggs in a terrarium find that, to maintain the right conditions, it is necessary to give them almost daily attention. This is something that the snakes themselves seldom do, for parental care of the eggs is a rare occurrence, and they rely on an instinctive selection, usually of damp but well-drained soil, in which the eggs are buried at a sufficient depth to protect them against over-heating by the midday sun. In Britain Grass-snakes usually lay their eggs about two months after mating, i.e. during late June or early July, by which time embryonic development is well advanced, and the places selected may be in the soft earth of ploughland or similar situations. Very often, however, piles of sawdust, rotting leaves, hay ricks and manure or compost heaps are selected, where the heat of decomposition produces a uniform and higher temperature that materially assists the incubation. Existing holes may be used but if none are available the female burrows into the loose material with her snout and, by rolling into a ball, forms an enlarged cavity in which the eggs are laid and left. Given normal conditions the young are fully developed and ready to hatch during the latter part of August or early September, early enough for them to have an active feeding period of at least five or six weeks to accumulate food reserves before going into hibernation. To escape from their tough egg-shells the young snakes are provided with a special "egg-tooth," a small conical bony structure with a hollow base that fits onto the bone that forms the tip of the snout (the premaxilla). With this tooth two or three long rents are torn in the shell by slashing movements of the head which, after much struggling, emerges through the hole. Then a long breathing space ensues, sometimes a whole day, before the young snake crawls out to begin its active and independent existence; the egg-tooth drops off a few hours later. On hatching young Grass-snakes vary from about $6\frac{1}{4}$ to $7\frac{1}{2}$ inches in length, an almost incredible size to emerge from an egg barely an inch and a quarter long.

The pattern of laying, development and hatching in most other oviparous snakes is similar in essentials to that of the Grass-snake though there may be differences in timing in different species, especially in the length of the interval between laying and hatching. This period, often incorrectly called the incubation period, varies not only with the temperature but very much more with the state of development of the eggs at the time they are laid, i.e. to the interval between fertilization and laying. Some snakes lay very soon after the eggs have been fertilized but in others the time lag is even greater than the two months of the Grass-snake, and it seems safe to predict that when more information becomes available it will be found that there is an almost complete gradation between forms in which the whole development takes place outside the mother's body and the other, ovo-viviparous, kinds where it all takes place inside the oviducts.

As already mentioned, the Grass-snake has a predilection for nesting sites in which the temperature is not wholly dependent on the sun's heat; and it also, on occasions shows some parental care, for the female may remain on or near the nest for a time after the eggs have been deposited. Although such behaviour is unusual in egg-laying species, one or two forms show similar reactions. The Aesculapian Snake also favours nesting sites where the temperature is raised by the heat of decaying vegetable matter, but the Hamadryad is not content with sites where such conditions already exist, but creates them. Loose vegetation and dead leaves are scooped up into a mound by loops of the body and the eggs, to the number of twenty to forty, are laid in a compartment at the bottom of the pile whilst the mother coils up in a second compartment over the eggs and remains there, with short periodic excursions away from the nest, until the eggs hatch; and the male may also remain near at hand. Construction of a definite nest and attendance on the eggs is also practised by the harmless North American Mud Snake which excavates a flask-shaped chamber in damp soil, the neck of the flask being a vertical passage which the mother uses to enter and leave the nest whilst the eggs are incubating. Here there is no supplementary heat from decomposition, but it is possible that the female's body, warmed by the sun during her excursions to the surface, may maintain the nest fractionally warmer than the surrounding soil. It has been claimed that pythons, which also coil themselves over their eggs (though these are laid on the surface and not underground), have an increased body-temperature during this incubation period; measurements made on captive specimens showed temperatures from 7° to 12° F above that of the surrounding air. But, as pointed out in an earlier chapter (IV), a snake's body temperature is almost always different from that of the air, and these temperature differences were measured in heated cages where conduction or radiation from nearby objects could well have accounted for them; so the claim is open to doubt. Coiling around the eggs which is also practised by several cobras and kraits and some pit-vipers (e.g. the Malayan Pit-viper) assists incubation by interposing a thermal insulation layer and so maintaining a more uniform temperature, but its major advantage undoubtedly lies in the protection it gives against marauders.

This advantage obviously also accrues when the eggs are retained in the oviducts, but there are many other and even more important benefits. Humidity remains constant and the mother can take active measures to regulate her own temperature by seeking sun or shade, and can maintain it many degrees above that of the air and thereby shorten the incubation period. So, retention of the eggs by the mother must be especially advantageous in climatic zones where the summer is short or where temperatures are lower. This effect is, indeed, very marked and ovo-viviparity is almost invariably found in species of the far north or of higher altitudes; all the species mentioned in Chapter IV as record holders for altitude or incursion into the arctic regions have this method of reproduction. For mainly aquatic species, too, it is an advantage since hazardous journeys into an alien environment for egg-laying are not necessary; nor do the young have to migrate back from the land with all the perils that entails. The only obvious disadvantage associated with ovo-viviparity is that the mother is handicapped by loss of agility during the period of pregnancy, with an increased risk of falling a victim to enemies and an impaired ability to obtain food. In some other groups of animals the handicap of lost agility is minimized by reducing the numbers of young that are carried, but this expedient has been adopted only to a limited extent among snakes where some ovo-viviparous forms are at least as prolific as any that lay eggs. The Puff-adder, for example, often has litters of sixty to seventy or even more, some rattlesnakes have as many as sixty and the Common Garter-snake has been recorded as producing seventy-eight. On balance, though, there is a tendency towards reduction compared with egg-laying forms. Amongst the British species, for instance, the Adder has litters of from six to twenty and the Smooth-snake from four to fifteen, compared with the mean range of thirty to forty eggs produced by Grass Snakes of the same size. The greatest reduction in numbers is found amongst the Sea-snakes, where some species bear only one or two young, and it seems probable that the reason why more species have not followed the same path is that ovo-viviparity is a comparatively recent development among reptiles and one that has not yet been fully exploited. How recent it is may be indicated by the fact that the egg-tooth, a structure that is not only unnecessary when there is no longer a protective egg-shell to be cut open but which may also be a menace to the delicate maternal tissues, persists in most, if not all, ovo-viviparous forms. In the Adder the danger to the mother is minimised by the shape and position of the tooth which points downwards or downwards and backwards, but it remains as a functionless organ that is not shed until some weeks after birth.

Young snakes are self-sufficient from the time of birth or hatching and can lead an independent existence without parental care or attention. Most of them begin life with some food reserves in the form of unexpended egg-yolk, for the yolk sac and its diminished contents are absorbed into the body-cavity and finally into the intestine a few days before birth. This leaves a slit-like umbilical scar on the middle of the belly just in front of the vent and though it eventually disappears completely its presence is a hall-mark by which a newly born or freshly hatched snake may be recognized. The amount of yolk left over varies and may, in some instances like the Smooth Snake, be sufficient to enable the young creature to live in hibernation through the winter and even to grow a little. In most cases, though, the young commence foraging almost at once, their food, determined by their size, usually consisting of small invertebrates. Their rate of growth is, of course, greatly affected by circumstances such as climate and topography and the availability of food, as well as by inherent differences between species, so that it is impossible to relate size and age except in the most general terms. It is, however, clear that growth proceeds in a series of steps, being negligible during periods of hibernation and greatest during middle and late summer, June to September in Britain, and that there is no abrupt reduction or cessation of growth, with the attainment of full sexual maturity, as there is in birds and mammals. Instead there is peak growth during the early years with a progressively gradual diminution thereafter but, in many cases, no complete cessation. With this pattern of growth the rate of increase is like compound interest in reverse and for each species there is a theoretical upper size limit which would only be reached at infinity but which is approached in comparatively few years. Precise figures for the rates of growth of wild snakes are difficult to obtain, but during their early years when the rate is at its maximum there is little or no overlap in the sizes of successive "year classes," so that average figures can be obtained. Figures for the Adder obtained in this way in Denmark indicate that the annual increase in length diminishes by about a fifth each year. At birth the young snakes average 150-160 mm. in length and during their first year males increase by about 80 mm. and females by 100 mm. With each successive annual increase diminishing by one fifth the theoretical average sizes of males at the end of their first to fourth years would be about 240, 305, 357 and 399 mm., figures which agree closely with the observed averages of wild-caught samples of year-classes which were 240, 310, 360 and 400 mm. On the same basis they would reach a length of 550 mm. in fifteen years, but their annual increase then would be less than 3·5 mm; their theoretical upper limit is 565 mm., or just over 22 inches. This, however, is an average figure and specimens exceeding this length are to be expected; the five largest males recorded in Britain were 547, 549, 552, 590 and 606 mm., i.e. averaging 569 mm., which is very close to the theoretical value. Similarly with females where the theoretical average sizes at the end of the first four years are 260, 340, 404 and 455 mm., compared with observed sizes of 260, 350, 430 and 470 mm; the theoretical average maximum is 660 mm. compared with an average for the five largest British specimens of 605 mm. This low observed average may reflect a higher mortality rate due to the hazards of reproduction, which would result in fewer females than males living to an advanced age. The largest Adder ever recorded, a female from Sweden was considerably above the average maximum; it was 1,040 mm. (41½ inches).

The growth pattern of most, if not all, snakes will probably be found to be similar to that of the Adder, but there are wide differences in the proportional increases in the early years and in the extent to which they diminish year by year. For example, whereas male Adders increase by 50 per cent in the first year, Red Diamond Rattlesnakes increase by more than 100 per cent, growing from about 300 mm. at birth to 670 mm; but the rattlesnake's second year increment is only about 60 per cent that of the first (670 to 870 mm.) whereas the adder's is 80 per cent. And, again, an Indian python has been recorded as increasing by more than 170 per cent in its first year, with the second year's increment 70 per cent that of the first. Differences such as these occur not only between different species but also, at times, within the same species. Thus, on small or barren islands with a poor food supply the local population is often dwarfed, and, as mentioned in an earlier chapter (IV) dwarf races frequently exist at high altitudes where low temperatures restrict the length of time in which a snake is active enough to hunt and feed.

One of the most important factors that determines the success or failure of any animal is its reproductive capacity relative to its mortality rate and the former depends not only upon the numbers in each brood but also upon the number of broods produced, i.e. upon the length of life after sexual maturity has been attained. Unfortunately there is very little information available about the duration of life in snakes, though there is a general and widely held belief that they reach great ages. In captivity, where conditions are necessarily artificial, some species do attain a considerable age, though nothing comparable with the records of longevity in other reptiles such as tortoises and crocodiles. Thus a Black-necked Cobra and an Anaconda have both lived for twenty-nine years, a Boa Constrictor for nearly twenty-five, a Leopard Snake for twenty-three and an Indigo Snake for twenty-five; but ages exceeding twenty are exceptional. The onset of sexual maturity is probably related to the potential life-span and, like it, is also subject to environmental conditions. Thus, rattlesnakes in the southern parts of their ranges seem to be mature at three, but farther north where reproduction is biennial instead of annual, the Prairie Rattler, Great Basin Rattler and Northern Pacific Rattler do not reproduce until they are four, or even five, years old. And male adders reach maturity in Denmark and Britain when about 400 mm. long, i.e. when four years old, and females also begin to develop eggs during their fourth year and produce the first litter during their fifth year when about 470 mm. long; but further north, in central Sweden, males are about 470 mm.

and females 555 mm. before maturity is reached. The other two British snakes, the Grass-snake and the Smooth-snake resemble the Adder in producing their first eggs or young during their fifth year, but many tropical species begin breeding much earlier in life and the most precocious of all, one of the oriental thirst snakes, *Pareas carinatus,* has been reported to reach maturity at eleven months.

VIII

The Colubrid Snakes

The total number of different kinds of animals living in the world today is estimated to be about 1,120,000, of which approximately 3,000 are snakes. It may cause surprise that more precise figures cannot be given since only comparatively small areas of the world remain to be explored, but the uncertainty arises from the difficulties of distinguishing between species and variants that arise from other causes such as climate, nutrition, and individual or, above all, geographical. variation. It is common knowledge that in any one area of limited extent the different animals sort themselves out into self-recognizing, self-perpetuating kinds, or species, and that hybrids are few and far between or non-existent; if any do occur they are usually sterile and leave no progeny. But if one moves from place to place over wider areas, and especially over physical barriers such as high mountains or arms of the sea, into regions where climate, geology and other features of the physical environment are different, the animals (and plants) change. Almost always new forms are found that are totally unlike any creatures previously encountered, but very frequently an old, familiar type is replaced by one which is similar but yet recognizably different. Is this a different kind of animal? Do the two forms maintain their separate identities when they meet, or do they intermingle freely and grade imperceptibly the one into the other? The answers have to be sought and are often far from easy to find. Often there is no clear-cut answer, for there are all manner of complications; as when two "forms" treat each other as distinct species in some places where they meet but mingle freely in others. The magnitude of the problem may be appreciated from the fact that, whereas fifty years ago it was believed that there were some 19,000 different kinds of birds, it is now accepted, as a result of closer and more intensive studies, that there are probably not more than 9,000. Snakes have not been so intensively studied as birds and many fewer "new species" were described during the eighteenth and nineteenth centuries when the tide of geographical exploration was at its peak and when there was intense competition among dilettante naturalists to find and describe "new" creatures. So, a similar proportional reduction in the number of recognized species of snakes is not to be expected, though there will undoubtedly be some diminution despite the occasional discovery of species that have been previously overlooked. In America where reptiles have been more intensively studied in the past few decades than in any other area of comparable size, 139 different species of snakes were listed for the United States and Canada thirty years ago, but the latest list recognizes only 115.

The known species of animals are arranged by zoologists in groups according to what is believed to be the degree of kinship between them, and the smallest grouping for most practical purposes is the genus; the species placed in any one genus are believed to be so much akin in their evolutionary descent that the nearest relative of any one of them is also a member of the same genus. Naturally there is no uniformity in the number of species that constitute genera; where evolution has been rampant large numbers of closely related species have been produced, but at the other extreme where evolution has been slow or extinction rapid, there are species with no surviving close kindred and these are placed in genera by themselves. Altogether some 400 genera of snakes are currently recognized and these are grouped together, according to kinship, into families.

The largest of these family groups is the Colubridae, which consists of the typical, mostly harmless snakes that form the bulk of the snake fauna of all the continents except Australia. Out of the thirty-three kinds of snakes found in Europe 63 per cent are Colubrids and the percentages in the other continents are, roughly: Asia 70; North America 80; South America 78; Africa 65; Australia 13. At this point it may be opportune to mention that there are no snakes in New Zealand, presumably because it became separated from the main Asiatic and Australian land masses in mid-Cretaceous times before the snakes,

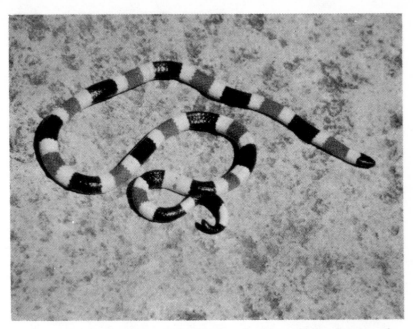

9(a)   The venomous Sonora Coral-snake has warning colours of red, black and yellow. (*Courtesy* American Mus. Nat. Hist.)

9(b)   The harmless Sonora Shovel-nosed Snake has the same colouring as the venomous snake in the other photograph. (*Courtesy* Arizona-Sonora Desert Mus.)

10(a)   Head of an arboreal pit-viper. The pit, between the eye and the nostril, is a sense organ that detects heat rays. (*Courtesy* Dr. R. Mertens)

10(b)   Malayan Pipe-snake, a harmless species, waving its red tail aloft as if it were the head about to strike. (*Courtesy* Dr. R. Mertens)

which were then evolving in the northern hemisphere, had been able to penetrate so far south.

The characteristic features of the group are the absence of any traces of limbs and of the left lung; the bones of the skull, except those enclosing the brain, are loosely articulated and the jaws capable of wide distension; the upper jaw bears a row of teeth which are not perforated to act as poison fangs though the hindermost two to four or five may be enlarged and provided with a surface groove from base to tip; the venom, except in one or two instances, is not dangerous to human beings. The lower jaw consists of only two bones the anterior of which bears teeth, and there is usually a single row of transversely enlarged plates across the belly, each corresponding to a single vertebra; the upper surface of the head is normally covered by a series of nine enlarged plates (Figure 9), which are remarkably constant in shape and proportions in each species, and there is a circular, transparent scale (the spectacle) covering the eye. Not a single one of these characters is alone diagnostic of the family and it is not possible to frame a short and simple diagnosis to which there are no exceptions, because of the very large number of forms involved (about 2,500 species) and their diversity. There are, however, within the family, seven smaller groups of genera that are more homogeneous and more easily recognizable despite the fact that they grade into one another.

The thirst snakes (Sub-family Dipsadinae) form one such group. There are some seventy or so species in south-eastern Asia and Central and South America and their general appearance is that of typical snakes, with enlarged belly scales and nine enlarged plates covering the top of the head. For the most part they are of slender proportions, but the head is large and the snout very short, the upper jaw bone being consequently equally short and provided with comparatively few teeth, sometimes no more than four or five. Their method of extracting snails from their shells, however, (Chapter V) requires a very long lower jaw, to act as a winkle-pin, and it must also be capable of being thrust forwards into the snail's shell far in advance of the upper jaw. This combination of a short upper jaw and a lower one perhaps three times as long, is achieved by a lengthening of the quadrate bone (Figure 1) on the lower end

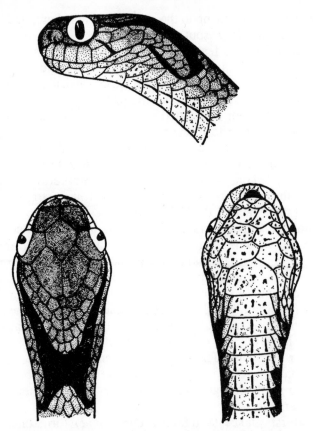

Figure 9. Head of a Thirst Snake. The nine enlarged plates covering the top of the head are typical of most Colubrid and Elapid snakes. The absence of a groove beneath the chin is a characteristic of the Thirst Snakes. A large eye, with a vertically contractile pupil is found in many nocturnal forms. (*After* M. A. Smith)

of which the lower jaw hinges. The quadrate can itself swing in an arc about its upper end and, as it does so, the lower jaw is carried forwards or drawn back. When the mouth is closed the quadrate is swung backwards so that the hinge of the lower jaw comes to lie behind the back of the skull and the animal's chin is level with the end of its snout; but if the mouth is slightly opened and the quadrate is then swung forwards the lower jaw is pushed into a prognathous position with its tip a long way in front of the end of the snout. Another feature of the group, also associated with their food, is to be seen under the chin. Most snakes that feed on bulky prey, where the two halves of the lower jaw have to be widely separated in the act of swallowing, have a deep longitudinal groove in this region. The groove is, in effect, a pleat that provides distensibility; but the thirst snakes, eating only the soft parts of snails and slugs, do not need any such provision and the groove is absent or nearly so. Most of the species are nocturnal or crepuscular and have very large eyes, with vertically contractile pupils. Many of them are arboreal and are exceedingly slender with long tapering tails that may account for as much as a third of the total length; one of the more abundant American species, *Sibon nebulatus*, which ranges from Mexico to Ecuador and Brazil, is known in Trinidad as the Fiddle-string Snake. When molested this snake reacts with such a purposeful withdrawal of the head prior to striking that it has acquired the reputation of being extremely dangerous. In fact it is, of course, quite harmless and when it strikes it does so with the mouth closed. It spends most of the daylight hours rolled up in the cup-like bases of wild pines (bromeliads), in bushes, or under dead vegetation and only emerges at dusk to hunt slugs. When it finds one it approaches slowly with raised head and arched neck until within striking distance and then lunges forward to seize the victim, which may be almost completely engulfed in a single bite. As a slug eater the Fiddle-string snake has a relatively long upper jaw and in this respect links the thirst snakes with the more typical Colubrines.

The Wart Snake subfamily (Acrochordinae) consists of only two species and is very readily distinguishable. Found in the coastal waters, estuaries and rivers of the region from India and Ceylon to northern Australia, the snakes are completely aquatic. Their salient features, many of them associated with their life in water, are the absence of any enlarged belly scales, a small head with tiny eyes and nostrils situated on the top of the snout, and gross, obese bodies with loose baggy skin and very small rough scales that do not overlap. They have no enlarged or grooved teeth and they can exclude water from the mouth and lungs by a cartilaginous flap on the roof of the mouth, which covers the internal openings of the nasal passages.

The better known of the two species is the Elephant's Trunk snake whose skin is the karung of the leather trade. It is a comparatively large snake, five to six feet long, with a girth of nearly a foot, and is restricted to the area from Siam and Viet Nam southwards and eastwards to Queensland. Sluggish in disposition, it is almost helpless out of its element, progressing slowly and laboriously more like a large and bloated worm than a snake; even in the water it can scarcely be induced to move in daylight but becomes more active at night. Only under great provocation does it attempt to bite, but if it does its large sharp teeth, admirably suitable for catching the fish on which it lives, can inflict severe lacerations. It is a prolific creature producing twenty-five to thirty-two young in a single litter. The second species, sometimes known as the File Snake (but not to be confused with the African File Snakes), is smaller (four feet) and not markedly different in habits, but the hinder part of the body and tail are slightly compressed from side to side, producing a paddle-like shape, and along the middle line of the belly there is a raised ridge of skin resembling a long narrow fin. These modifications may be expected to result in greater swimming efficiency and this is reflected in the fact that the species is almost exclusively marine and has achieved a wider distribution, from India and Ceylon to the Solomon Islands and Australia.

The Homalopsine Snakes (subfamily Homalopsinae) resemble the wart snakes in being aquatic but appear to be the outcome of an independent evolutionary development. They occur in the same geographical region, but are seldom found in the sea and have not severed their connection with the land to the same extent, for they have enlarged belly scales suitable for terrestrial locomotion and are often to be found on shore, though always near water. The skin and scales resemble those of typical terrestrial snakes but in connexion with aquatic life they have small upwardly directed eyes and nostrils with arrangements to exclude water from the wind-pipe and lungs. The nostrils themselves are crescentic and valvular so that water can be completely excluded whilst the animal is submerged; but to enable it to breathe with only the nostrils showing, the glottis can be pushed forwards and fitted into the internal opening of the nasal passages on the roof of the mouth, thus forming a tube directly from the nostrils to the wind-pipe and lung. Unlike the wart snakes, the Homalopsines are technically venomous, for two, or sometimes three, of the teeth at the hinder end of the upper jaw are enlarged and have a groove on their outer surface to act as a channel for the conduction of the products of a venom gland. The venom, however, is not known to be dangerous to human beings though toxic enough to the cold-blooded creatures, mainly fish and frogs, which form the usual diet.

Of the two dozen or so species known, the most unusual is the Fishing Snake to which reference has been made in earlier chapters (V and VI) in connexion with the use of a pair of tentacles as lures to attract prey and the defence reaction that has gained it the vernacular name of "snake like a board." It is an inhabitant of the fresh waters of Siam, Cambodia and neighbouring countries, reaching a length of nearly three feet, and having small, strongly keeled scales that give its skin a rough texture. Like all the other members of the subfamily it is ovoviviparous and produces nine to thirteen young at a litter.

The other species, which range in size from about a foot to four feet six inches, lack any tentacles and are all rather similar in general appearance. The largest, and perhaps the commonest, is the one that gives its name to the group, *Homalopsis buccata,* which is found from about 17 deg. N. latitude in Burma to Borneo and Celebes. It is a stout, heavily built snake with a very broad flat head, and shows a considerable amount of colour change with age. Young specimens are blackish, with narrow white cross-bars, and the head is white with regular dark markings in the form of a triangular spot on the tip of the snout, a stripe on each side of the head and an oval or inverted V-shaped spot on the crown. With age these markings become progressively less distinct and adults are dark olive-green, or plum-coloured, with the cross-bars dull yellow, edged with black. It is sluggish and docile in disposition and, at least in captivity, spends much of its time out of water or buried in mud. Its scales, like those of the Fishing Snake and several others are very small, arranged in numerous rows, and are strongly keeled, giving a very rough texture to the skin; but others again have smooth scales, amongst them the White-bellied Water-snake which was briefly mentioned in an earlier chapter. It is one of the five species of

the group that occur in northern Australia, whence it extends
northwards to Burma and Bengal, and is one of the most
variable, and sometimes colourful, of water snakes. In the
north of its range all specimens are uniformly grey or brownish when adult, but south of the equator various other liveries
occur as well; it may be black with large yellowish spots that
can be sufficiently numerous to restrict the black ground-colour to a mere network, or it may be reddish with a black vertebral stripe, or brown with black spots. And in its habits, too,
it may be equally variable, for in Australia it is reported to
subsist mainly on fish and frogs whereas in Java it commonly
lives in the burrows of crabs that form its main diet. Of the
other four Australian Homalopsines, three are native there.
One of them, Macleay's Water Snake is smooth-scaled, black
in colour, with a yellowish white stripe along each flank, and
is almost entirely aquatic and restricted to fresh water, but the
Bockadam is rough-scaled, spends much of its time basking on
mud flats and may be found at sea or in brackish as well as
fresh waters.

A small group of genera without poison fangs, four in the
Indo-Chinese and Malayan regions and one in Central America
(Nicaragua to Ecuador) form a rather ill-defined subfamily
(Nothopsinae) about whose status and relationships there is
considerable doubt. They may, conceivably, be a connecting
link between the typical Colubrines and the Wart Snakes,
though, not being aquatic, they have none of the specializations
of the latter. They resemble the Wart Snakes in having a supra-
orbital bone (absent in the Colubrines) and in some of them
the scaly covering of the body is unlike that of any other snakes
and most nearly approaches that of the Acrochordines. For
example, in *Xenodermus*, a semi-burrowing snake from the
Malay Peninsula, Java and Sumatra, the upper surface of the
head is entirely covered with small uniform scales, with no
traces of the enlarged plates which all Colubrines have, and the
scales of the body are more lizard-like than snake-like. As
shown in the sketches (Figure 10) the central region of the back
is covered with small granular, non-overlapping, scales amongst
which there are three rows of enlarged keeled scales, the central one being complex and the other two simple. Other forms
show a series of transitional steps towards enlarged head-plates,

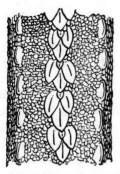 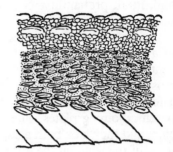

Figure 10. The unusual, rather lizard-like scales of the back and flanks of the Malayan and Indonesian snake *Xenodermus*. (*After* M. A. Smith)

and all of them have enlarged belly scales; the scales of the back and flanks, too, approach the normal Colubrine condition, being larger and arranged in regular linear series, though they barely overlap each other. Very little is known of the habits of any of the group. *Xenodermus* is nocturnal and lives in the loose, wet earth of cultivated fields, feeding on frogs; its movements are very slow and deliberate and it is oviparous, laying no more than two to four eggs. Most of the other Asiatic species, all of which are less than two feet six inches in length, seem to be inhabitants of hilly country clothed with low vegetation; some, at least, prey on earthworms and it would be extremely interesting to discover whether there is any connection between this diet and the fact that, in all of them, the margins of the scales bordering the lips are more or less distinctly everted. This curious arrangement reaches its maximum development in *Fimbrios* which lives at high elevations (3,000—5,000 feet) in Viet Nam and Cambodia; here the edges of the scales project to such an extent that a series of pits results, recalling the sensory pits of some boas and pythons.

The egg-eating snakes form a small subfamily, the Dasypeltinae, easily distinguishable from all other snakes by their unique egg-breaking "teeth" that have been described in some detail elsewhere (ChapterV). In other respects the African species, that have no grooves on the upper jaw teeth, are typical Colubrines and the Indian form, that has grooves, is a Boigine. This, however, is a distinction of no real significance and, in all probability, both types are the product of a single evolutionary line.

More than half the snakes of the world are grouped together in a single subfamily, the Colubrinae. They all have enlarged ventral scales, and large plates covering the top of the head; most frequently there are nine of these (Figure 10) though in a few instances the number may be less because of fusion between adjoining plates. There is a median groove beneath the chin, and they lack both a supra-orbital bone and poison fangs; some of the teeth on the upper jaw may be enlarged and appear fang-like but there is no channel through them, nor groove, for the conduction of venom. The secretion of the salivary gland may sometimes, as stated in Chapter V, be toxic and even lethal for the animals on which they prey, but is virtually innocuous for human beings. None of the group is exclusively marine and few are adapted to life in very arid surroundings, but otherwise they have colonized environments in every climatic zone on all the continents (except Australia, where there are only five species). They exhibit great diversity, but one of the commoner and better known species, the European Grass-snake (Plate 2) may be taken as a typical, unspecialized representative of the whole group. This snake has a very extensive geographical range, extending all over Europe, eastwards into Asia at least as far as the Lake Baikal region and southwards to Asia Minor, Cyprus, and north-western Africa (Algeria, Tunis and Morocco). Its upper montane limit in the Alps is in the neighbourhood of 7,500 feet and it extends northwards, crossing the Arctic circle to 67° N. in Sweden. Although it is common in most parts of England and Wales its distribution in Scotland appears to be patchy and uncertain, and it is, of course, absent from Ireland. Although this has been picturesquely ascribed to the beneficent ministrations of St. Patrick, the more prosaic explanation seems to be that the Grass-snake arrived in Britain too late to make the crossing before the last land connexion to Ireland was severed. During the last Glaciation when the whole of Britain, except the extreme south, lay under an ice sheet the climate in both Britain and Ireland was too severe for any reptile to tolerate and it probably remained so until less than 10,000 years ago. At that time the general level of the sea was probably 300 feet lower than it is today, so that most of the English Channel was dry land and reptiles that could withstand near-arctic conditions would have been able to migrate northwards into southern England. For a time they would have been able to cross to Ireland, also, since certain parts of the Irish Sea, notably a belt from the Lleyn Peninsula to Wicklow, were also dry. With the climate growing progressively milder, however, the ice-caps were melting and the sea-level rising, perhaps by five feet a century or even more. So, although the land connection with France remained unbroken until the Straits of Dover were cut some 6,000 years ago, the causeway to Ireland (where there is now more than 240 feet of water) must have been partially submerged very much earlier. An overland route seems to have been available for less than a thousand years after conditions became tolerable for even the hardiest of reptiles and the snakes were too late; only the Common Lizard made the crossing.

The Grass-snakes that colonized Britain are, as might be expected, indistinguishable from those of France and the same geographical race extends into western Germany, Switzerland and northern Italy. The colour pattern of this subspecies consists of an olive-green to olive-brown background with black spots forming vertical bars on the sides, and there are two rather irregular rows of smaller blackish spots down the back; the upper lip is white or yellow, with black bars outlining the scales, and the iris is reddish brown with a golden circle round the pupil. Across the nape of the neck is a very characteristic light marking, which may be any shade of yellow from the very palest to bright orange and this yellow "collar" is, more often than not, broken on the middle line and is bordered behind by two triangular or crescentic black blotches; the lower surfaces are checkered black and grey, the black often predominating. Variations from this general scheme occur in different parts of the snake's wide geographical range and nine subspecies can be recognized. Thus, for example, in the Iberian Peninsula the collar is present only in young individuals, adults often being uniformly olive with no dark markings, whereas another form, common in Italy, south-eastern Europe and Asia Minor not only has a well-marked collar but also has a pair of longitudinal stripes of the same colour, one on each side of the back. In addition to differences of this kind in the colour and pattern

there are also minor differences in the numbers and arrangements of the scales and also in size; the largest British specimen,
from Wales, is a female that measured five feet nine inches, but
much larger individuals have been recorded from other
countries, up to six feet eight inches.

The Grass-snake is a typical Colubrine in its general appearance and habits, though in regard to the latter it is, perhaps,
rather more aquatic than most. Frequenting damp areas where
its main food, frogs and other amphibians, is to be found, it
takes readily to water, even brackish or salt water, and on one
occasion a specimen was encountered twenty-five miles out to
sea. Other members of the same genus (*Natrix*) are even more
aquatic; the two other European species, the Tessellated Water-
snake and the Viperine Water-snake are seldom found far from
water and, more frequently in it, whilst the North American
species, ten in number, are all known as water-snakes. Most of
the American species obtain their food, consisting of frogs,
salamanders, fish, crayfish and so on, near or actually in the
water and if they are alarmed whilst on land they will frequently dive into water for refuge; because they are fierce and
aggressive, biting viciously when cornered, the larger and
stouter species are often confused with the venomous, semi-
aquatic vipers sometimes called Cottonmouths. At least half the
very numerous species of *Natrix* (found throughout the northern hemisphere and also southwards through Indonesia to
Papua and Australia) are water-loving creatures, but there is
every gradation between species that are predominantly aquatic
and others that are seldom to be found in, or even near, water.
Indeed, with snakes of all kinds the type of habitat may vary
from place to place according to the climate. Thus, for example, some of the American garter-snakes are often restricted
to the neighbourhood of lakes, ponds and streams in the drier
western half of the United States, but in the more humid east
may be found almost anywhere, even far from permanent
water. It is, of course, impossible to assign all snakes to a
limited number of ecological categories; there is every gradation between aquatic forms and terrestrial burrowers in the
species that dwell in mud of varying consistencies; and there
are species that are aquatic-arboreal, or terrestrial-arboreal and
so on. But on every continent where many Colubrine species

occur there are forms that are pre-eminently associated with, and restricted to, particular environmental niches, and the association is reflected in their appearance and physical characteristics.

The more thoroughly aquatic forms are usually of medium size and heavy build, often with broad, flat heads, small eyes, nostrils directed upwards rather than sideways, and a general superficial resemblance to the Homalopsines; their diet usually contains a large proportion of smooth, slippery animals, such as fish and frogs, and for seizing and holding these they have very numerous needle-like teeth. Examples of this type of snake are found in such genera as *Helicops* in tropical America, *Atretium* in the Indian region and *Grayia* in Africa. The most widely distributed species of the first-mentioned genus is the one known in Trinidad as the Water Mapepire which occurs over almost the whole of the Amazon basin southwards to Paraguay; it is a snake of about two feet six inches that passes most of its life in stagnant waters or slow-running streams, kills its prey by constriction and has an unexpected agility in defence; when taken from water it coils and at the same time flattens its body and from this position springs vertically upwards when striking at its assailant. The Olivaceous Keel-back, of India and Ceylon, is so similar in structure to this American species that until recently it was thought that the two were closely related; but it is now believed that their similarity arises from convergence, i.e. the acquisition of the same characteristics in response to similar needs, rather than from genealogical reasons. The African Grayias, however, though conforming with the general aquatic pattern, are distinctive; they are much larger, up to seven feet in length and, instead of being rough-scaled like the others, they are very smooth and highly polished. Four species are known, with a joint distribution from West Africa to the Upper Nile southwards to Angola and Tanganyika, and in some localities, particularly in Lake Victoria, they are extremely abundant and take a heavy toll of commercially valuable fish. Adult individuals are generally coloured a mixture of various shades of brown, but there are often traces of cross-bars of black, speckled with yellow or buff, which are the persistent traces of a handsome juvenile livery where dark bars contrast strongly with a lighter ground colour. A pattern of this nature, usually in subfusc hues, is of common occurrence in water snakes of all kinds, whilst vivid colours are exceptional. One such exception is the water-snake known in Trinidad as the Water Coral, which is purplish brown on the back, red on the sides and white below, with a series of black rings that are sometimes broken on the middle line of the back, the two halves then having a staggered arrangement. Its local name is the result of confusion with the true, and very venomous, coral snakes that are even more brilliantly banded in black, red and yellow; significantly the innocuous banded Grayias are also frequently confused with the banded water cobras.

The terrestrial forms, i.e. those which normally live at ground level, are of slimmer build than the aquatic forms and usually have a distinct neck, larger eyes and laterally directed nostrils. Since their environment may be so varied in regard to physical conditions, vegetation, food and so forth they show correspondingly greater diversity and the number of species is far greater than that of the aquatic, arboreal and burrowing types combined. Typical of the more active members of the family are the Bull Snakes and Gopher Snakes (Plate 12) of North America, and the Whip-snakes, Racers, Rat-snakes, Fox-snakes and Corn-snakes, which are widespread throughout the northern hemisphere, not to mention hundreds of others in Africa and South America. Most of them are constrictors and many are good climbers, seeking refuge in bushes and low trees if their speed in flight does not carry them clear of danger. The largest non-poisonous snakes, apart from the boas and pythons, are to be found amongst the terrestrial types and these larger forms are, not unnaturally, the ones that attract most attention. Thus in the New World, the Indigo Snake, which holds the record with nine feet eight inches and has a wide geographical distribution from the southern United States to Brazil, is the favourite of the "snake-charmers" of travelling circuses and carnival side-shows. In the Old World the Keeled Rat-snake, of Indonesia and Malaya, is even longer, up to twelve feet, and is one of the many snakes that have adapted themselves to the altered conditions resulting from human activities; in wild and unpopulated areas it is essentially a diurnal snake but the large numbers of rodents in and around farms and villages present a special attraction and in these areas it becomes almost entirely nocturnal.

Although there are almost innumerable other instances of close association with man-made conditions, there are almost as many cases where the opposite holds good and snakes can only find their preferred conditions in areas unsuitable for human exploitation. Large desert areas are an extreme example of this (though, strangely enough, few colubrine snakes are to be found in this environment) but in other cases the linkage which restricts a snake to particular areas is less easy to understand. The Smooth-snake (Plate 5), for instance, although it has a wide geographical and climatic range from the Iberian Peninsula to the Caucasus and northwards almost to the Arctic Circle in Scandinavia, has a very restricted and patchy distribution in Britain; it is found only in a comparatively narrow belt along the borders of Surrey with Berkshire, Hampshire and west Sussex and, farther west, in the New Forest area and the adjoining parts of Wiltshire and Dorset. These are areas of heath and woodland, mostly on sandy soil that does not lend itself to intensive agriculture, and they are not highly industrialized. At one time it was believed that the snake's occurrence only in these places was caused by a narrowly restricted food-preference—that it could only exist where Sand Lizards were abundant. But this cannot be the whole explanation since this particular species of lizard occurs in other areas, though less abundantly, and the snake is far from being so single-minded. Its diet includes other lizards, small snakes and a variety of small mammals such as field mice, voles and shrews that are held by constrictor-like coils of the body though there is no actual killing of the victims by constriction. It is much rarer than either of the other two British snakes but, because of its secretive ways and semi-burrowing habits, it appears to be even less abundant than it really is, and has been less intensively studied in consequence. To judge by what has been observed in other countries where it is more abundant it mates in spring and the young ones, four to fifteen in number and about seven inches in length, are born in the latter half of August or early September, their egg-teeth being shed a day or two later; the first moult takes place ten to twelve days after birth and the young ones have a sufficient reserve of yolk and fat to carry them through hibernation. Females are sexually mature at four years of age, when they are about nineteen to twenty inches long, and the maximum recorded size is a little over two feet.

Although the Smooth-snake spends much of its time burrowing in soft earth or under vegetation it is not a typical burrower. Those best adapted for this kind of existence are generally small in size, not unduly elongated, short in the tail, and small in the head, with very small eyes and no apparent neck. No snake has any means of excavating a burrow by removing the soil and all of them rely on making a passage by main force, the head taking the brunt of the work; in consequence, the snout tends to be acute in shape, often sharply pointed or wedge-shaped, and the scale covering its tip (the rostral shield) is frequently thickened and enlarged to cover a large part of the head. Exceptional in regard to size is the African Hook-nosed Snake that reaches a length of more than five feet and which is found across almost the whole of equatorial Africa from Guinea and the Congo to the Sudan and Eritrea. Here the rostral shield is enormous and, as the name implies, forms a hooked beak with a sharp, horizontal cutting edge; to prevent soil being forced into the mouth during burrowing, the lower jaw fits snugly inside the margins of the upper lip, like a valve, and there is also a small, horn-like prominence on its tip that can be used to close the notch in the upper jaw through which the tongue is protruded. Other, and more typical, burrowers are the African Prosymnas of which there are about fourteen species that occur throughout the wide range of climatic conditions existing between the humid West African countries, the arid Somali Peninsula and Natal. None of them is much more than a foot in length, the snout is flattened and wedge-shaped, with a cutting edge, and the tail is short, ending in a horny spine. They are, apparently, mainly insect eaters and this hard-shelled diet is associated, as in the egg-eating snakes, with a reduction in the number of teeth; there are none at the front of the upper jaw, the first being situated at the level of the eye, nor are there more than a few very small ones on the palate and lower jaw. But, for perforating the tough shell of the prey, the hindermost of the few teeth in the upper jaw are relatively enormous and have the form of curved, dagger-like, flat blades. Hook-nosed Snakes, Shovel-nosed Snakes, Long-nosed Snakes and Leaf-nosed Snakes, all as their names imply, with similar hooked, wedge-shaped or pointed snouts for burrowing are found in the more arid regions of the western United States and Mexico, and some of the last-mentioned are so similar to a group of species (*Lytorhynchus*) found in the countries bordering the Saharo-Sindian desert belt that for many years they were all placed in the same genus. It is, however, clear that their similarities are another instance of evolutionary convergence, the parallel development of burrowing modifications in different stocks at different times and places.

As noted in earlier chapters a long body and tail have considerable advantages for climbing snakes, whilst good vision, preferably binocular to help in judging distances from branch to branch, is also needed. So, the arboreal colubrines are usually slender creatures with long tails, large heads and prominent eyes, as in the Malayan Bronze-back shown on Plate 13(a). Snakes with these general characteristics (though frequently with much longer and more pointed snouts than in the illustration) are abundant in the tropical regions of all the continents but are less numerous in the temperate zones. Many of them also have two other features; the belly scales have a pair of low ridges (keels), parallel with the axis of the body, one on each side, and the scales of the flanks overlap one another more than usual and are arranged obliquely so that they slope backwards and downwards towards the belly. The keels of the ventral scales serve as anti-skid devices that stop the snake slipping sideways off the twigs and branches on which it may be crawling, but the significance of the oblique arrangement of the scales on the flanks remains obscure. It will ensure that less unprotected skin between the scales is exposed when the body is inflated or distended, than with the more usual longitudinal arrangement, and since it is almost invariably associated with great slenderness which involves much distension during feeding, this may be its function. The Bronze-backs are mainly frog-eaters and they and others like them have a very simple dentition consisting of numerous exactly similar sharply pointed thorn-like teeth. Some others, however, whether climbers or not, that take tougher and more active prey such as lizards, birds and mammals have specialized teeth. An extreme modification is found in the Oriental Wolf-snakes which are largely arboreal and prey on hard-shelled scincid lizards almost exclusively. The upper jaw is hooked downwards in front and the lower jaw curved upwards to meet it, so that the two form a pair of pincers; the ends of the pincers have much enlarged, almost canine-like tusks, but the teeth on the hinder parts of the jaws are very much smaller. This arrangement, recalling that of raptorial mammals, provides the largest and strongest teeth at the point of maximum mouth-opening and is found in a number of other non-venomous species such as the African Wolf-snakes, whose preference is also for scincs, and the snake-eating African File-snakes.

In the same way that most of the Dasypeltine Egg-eaters lack poison fangs entirely but one species has the primitive grooved type of fang at the hinder end of the upper jaw (see Chapter V), so there is a whole series of snakes that differ from the colubrines only in the possession of similar fangs. There is no scientific reason why these back-fanged snakes should be relegated to a separate and distinct sub-family, since the development, or loss of, the groove has probably occurred many times. In some instances, e.g. one of the false coral snakes of South America, grooves may be present or absent in different individuals of the same species, and there are several instances of pairs of "genera" e.g. *Coniophanes* and *Rhadinaea,* both South American, that have teeth almost identical in size and arrangement but where one has grooves and the other not. Nevertheless, since those with grooves are, at least technically, venomous it is convenient to maintain a distinction and the poisonous ones are then classed as the subfamily Boiginae. There are only about a third as many Boigines as Colubrines but the relative proportions of the two groups vary greatly in different continents; in Africa their numbers are nearly equal but in South and Central America there are only half as many Boigines and in Europe, Asia and North America the proportion falls to between one sixth and one eighth. Their habits and environmental adaptations are similar to those of the Colubrines in almost every respect—except that there are few constrictors amongst them because immobilization of the prey is catered for by the venom. There are, however, considerable numbers of arboreal and climbing forms such as the Flying Snake (Plate 14), and whip-snakes of the oriental region, and the African Twig-snakes already mentioned in earlier

11(a) An angry tree-snake inflating its body as a threat. (*Courtesy* Dr. L. Brongersma)

11(b) A Thirst Snake extracting a snail from its shell. (*Photo.* Hans Rosenberg)

12 Sonora Gopher Snake, a typical harmless terrestrial Colubrine Snake. (*Courtesy* American Mus. Nat. Hist.)

chapters as amongst those best adapted for arboreal life. Another African tree-dweller, the Boomslang must, however, be mentioned for a very different reason; it is highly dangerous. The majority of Boigines are not dangerous to human beings because their fangs are so inefficient and their venom, consisting mainly of tissue destroying agents, is slow in action though it may cause considerable pain and severe local symptoms. The Boomslang, however, is not only a comparatively large snake, up to five feet in length, but it also has a phenomenally wide gape which allows the fangs to be driven straight into comparatively large objects, without any of the preliminary chewing movements which most other members of the group have to employ to get their fangs into action; its venom, moreover, contains a higher proportion of nerve poisons and substances that destroy the linings of the blood vessels to produce copious internal bleeding. In consequence, its bite (and it is irascible and easily provoked) is always dangerous and has resulted in many tragedies. Although any large Boigine should be regarded as potentially dangerous, size alone is not the main consideration. Even a very small Boomslang has been known to kill a man, yet there are no recorded fatalities from the bite of such a large species as the six foot Montpellier Snake of the Mediterranean countries. How variable the venom can be within the group is shown by comparing this snake with another equally large one, the Mussurana of central and tropical America and the West Indian islands of Trinidad, Grenada, Sta. Lucia and Dominica. The Montpellier Snake's venom is neurotoxic, killing small mammals in a matter of minutes, and the snake itself must have some immunity to venoms of this type; but it has no resistance to viperine venom and is preyed on by the Sand Viper. The Mussurana, on the other hand, has no immunity to the neurotoxic venom of coral snakes, and succumbs to their bites, but regularly feeds on vipers, even such large and dangerous ones as the Fer-de-lance, killing them by constriction and being unaffected by the many bites it receives whilst doing so.

The maximum development of the Boigine fang is found, strangely enough, in the smaller secretive and burrowing forms that are especially numerous and varied on the African continent. In genera such as *Miodon, Polemon, Micrelaps, Brachy-*

ophis and *Macrelaps*, all typical burrowers with small heads, tiny eyes and stumpy tails, there are not more than two to four tiny teeth at the front of the upper jaw. These are followed by one or two relatively enormous fangs which, because the jaw bone is so short, are situated no farther back than the eye or maybe even be in front of it. This position is obviously more practical than the usual one closer to the angles of the mouth, especially when the mouth itself is very small, and it is possible that the shifting of the fangs forwards is an essential accompaniment of the acquisition of a burrowing head; without it the venom apparatus would become almost useless.

IX

Dangerous Snakes

"We are all as God made us and many even worse" (Don Quixote). Without question the "worst" snakes from the point of view of humanity are the *élite* when considered as animals adapted to a particular mode of life; they are the ones with the most efficient methods of securing their food and defending themselves. As noted in a previous Chapter (V) it is the vipers and the cobras that possess the most virulent venom and the best means of delivering it, and although they may be no more aggressive than other snakes they are all potentially dangerous. Fortunately they are not especially numerous in species, despite widely held beliefs to the contrary, and they constitute less than nine per cent of the known serpents of the world. Both groups have their poison fangs at the front of the mouth, the most advantageous position, but whereas the vipers have no other teeth on the upper jaw (though there are two rows of them on the palate) and can fold their fangs, the other group has only slightly movable fangs and their longer upper jaw generally has a few other teeth as well. In addition, the fangs of the cobra family have a furrow on their surface, from base to tip. This may seem a trivial point but it is of interest because it indicates the evolutionary origin of the venom canals inside the teeth from open surface grooves like those of the Boigine snakes; in the vipers, except the Night Adders, all traces of the groove have disappeared.

The cobra tribe is usually divided into two families, the aquatic sea snakes (Hydrophidae), and the Elapids (Elapidae) comprising the cobras, kraits, coral snakes, etc. The latter group has no characters, other than its venom apparatus, to distinguish it from the Colubrine and Boigine snakes and, having precisely similar environmental modifications, there is not one

131

single external and easily seen character that will distinguish any Elapid from any Colubrine on sight; nor even any simple combination of characters. So, recognition of the dangerous snakes becomes a matter of recognizing individual species, no easy task but, fortunately, not completely impossible since, in most areas of limited extent, the number of dangerous Elapids is small. There are none at all in Europe or Madagascar and North America has only four; in Asia and Africa they account for less than a tenth of all the species and it is only in Australia and the Papuan region that they are as numerous as the harmless types; even there, however, many of the species are temperamentally placid and so small that they are seldom very dangerous.

The best-known members of the group are the true cobras, with two or three species in Asia and Malaya and four more in Africa; they all have the same defence reaction, rearing up and spreading a "hood" by means of long, mobile ribs. The largest of them, and the largest of all venomous snakes, is the Hamadryad which has been recorded up to eighteen feet four inches in length and whose nesting and feeding habits have been described in earlier chapters. Throughout its wide geographical range, from southern China and the Himalayas southwards to Bali, Celebes and the Philippine Islands, it is nowhere common though most likely to be encountered near jungle streams. Of the other true cobras, which are all relatively large and terrestrial in habits, the best known is the Indian, or Spectacled Cobra, the stock-in-trade of the oriental "snake charmers." It is an abundant species everywhere within the area from Transcaspia eastwards to southern China and southwards to Bali, and within this area it shows a great deal of geographical variation, especially in the markings on the hood. The well-known spectacle marking, on the back of the hood only, is typical of western Pakistan, India and Ceylon, but to the east of a line between western Nepal and Bengal individuals with only a single ring-like marking occur and this type increases in frequence and finally becomes universal to the east and south of Assam; in the north-west, from the Punjab and Kashmir to Transcaspia, the spectacle mark is replaced by black transverse bars that extend across both the back and front of the hood. Although the species will sometimes eat frogs and toads and, to a lesser extent, birds, eggs and other snakes, its main food consists of rodents. In searching for these it frequently invades human habitations where its presence results in a great many accidents; so much so that in the search for effective remedies its venom has probably been more extensively studied than that of any other snake. In addition to tissue-destroying agents, similar to digestive enzymes, which probably occur in all venoms, the main constituents are poisons that affect the brain and nerves, especially those which control movements, and other substances that reduce the clotting power of the blood.

The symptoms immediately following a bite are pain out of all proportion to the damage caused merely by the wounds, followed at once by much local swelling with blood and serum oozing from the fang punctures. These symptoms, produced by the tissue-destroying and anti-coagulant substances, may appear within thirty seconds, and they spread as the venom disperses through the body, with haemorrhages developing at other points. Simultaneously the nerve poisons begin to take effect; weakness of the legs, drooping of the head and eyelids, paralysis of the tongue, lips and throat so that speech becomes slurred, nausea and increasing difficulty in breathing follow in succession with, though not inevitably, death from respiratory and heart failure. The final outcome naturally depends upon the amount of venom received, the victim's powers of resistance and the nature of the counter measures that are taken. Clearly the immediate objectives in first aid (in all cases and not merely for cobra-bite) must be to remove as much as possible of the venom that has been injected and to prevent the remainder from spreading; so prompt and speedy actions are called for. To localize the poisons a tourniquet should be applied between the bite and the heart, about two inches from the wounds, and this must be tight enough to impede the circulation but not to stop it entirely as this would result in additional damage to the tissues; if the tourniquet is on soft muscle it should not be so tight that a finger cannot be forced underneath it and if the tissues around it begin to turn blue it should be released for about twenty seconds. In any event this should be done about every quarter of an hour. To reduce the amount of venom, suction should be applied to the wounds and the quantity removed will be increased if the fang punctures can be enlarged by an incision, preferably about half an inch long and an eighth to a quarter of an inch deep, running from the puncture towards the ligature. Suction in most instances will have to be by the mouth and if there are lesions in the mouth there is some risk of poison entering the blood stream through them. This is, however, a risk that must be accepted and it will be minimized if a copious flow of saliva can be maintained, with frequent expectoration; swallowing the venom is not, in itself, dangerous.

Additional measures to reduce the spreading of the venom are indicated by common sense; anything that tends to raise the pulse rate must be avoided and this includes excitement, exercise and alcoholic stimulants of any kind. If the appropriate antivenin is available it should be administered in accordance with the instructions supplied with it and if steps have not already been taken to obtain medical assistance it should be summoned forthwith. If wheeled transport is available it may be quicker to take the victim to the nearest medical post, but any exertion on his part should be avoided. It is also important that the identity of the snake shall be established if this is at all possible; there is no such thing as a universal panacea and antivenins are effective only against the bites of single species of snakes or groups of snakes with similar venoms (see Appendix).

Amongst the African cobras the three best known are the Egyptian, the Black and White and the Black-necked. The first mentioned occurs from Morocco to Arabia and thence southwards to northern Rhodesia and Southwest Africa, and is a creature of the arid and hotter places. Unlike the Indian Cobra it is not a rodent eater, but subsists mainly on toads, with birds and their eggs as subsidiary items of diet; its venom, predominantly neurotoxic, is far more lethal to birds than to mammals and consequently, despite the large amount secreted by an adult snake, there are singularly few recorded instances of human fatalities. In the forested regions of West Africa, the Congo drainage and neighbouring countries, from Gambia to Kenya, Nyasaland and Angola, a commoner species is the Black and White. This is similar in length to the Egyptian Cobra (up to about eight feet six inches) but needs a more humid environment; it is often found in or near water and fish are included in its diet together with other cold-blooded animals and small mammals. The commonest and most widespread of all, however, is the Black-necked Cobra which is found throughout the savannahs of the continent from Senegal to Somalia and southwards to the Union of South Africa. Largely nocturnal in its habits it is seldom found far away from water and is very catholic in its feeding habits; it is particularly dangerous on account of its ability to "spit" its venom.

With the exception of the oriental Kraits and New World Coral Snakes, the other terrestrial elapids are mainly Australian. The Kraits, of which about a dozen species are currently recognized, are all very similar in general appearance and scale-pattern; they have small, flat heads and tiny eyes in which the iris is black, like the pupil, there is no neck, the body is rather triangular in section and the scales of the central row down the middle of the back are larger than the others. All the species are nocturnal and they feed principally on other snakes. Their venom is neurotoxic but their venom glands are relatively small and this, coupled with their inoffensive disposition, makes them less of a menace to human beings and fatalities appear to be rare. So far as is known all the species lay eggs, depositing them under dead leaves or in holes, and the mother guards them until they hatch.

Most of the Australian Elapids, on the other hand, give birth to their young. The largest, and potentially most dangerous, of them is the Taipan that rivals the Hamadryad in size, reaching a length of over ten feet, and which has very large poison glands and fangs up to half an inch in length. Fortunately it is not a very common species and is restricted to the less densely populated parts of Queensland, so that casualties are not numerous. Its close relative the Australian Copperhead, though much smaller (up to about five feet) may be a greater menace, since it occurs in the more populous states of Victoria and New South Wales, as well as in Tasmania; it is biologically interesting as one of the few terrestrial snakes where the developing young are not wholly nourished by the yolk of the eggs but receive additional food material, or at least oxygen and water, directly from the mother through a primitive type of placenta (see Chapter VII). Another of the dangerous Australian snakes is unusual and interesting from a different point of view; the

Death Adder is not a viper as its name might suggest, but an Elapid that looks like a viper in a continent where there are no vipers. It has a broad, flat, triangular head on which the usual nine plates are hardly enlarged at all; the scales above each eye are often upturned and those on the body are rough and keeled, whilst even the tip of the tail resembles that of some vipers in being slightly compressed from side to side and ending in a long spine. Its behaviour, too, resembles that of sluggish forms such as the Puff-adders; it relies on its cryptic coloration to escape observation and lies so very still that people easily step on it without being aware of its presence. Other large and dangerous snakes are the Black Snake and the Tiger Snake, the latter being probably the commonest of them all and, being aggressive in disposition, is responsible for many accidents. The Common Brown Snake, an egg-laying species, is also abundant in many areas, especially in New South Wales, and is a source of fairly numerous casualties. It is interesting, too, in its colour-habitat associations. Young ones have a livery resembling that of the Tiger Snake, sepia cross-bars on a lighter ground colour, but this is lost as age increases and is replaced by a uniform olive or light tan colour, the former being found predominantly in bush country and the lighter tan in more arid areas such as the treeless plains and deserts.

Vividly contrasting "warning" colours are best exemplified among Australian elapids in some of the species of *Vermicella*, notably by the Common Bandy-bandy whose habit of "threatening" by holding its body vertically erect has already been mentioned. This small snake (twenty to thirty inches) is banded with sharply defined rings of black and white and although not a true burrower it has many of the characteristics of fossorial snakes, viz., a small head, tiny eyes and short, stumpy tail. "Warning" colours, usually red, black and white or yellow are, for some hitherto unexplained reason, often associated with burrowing or secretive habits and the name "coral snake" is popularly applied almost indiscriminately to a great many unrelated species which have these colours, especially when they are arranged in alternate rings round the body. In Australia, for instance, some eight or ten species of the genera *Brachyurophis* and *Rhinelaps*, all burrowers with wedge-shaped digging snouts, are red or yellow in colour with black cross-bars and are often called coral-snakes; and so are various nocturnal snake-eating species of the genus *Callophis* in the orient and *Elapsoidea* in Africa. The true coral-snakes, however, are confined to the Americas, mainly Central and South America, but with two species in the United States. One of these, the Sonora Coral-snake, is illustrated on Plate 9(a) which shows a fairly typical pattern in which black and red bands are separated from each other by narrower yellow ones. Each of the thirty to forty other true coral-snakes has its own distinctive pattern based on some combination of rings of these colours though yellow may be replaced by white, or, in a few instances, eliminated entirely. In one of the commoner patterns the whole snake appears to have a back-ground colour of sealing-wax red with, at intervals, black bars in groups of three separated from each other by white or yellow. All the species are secretive and they feed to a large extent, but not exclusively, on other snakes; lizards and frogs are also taken. Most of them have the "head-mimicking" habit, thrusting the tail upwards with its tip curled over, when they are alarmed.

Another burrowing elapid snake, *Ogmodon*, presents a puzzle to students of the distribution of animals for it is found only in the Fiji Islands, a thousand miles from its nearest relatives in the Solomon Islands. It seems highly improbable that a small burrowing snake could have swum this great distance; transport by human agency is ruled out of consideration unless one makes the equally improbable stipulation that the original stock has become extinct in its homeland; and transportation on a raft of drifting vegetation is almost equally unlikely since the prevailing trade winds and the ocean currents of the area both set in the wrong direction—from the east. A possible explanation, however, seems to be that the creature may have been carried by air in a hurricane. Violent storms of this nature are prevalent in the western Pacific and the wind in those which occur south of the equator blows in a huge clockwise circle. So, in the northern half of any such system the wind is always blowing in a semi-circle from west to east and with a velocity capable of lifting large masses of loose vegetation over considerable distances. A small burrowing snake could easily be carried away in this manner and although a hurricane with a radius of more than 500 miles must be a rare event it is presumably not impossible and the circumstances do not require that it shall be an every day occurrence. A very few in every million years would be enough, and even one might suffice; and that one sufficiently long ago for the transported snake to have lost its original identity in its isolation. Some other facts lend support to the theory. For instance, the eastern limit of the hurricane belt is the Tonga region, and the islands of Melanesia to the west of Fiji have a much more abundant fauna than those of Polynesia to the east, which lie outside the hurricane area. And again, frogs of the genus *Cornufer,* but no others, are also found in Fiji a thousand miles to the east of any other islands where similar frogs occur. Frogs are notoriously intolerant of salt water so that transport by sea over these distances is incredible. But *Cornufer* is most unusual in having no tadpole stage; instead, the whole of its development takes place inside large, tough-shelled eggs that are laid among decaying leaves and similar débris, i.e. in precisely the type of material that a hurricane could whisk away with ease. Is it a mere coincidence that all the truly native frogs of the Antilles, also in a hurricane zone, either have an exactly similar type of egg or live in the leaf-bases of bromeliads, which are almost equally likely to be detached and become air-borne in hurricane force winds?

There are only two small groups of arboreal elapids, the African Tree Cobras (*Pseudohaje*) and the mambas which are popularly divided into two types, Black and Green. Actually there are five species, of which only one is black or, to be more accurate leaden grey to black, and all of them have the slender form and long tail typical of arboreal life. They have a very evil reputation that is not wholly unmerited, for they are uncannily swift to strike and have a particularly toxic venom. Many hair-raising stories of their attacks, with tragic consequences, have been told and re-told so often that the picture built up is probably exaggerated, though they are nevertheless among the most dangerous of all snakes. At one time it was believed that the Black Mamba was the adult stage of the Green Mamba, but this has now been disproved; the Black is a distinct species, somewhat larger and not quite so arboreal in habits as the Common Green. Both have a wide distribution from Senegal to Somalia and southwards to the Transvaal and Natal and they both prey on small arboreal mammals, especially squirrels, and birds. Neither of them is a forest form, but the other three species, all green, are found in the damper forested areas of West Africa and the Congo River drainage. Not only have the elapids failed to colonize the trees very effectively despite their fifteen million years of existence (since the end of the Miocene) but they have produced singularly few amphibious types; almost the only ones are the large (eight feet) Water Cobras of the central African region, from the Cameroons to Nyasaland. Even these have no special modifications for aquatic life though, as fish-eaters, they are restricted to the neighbourhood of water; when menaced they behave in true cobra fashion, rearing up and spreading a small hood, but little is known of their venom or whether they constitute a real hazard for the fisher folk.

In spite of the paucity of water-loving amphibious species amongst the elapids, the front-fanged snakes have made at least one, possibly two, major and successful incursions into a very alien environment, the sea, and the rather drastic modifications they have undergone to fit them for life in this medium have been outlined in previous chapters. The sea snakes (family Hydrophidae) number about fifty species and all of them, with one exception, occur in the area from the Persian Gulf to Japan southwards to Australia and Polynesia. Their most obvious character is a vertically compressed paddle-shaped tail, with some side to side flattening of the hinder part of the body, and most of them also have valvular nostrils situated on the top of the snout and very short tongues. Two sub-groups can be recognized, the one less fully equipped for aquatic life than the other. The dozen or so species of the former are never found far from the shore, which they have to visit periodically to lay their eggs, and they may lack upwardly directed nostrils; they all have the comparatively large belly shields that are characteristic of life on land. The species of the other, more fully aquatic, group have no need to go on shore, since they bring forth their young alive, and their ventral plates, being obsolete for locomotion, are very much reduced in size or completely absent. The reduced size of the tongue, too, may also be ascribed to obsolescence, for a sense of smell that can only function in air must be of very limited value to an animal that spends most of its time under water. The valvular nostrils, however, are an essential modification for life in this medium and they are associated, as in the Homalopsinae, with an arrangement that allows the glottis to be plugged into the internal opening of the nasal passages to form a continuous water-tight tube from the nostrils to the lung.

There are as many different types of habitat below the surface of the sea as there are on land; an off-shore pelagic life, the quiet waters of lagoons, a rock-bound coast, sandy shores, shallow weedy estuaries and different types of prey must all make different demands and much of the diversity of the sea-snakes is probably connected with such differences. Unfortunately, however, so little is known of the habits of the different species that it is impossible even to speculate about the significance of such features as a spine on the end of the snout, thorn-like scales above each eye, large, leaf like overlapping scales or small, warty, non-overlapping scales, and so forth, which may be found amongst different species even from the same geographical area. Almost the only correlation that has been established is that forms with very small heads and very long slender "necks" (i.e. the anterior half of the body) but much fatter hind-quarters feed exclusively on eels. Many species are transversely barred with brown on a dun or grey background, a type of procrypsis that suggests a habitat where light and shade alternate, as amongst waving fronds of sea weed. But a pelagic species, living in the surface waters of the open ocean, will require a different livery. Subjected to strong and unshadowed light from above it will need "obliterative shading" with dark colours over the illuminated surfaces and lighter colours below to offset the dark shadow over its lower surface. The only truly pelagic form, the Yellow-bellied Sea-snake that ranges from South Africa to the west coast of Mexico, has exactly this type of pattern; the back is nearly black and the belly pale brown to yellow, the two colours being sharply demarcated, sometimes even to the extent of separation by a narrow yellow line, whilst the tail, which will be in constant motion and throwing wavering shadows, is dappled black and yellow.

The majority of the sea-snakes are in the four to five foot size range, and even the largest of them, perhaps nine feet long, would hardly qualify for consideration in connexion with the Great Sea Serpent controversy unless a mass of them squirming on the surface was obscurely seen and mistaken for a single animal. This is not entirely a far-fetched possibility for incredible numbers have from time to time been seen massed together at the surface. One observer on a steamer in the Malacca Strait saw a ten-foot wide belt of them writhing together at the surface and this belt was kept in sight for sixty miles! The number in this assemblage must have been quite astronomical, but there is no reason to doubt the story since there have been other, similar observations. It is suspected that these vast concentrations may be connected with some phase of the breeding cycle, but whatever the explanation may be they indicate very clearly how abundant the animals are. In spite of this, however, there are relatively few records of fatal casualties amongst fishermen who find them in their nets and often get bitten. There is probably a great deal of variation in the toxicity of the venom from species to species, especially for human beings, and the professional fishermen may acquire an immunity to the one or two forms they most frequently encounter.

The remaining dangerous snakes, the folding-fanged vipers (family Viperidae), fall conveniently into two groups; the Crotalinae that have a heat-radiation detector embedded in the side of the head between the nostril and the eye (Plate 10(a), Chapter III) and the Viperinae which lack this device. None of either occurs in the Australo-Papuan region or in Madagascar and the Viperines are confined to the rest of the Old World; the Crotalines are essentially a New World group, though about thirty species are found in eastern Asia with one extending as far west as the region of the mouth of the Volga river.

The Common Adder, (Plate 15), already mentioned on numerous occasions in previous chapters, is a typical, terrestrial, viperine snake short and stocky in build, with a flat, broad, triangular head covered with numerous small scales. These features, together with its vertically elliptical, cat-like pupil distinguish it from the other two British snakes, but since they can only be appreciated by close examination at short range its colour and pattern have to be relied on for distant identification. The general ground colour is normally some shade between grey through brown to brick red, the greyer tones being typical of males and the redder of females. Superimposed on the ground-colour are markings of dark brown or black and these are, typically, as shown in the plate; the marking along the middle of the back may be straight instead of zig-zag, but this is comparatively rare in Britain, as are uniformly black (melanic), red (erythristic) or creamy white (albino) specimens. Its wide geographical and altitudinal range in Europe has been mentioned already and in Great Britain it occurs almost everywhere from Land's End to John O'Groats, though not in the Outer Hebrides, Orkney, Shetland or the Isle of Man. Because of its secretive ways and almost nocturnal habits it is comparatively seldom seen, and appears rarer than it actually is; in fact it is the commonest British snake and how abundant it may be is indicated by the fact that no less than 2,400 were killed in a few years on a sixty-acre reclamation scheme on Solway side at the end of last century. Its abundance coupled with its quiet ways naturally results in a number of accidents every year but fortunately relatively few end fatally because, although the venom is toxic enough to kill a lizard in thirty seconds, the amount injected at a bite is not large in relation to a man's size. Nevertheless a bite is not to be trifled with; the symptoms vary, but there is usually much local swelling and pain, accompanied by more general effects such as vomiting, diarrhoea, giddiness and prostration. First aid precautions, on the principles outlined earlier in this chapter, should be taken.

The Adder has eleven close relatives (all members of the same genus, *Vipera*), seven of them occurring in Europe. Three of these show progressive stages in the development of an upturned scaly prominence, of unknown function, on the tip of the snout and yet another species can erect the scales above its eyes. The most impressive of them, however, is the notorious Daboia or Russell's Viper which ranges from the Himalayas southwards to Ceylon and the Indonesian island of Komodo. This is a large species, up to five feet six inches in length and very robust, with a strikingly handsome colour pattern consisting, as a rule, of a light brown background with three longitudinal rows of large round or oval blotches that are a rich reddish colour in the centre but are margined in black with a fine white line around them; sometimes the blotches are partly confluent to form three chains and there may be some additional dark markings between the chains. It has a curiously irregular distribution being abundant in some districts but rare or completely absent in others and the reasons for this are not known. Wherever it occurs in numbers it is a menace to man and his domestic animals despite its rather docile nature, for it can inject very large doses of a venom that contains not only large amounts of the tissue-destroying agents and anti-coagulants that characterize most viperine venoms but also considerable quantities of nerve poisons. The result is that even if the effects of the neurotoxins are successfully resisted or countered there may be persistent haemorrhages as well as extensive ulceration and necrosis around the fang punctures.

Something has already been said about the more conspicuous of the other terrestrial vipers, such as the Puff-adder (Plate 8(a)), Gaboon Viper (Plate 8(b)), River Jack and the Night Adders, as well as of desert-dwelling types like the Horned Asp, Saw-scaled Viper and Dwarf Viper, but the burrowing and arboreal forms have their own special interest. The African and Arabian Mole Vipers are small rather insignificant snakes, many of them coloured a uniform brown or leaden black; but their adaptations to subterranean life so exactly parallel those of the burrowing colubrids that they can scarcely be recognized as vipers except by detailed examination of their teeth, and the parallelism even extends to these. The upper jaw teeth of the Mole Vipers are, of course, poison fangs that fold away when the mouth is closed, but they are inordinately long in relation to the size of the mouth, and this invites comparison not only with the disproportionately long fixed fangs of the Boigine burrowers *Miodon, Polemon,* etc., but also with the enormous dagger-like teeth of the harmless Colubrine burrowers of the genus *Prosymna* (all mentioned in the previous chapter). Why these small, burrowing African snakes, some venomous and some not, should all need such huge teeth remains to be explained, but as previously suggested, it may be connected with a diet of hard-shelled prey, such as insects, or hard-scaled burrowing lizards and blind-snakes which are said to be the principal food of the Mole Vipers. The venom of these vipers, though not extensively studied, is reported to be particularly dangerous and so much is it feared that the vernacular name of one of the species found in the Sudan means "Father of ten minutes," this being the supposed duration of life after being bitten. This is certainly a gross exaggeration, but the snakes are undoubtedly dangerous, the more so because of the ease with which they can be confused with one or other of the harmless *Prosymnas*.

Adaptation of the vipers to an arboreal existence has not followed the usual colubrid and elapid pattern of great elongation. The head remains typically viperine, broad, flat and triangular; the body is not unduly slender and the tail, instead of acting as a counterpoise, is short and prehensile. There are only five species, all found within the African equatorial forest belt that extends from Liberia to Tanganyika and Angola, and most of them are cryptically coloured in green, with or without golden and black flecks, to harmonize with the leafy trees and bushes in which they live; they also enhance their resemblance to leafy twigs by adopting curiously un-snake like postures, with the neck or body held stiffly at odd angles, and these attitudes are held completely motionless even when the snake is approached quite closely.

Whilst there are no distinctly aquatic vipers two of the Crotalines, the North American Cottonmouth and Copperhead, are amphibious, always frequenting the neighbourhood of water and feeding to a large extent on fish and frogs, but lacking any modifications for aquatic life. Most of the other pit-vipers are terrestrial or arboreal or transitional between the two. Their adaptations for climbing are similar to those of the African tree-vipers, a prehensile tail being the principal feature, but whereas only a few of the true vipers have succeeded in establishing themselves in this environment, the Crotalines have been more successful and they have proliferated into a number of forms. In the Oriental and Malayan regions there are about two dozen "species" of the genus *Trimeresurus* some arboreal and some terrestrial; some laying eggs but others viviparous; some easily recognizable but others where the females are indistinguishable though the males are different; and yet others again where the barriers between species appear to be incomplete and mixed populations occur in certain areas. Evolutionary development is clearly in a state of flux in these snakes and they present many problems requiring further investigation. Almost all of them are very docile, so that casualties are rare, and one species, the Temple Viper, is protected and encouraged as a sacred animal; sometimes as in the well known Chinese temple

13(a) A Malayan Bronze-back. Slender bodies and large eyes are characteristic of many tree-dwellers. (*Courtesy* Dr. L. Brongersma)

13(b) The Desert Thread Snake. Nearly cylindrical bodies, small heads, short tails and tiny eyes are characteristic of burrowing snakes. (*Courtesy* American Mus. Nat. Hist.)

14 The Flying Snake, an arboreal snake that can glide through the air. (*Photo*. Hans Rosenberg)

on the island of Penang, it swarms everywhere throughout the precincts but without any apparent risk to the worshippers.

An equally complex, but larger, group of pit-vipers occurs in Central and South America. In this genus, *Bothrops*, there are the same gradations between arboreal, prehensile-tailed species and strictly terrestrial types, but far from being a docile and inoffensive assemblage it contains such notorious snakes as the Fer-de-lance and the Jararaca which are jointly responsible for a very high proportion of the annual casualties in tropical America. These are both large and powerful species, between five and six feet long, and though they have their value as destroyers of rodents they are a great menace, especially in sugar-cane plantations and similar places where there is dense cover that conceals them from the workers engaged in cultivation or harvesting. Another, and perhaps even more dangerous snake, is the Bushmaster, the largest venomous snake of the New World, with a length of eleven or twelve feet. It is an inhabitant of damp tropical forests from Costa Rica to Brazil (including Trinidad) and is unique amongst the vipers of the New World in being oviparous; all the others, including the rattlesnakes, give birth to their young.

The rattlesnakes are a predominantly North American group, only two of the twenty-nine known species occurring south of Mexico. They have been more extensively studied than, perhaps, any other group of snakes and this is reflected in the frequency with which they have been mentioned in previous chapters to illustrate phenomena of general interest. They are chiefly at home in the drier areas of the western and south-western parts of the United States, but some of the species have invaded very different environments though none are aquatic or arboreal. The Cascabel, for example, ranges over the whole of the tropical parts of Central and South America east of the Andes; it is the only South American species and is probably the most dangerous of all the rattlesnakes for its venom contains an unusually high percentage of nerve poisons. Amongst the North American rattlers the most obviously specialized species is the Horned Rattlesnake or Sidewinder whose manner of locomotion, method of burying itself in loose soil and general appearance recall certain of the Old World vipers, such as the Horned Asp, which are also desert dwellers.

Under what conditions and circumstances the rattle came to be developed is uncertain. It was once suggested that a warning device of this nature would be particularly advantageous in open country where big herds of large, hoofed mammals grazed as they used to do in earlier days over the prairies. Under those conditions a rather sluggish and well camouflaged snake would have had a poor chance of escaping the ponderous hooves, but a warning audible at a sufficient distance would have prevented many a mutually disadvantageous encounter. Unfortunately, however, it is far from certain that comparable circumstances existed in the days when rattlesnakes came into being, for this must have been more than a million years ago.

X

Boas and other Primitive Snakes

Approximately eighty-five per cent of the known snakes belong to the four families considered in the two previous chapters, but the remaining fifteen per cent, all non-poisonous, are more diversified; so much so that they are usually split up into at least six other families. The differences between these families are sometimes not at all obvious from external appearances but their interest lies in their being features that reveal the links between snakes and lizards. The best known group, the family Boidae, comprises both the boas and the pythons which, like the colubrid snakes, are fitted for life in a wide range of environmental conditions; they further resemble the colubrids in having a flexible skull and jaws suitable for swallowing bulky prey and in having enlarged scales across the belly, one to each vertebra. Unlike the typical snakes, however, most of them have two large, though unequal, lungs and vestiges of a pelvis and hind limbs. The pelvis is composed of the same number of bones as in lizards, though they are smaller and not connected to the backbone, but the hind limbs are represented by only one, or at most two, very small bones that are enclosed in the horny claws which project, one on each side, just in front of the vent; these are not used in locomotion but males, at least, use them during courtship. Yet another primitive feature of their skeleton is the presence of an additional bony element, the coronoid bone, in the lower jaw. In lizards this bone is always present and plays an important part in locking the other bones together so that the jaw is almost completely rigid. In those snakes where the jaw has to be flexible, the coronoid bone has lost its function and in most of them it has disappeared entirely; vestiges of it persist, however, in the boas and pythons as well as in the primitive burrowing forms which have less flexible skulls. The family Boidae has a long history and fossils have been found dating from Paleocene times, about sixty to seventy million years ago. During this long period the group probably evolved into a far greater variety of forms than have survived to the present day and there are now so many missing links in the chain that it is difficult to see precisely how some of the survivors are related to each other. For convenience three sub-family groups (Boinae, Pythoninae and Bolyerinae) can be recognized, though this probably over-simplifies a complex situation.

The true boas (sub-family Boinae), as distinct from the pythons, are almost, but not quite, restricted to the New World where some thirty to forty species are found; there are also five species in Melanesia and Polynesia, three in Madagascar and a group of about ten small semi-burrowing species in the arid belt of the Near and Middle East and northern Africa. Popular literature contains many references to the "Boa Constrictor" as a giant constricting snake with many incredible attributes, but these accounts, even when they are not merely fanciful, are probably based on a confusion of species; any large snake of constricting habits is automatically called by this name. The species to which the name is strictly applicable (Plate 16(a)) is not by any means the largest in the world and actually ranks no higher than number five, with a maximum recorded length of eighteen feet six inches, and a more usual size range of ten to twelve feet. It is found from Mexico to central Argentina and shows a remarkably high degree of tolerance of the very varied climatic conditions to be found in those countries, from arid, semi-deserts to lush, humid, tropical forests. Its diet, too, is equally varied, consisting of large lizards, birds and mammals of various kinds, mostly rodents but also such fierce predatory creatures as ocelots and, on occasion, a mongoose. Although warm-blooded creatures predominate in this dietary the Boa Constrictor lacks any of the peculiar pits on the lips which, as mentioned in an earlier chapter, are thought to be heat-ray detectors to assist in discovering and locating objects with a temperature greater than that of their surroundings. Shallow pits of this type are, however, present in the Rainbow Boa. This species, which has almost the same geographical range as the Boa Constrictor, derives its name, not from colourful pigmentation, but from the wonderful iridescence of its scales. In its typical form it has a bold pattern of dull colours, consisting of a series of dark brown or black circles along the back and eye-like white centred blotches on the flanks, superimposed on a pale brown background; but when seen in sunlight the whole snake is a lovely shimmering mixture of green and peacock blue. Though not markedly arboreal in habits it has a long, somewhat prehensile tail and its diet includes bats in addition to the usual rodents and other small mammals. Possibly the heat detectors along its lips may be of importance in locating these creatures of dimly lit roosting places, and a closely related species which also has them, the Cuban Boa, is said to feed on bats almost exclusively. There is, however, no absolute correlation between labial pits and this diet, for the organs are even better developed in some of the distinctly arboreal boas in America and in the Madagascar Sanzinias, none of which are known to have any marked predilection for bats, though they may be taken occasionally. Most of these snakes are nocturnal, and the labial organs may be expected to be particularly helpful in locating warm-blooded animals that roost by night and which would otherwise escape observation owing to their lack of movement. Birds and squirrels, for example, form a considerable part of the food of species such as Cook's Boa, one of the commoner of the South American arboreal boas, and of the Amazonian Tree-boa.

These two species are also of interest on other counts. Cook's Boa, a seven- to eight-foot long and very docile creature of the Leeward Islands, Trinidad and northern South America has, when adult, a superficial resemblance to the deadly Fer-de-lance and this results in a two-fold persecution; the uninitiated slaughter it on sight and the initiated carry it around at carnival time to impress the gullible! Its biological interest, however, and that of the Amazonian Tree-boa too, lies in the range and extent of the colour-change undergone with increasing age. Adult Cook's Boas are cryptically coloured a pale yellowish or greyish brown with a double series of darker spots, but within a single litter of young ones, usually twenty to thirty in number, it is not unusual to find every colour from amber yellow to brick red and sepia. In the Tree-boa the changes are even more marked; adults are a brilliant emerald green with white or creamy spots and cross-bars which may form an irregular line down the back (Plate 6), but juveniles are yellowish, or rosy pink with the white markings edged with green or dark purple.

Other arboreal boas that lack heat-detectors on their lips, like the small rough-scaled *Trachyboa* of the region from Panama to Ecuador, and the various species of *Enygrus* which occur on the islands from Celebes to Tahiti probably feed principally, though not exclusively, on cold-blooded prey such as lizards, but most of the terrestrial or semi-burrowing types, which also lack the organs, feed on warm-blooded animals. Examples of these smaller forms are the Antillean Wood Snakes, and the North American Rosy and Rubber Boas which all have the ball defence reaction, with or without some head mimicking by the tail, and the Old World sand boas. The last-mentioned, of which there are seven species, are inhabitants of arid, but not completely desert regions and most of them not only have the appearance and proportions of typical burrowers but also have an enlarged digging scale on the end of the snout and slit-like valvular nostrils to exclude earth and sand from the nasal passages and lungs. Far from being passive in defence like their New World relatives, the sand boas are most aggressive and their method of attack is not a simple lunge and bite but a series of extremely rapid sidelong slashes which result in a number of deep lacerations that are apt to bleed quite alarmingly though, of course, not dangerously.

In marked contrast to these small burrowing and cryptozoic forms, none of which exceeds more than about three feet in length, is the semi-aquatic Anaconda which is certainly the largest snake of the Americas and probably of the whole world. It has a wide range, from Colombia to Paraguay, and is usually found in or near sluggish rivers, pools or swamps. In spite of the fact that it spends much of its time actually in the water it is not, predominantly, a fish eater but preys on the mammals and birds that come to the water to drink; dogs, deer, sheep, pigs, peccaries and even caymans figure in its diet as well as such smaller fry as coypus, ducks and geese. The great size of the Anaconda has inevitably attracted a great deal of attention from would-be "record" seekers, some of them none too scrupulous, and it is consequently difficult to arrive at the truth. Even when unsubstantiated "estimates" are rejected, dimensions obtained in all honesty from skins cannot be accepted unconditionally because of the uncertain amount of stretching that almost always occurs in their preparation; this may amount to as much as 25 per cent. Nevertheless, even with proper conservatism, it is fairly certain that in the northern parts of the continent, where the local subspecies is aptly named *gigas,* a length of at least thirty feet may be reached, perhaps even thirty-seven feet. The "record" of forty-six feet that has been claimed seems most unlikely although a fossil boa that lived in Egypt some fifty to sixty million years ago, is reputably calculated to have been about fifty feet long.

All the other giant snakes of the present day are pythons (Pythoninae), a group resembling the boas in almost all respects except that they have an additional pair of bones (supra-orbitals) in the roof of the skull and lay eggs. They and the boas are almost mutually exclusive in their geographical distribution; where there are boas there are no pythons, and vice versa. The tropical parts of Africa, Asia and Australia, excluding the desert regions, are the homes of the pythons, and the largest of them, the Reticulate Python which has been recorded up to thirty-three feet in length, rivals the Anaconda in length but is rather less heavily built. Like its rival it is a water-loving species, but is less catholic in its feeding habits, preferring comparatively small mammals. There is a single record of a fourteen-year-old child being eaten, but in spite of this it cannot be regarded as a particularly dangerous creature though it can be a great nuisance; it is a bold marauder and may sometimes be found even in the busier parts of large cities where it makes an easy living not merely from the local rodents but from domestic animals. The eggs which are "incubated" by the mother (Chapter VII) vary in number from ten to 100, according to her size, and hatch in from sixty to eighty days, the emerging young being between two and two and a half feet long. Another common species in south-eastern Asia is the Asiatic Rock Python which, though a smaller species (recorded maximum twenty-one feet four inches), prefers larger prey; an eighteen-foot specimen has been known to overpower and eat a leopard. It is a more heavily built and more sluggish species than its relative and, though equally at home in water, is somewhat

more arboreal, spending much of its time suspended by its prehensile tail in trees and waiting for some unsuspecting victim
to wander within range. Another and larger Rock Python, up
to thirty-two feet in length, occurs in Africa south of the Sahara.
The two are very similar in their appearance and habits but the
African species, though equally restricted to warm-blooded
prey, has a more extensive menu; any complete list of the
animals it will eat would be a lengthy one including, among
the more unusual items, porcupines. Like its Asiatic namesake
it has the reputation of being one of the more palatable snakes
and is a prized article of food for some tribes; others, however,
venerate it as a living symbol of the god of War or the god of
Wisdom. "Rock Pythons," so-called, are also to be found in
northern Australia and Papua and although they belong to a
different genus (*Liasis*) they are so like the true pythons both in
appearance and in habits that they call for little comment; the
largest of them, the North Queensland Rock Python reaches a
maximum length of twenty-three feet eight and a half inches
and lives to a large extent on wallabies. The Australian Carpet
Snakes, too, are essentially similar, but two other pythons from
the same general area, *Aspidites* and the Papuan Tree-python
are very different. The former, of which there are two races, the
one a coastal form ranging from Queensland to north-west
Australia and the other found farther inland, has the appearance of a burrowing snake and in this respect, and in the possession of large head-plates like a colubrid, resembles the North
American Rubber Boas. A similar parallelism with those
secretive boas is also shown by an African python, the Calabar
Ground Python (Plate 16(b)) a relatively small species (up to
three feet six inches) that spends most of its time underground
in rodent holes searching for mice and shrews; not only is it
superficially similar to the boas, but it also has the same
motionless-ball defensive posture. Even more striking, however,
is the similarity between the Green Tree-python and the Amazonian Tree-boa (Plate 6) for not only are the adults almost
indistinguishable superficially, with the same general proportions, prehensile tails, deep pits on the labial margins and an
emerald green coloration, but in both instances this colour
differs from that of the juvenile phase. In young Tree-pythons
the livery is brick-red with white markings, but with age the

red fades to yellow and then changes to green, whilst the white becomes yellow or cream.

From a zoologist's point of view some of the most interesting members of the boa family are two forms that occur only on a tiny island in the Indian Ocean, Round Island, close to Mauritius but nearly 500 miles away from Madagascar, the nearest place where any other boas live today. These two forms (sub-family Bolyerinae) differ from all other Boidae in lacking any traces of hind-limbs and in a greater reduction in the size of the left lung. In these features they form a link with two families of primitive snakes of the oriental region, the shield tails (Uropeltidae) and the sunbeam snakes (Xenopeltidae), but they also have some unique features of their own, such as a divided upper jaw bone that must give additional flexibility to the skull. It seems possible that the Bolyerines are "living fossils" persisting from early days before boas, pythons, shield tails and the sunbeam snake had gone very far along their separate evolutionary paths; they have been able to survive only because of their isolation, which resulted from the submergence of an ancient land-mass in the Indian Ocean that left only a few scattered islands, among them the Mascarenes and the Seychelles.

Another two peculiar species that were formerly considered to be pythons and, as such, the only representatives of that group in the New World, are the Mexican species of the genus *Loxocemus*. These are small typical pythons of the burrowing type in outward appearance and they have some of the normal python characters such as vestiges of hind limbs and paired lungs almost equal in size; but it has recently been found that several of their other anatomical features suggest that they may be links with the Sunbeam Snake which is itself in a unique position combining some features of the boas with others of the colubrid snakes. The Sunbeam Snake is a semi-burrowing creature, of the region from southern China and Burma to Indonesia, frequenting, more especially, rice-fields and cultivated land. Looking superficially like a typical burrowing colubrid, with large shields covering the top of the small head it also has other colubrid characters such as the absence of hind limbs, pelvis and coronoid bone. It resembles the boas, however, in possessing two well-developed lungs, although the left

is only half the size of the right. Its skull, however, lacks much
of the flexibility that is characteristic of both boids and colubrids; the upper jaw bones are firmly attached to each other,
the snout region is not loosely jointed to the cranium and the
supra-temporal bones, that play a major part in providing width
of gape in typical snakes, are short and firmly embedded in
the side walls of the cranium instead of being long and movable.
These features, which produce a more compact and rigid skull,
may be either an inheritance, with little change, from some lizard-like ancestor, or they may be a development from a typical,
flexible, snake's skull to provide an unyielding battering ram for
pushing a way into the earth. But whichever may be the correct interpretation there is no doubt that the Sunbeam Snake
is a conservative and only moderately successful animal because, although it maintains itself in competition with other
burrowing snakes over a fairly wide geographical area it has
neither proliferated into a variety of species nor has it colonized
any other environment. It is an inoffensive creature, preying
on other snakes, lizards and frogs, and so docile that it seldom
attempts to bite even when roughly handled, its sole "defence
reaction" being an extremely rapid vibration of the stumpy tail;
the name of Sunbeam Snake derives, not from its colour, which
is chocolate brown to black with the flank scales edged in white,
but from the very beautiful iridescence of its highly polished
scales.

The shield tails (family Uropeltidae) are also burrowing
snakes but they have an even more compact and rigid skull than
the Sunbeam Snake and differ in other respects. There is but
one lung and there are no enlarged scales across the belly, the
scales of the lower surface being similar to those of the back
with two transverse rows corresponding to each vertebra; such
an arrangement is found elsewhere among snakes only in the
blind snakes (Typhlopidae) and thread snakes (Leptotyphlopidae). There is also some resemblance to these two groups in the
extent to which the eye is reduced in size. In most of the shield
tails it is minute and, instead of being provided with its own
transparent watch-glass shaped covering (the spectacle) is situated beneath a larger scale, similar to the others which cover
the head. The group, containing some forty species, is confined to the Indian peninsula and Ceylon and its name arises

from the fact that the tip of the short tail is modified for use in the method of burrowing described earlier as "thrust creeping." The tail secures a firm anchorage to take the thrust when loops of the body are forcibly straightened out to drive the head forwards. Sometimes the modification consists in no more than an enlargement of the terminal scale, but in other species there are two or three spines and in the most specialized forms there is a circular area on which the scales are roughened or replaced by a single, much larger, spiny shield. All the species are small in size, seldom exceeding about a foot in length, and they occur most commonly in mountainous forest areas. Their rigid, non-distensible skulls preclude them from a diet of large or hard-shelled creatures and, though little is known of their habits they appear to subsist mainly on earthworms and soft grubs.

Another small group of about five species, the pipe snakes (family Aniliidae), are intermediate in several ways between the shield tails and the Boids. Resemblances to the latter are the persistence of a pelvis with vestiges of hind-limbs and distinct, though small, belly shields, with one to each vertebra, whilst the skull (text figure 2) is as rigid and compact as that of the shield tails. Other features, such as the lungs and eyes are intermediate; there are two lungs, but the left is less than fifteen per cent the length of the right and the eyes, though small, have "spectacle" coverings except in the case of the South American *Anilius*. This species is a reputed mimic of a venomous coral-snake, being brilliantly banded in red and black, and the best-known of the Asiatic forms, the Malayan Pipe Snake provides the classical example of a harmless snake "mimicking" the behaviour of a venomous species that uses its tail to simulate its own head (Chapter VI and Plate 10(b)). The Malayan Pipe Snake is not entirely a burrower but prowls above ground when searching for food and also takes readily to water. Although its skull is no more suitable for swallowing bulky prey than that of a shield tail it has an entirely different diet. Instead of being restricted to small, soft-bodied creatures that must, of course, be obtained in considerable numbers to provide adequate nourishment, it concentrates on larger, but slender, animals such as snakes and eels and the manner in which it can dispose of a meal longer than itself is almost incredible. The Asiatic members of the family are found in Ceylon and from Burma and Viet Nam southwards through Indonesia and all give birth to their young. In the Ceylon Pipe Snake the number in a litter is only two or three but they are sometimes disproportionately large; females attain sexual maturity when only ten to eleven inches long and produce offspring half their own length.

The remaining groups, the Blind-snakes and Thread Snakes, superficially resemble each other closely but are so different from all other snakes, at least in external appearance, that doubts have been expressed about their being snakes at all; they may have arisen independently from different lizard-like ancestors. They are burrowers without exception and the majority are almost completely restricted to subterranean life. In consequence they have all the usual burrowing modifications developed to the highest degree. As the photograph (Plate 13(b)) shows they are very attenuated and almost completely cylindrical, with tiny heads and minute, almost functionless eyes that lie deep below the surface, whilst their tails are so extremely short as to be almost non-existent, though they terminate in a sharp, needle-like spine. Perhaps their most salient feature is their very close-fitting and highly polished covering of scales that overlap one another to a greater extent than in other snakes; even on the head the plates are strongly imbricating, and the plate covering the end of the snout usually extends backwards at least to the level of the eyes (Figure 11). There is no special spectacle scale-covering for the eye alone, nor are there any enlarged belly scales; as in the shield tails the scales of both upper and lower surfaces

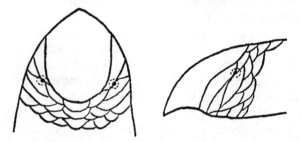

Figure 11. The head of a Beaked Blind-snake showing a much enlarged, hooked rostral shield and tiny, almost functionless, eyes.

are all equal in size and there are two transverse rows corresponding with each vertebra. There are usually vestiges of a pelvis, the skull is rigid and compact, the mouth not distensible and there is only one lung. Although the two families are so very similar in appearance, due to their adaptation to the same way of living, there are considerable structural differences between them. Thus, the Thread Snakes have a more complete pelvis with, in addition, a pair of claw-like vestiges of hind limbs, but in the Blind-snakes there are no traces of limbs and the pelvis is sometimes reduced to a single rod-like bone or may be absent entirely. More important, however, are differences in the jaws and teeth. In the Blind-snakes the upper jaw constitutes the principal feeding apparatus, the bones which compose it being only loosely attached to the rest of the skull and movable; they are short, forming an almost straight bar transversely across the front of the mouth and bear teeth, whilst the lower jaw is toothless (except in one instance, where there is a single tooth on each side). With the Thread Snakes, on the other hand, it is the lower jaw that is mainly used in feeding and carries a full row of teeth whereas the upper jaw has none at all and is, moreover, immovable, being firmly and rigidly attached to the rest of the skull.

The Blind-snakes (family Typhlopidae), of which there are perhaps two hundred species, have a cosmopolitan distribution throughout the warmer areas of the globe, though they have not reached the oceanic islands of the Pacific and are rather unaccountably absent from some of the older island groups such as the Seychelles. Only some of them, the four species of the genus *Anomalepis,* found from Mexico to Peru give any hint of linkage to other groups of snakes. As well as having a tooth on the lower jaw they have angular head plates not wholly unlike those of a pipe snake, whilst, as additional evidence of their primitive nature, there are vestiges of a skull bone (the jugal) that is not known to occur in any other snake. In all the other Typhlopids the scaly covering of the head is very different and conforms to the pattern shown in Figure 11, though there is much variation from species to species in the relative proportions of the various plates and in the shape of the snout, which, though merely bluntly rounded as a rule, may be even more beak-like than in the species illustrated. Most of the species, and all of those found in the Old World, belong to the one genus, *Typhlops*; few of them exceed ten to twenty inches in length and the majority are inconspicuous in colour, being uniformly pinkish brown to black above and lighter beneath. The largest species are African and some of these, up to thirty inches long, are more colourful with, for instance, black and yellow mottling (Blotched Blind-snake) or black with a yellow dot on each scale to produce a stippled or striped effect (Spotted Blind-snake). Little is known of their habits, except that they all seem to lay eggs and prey on small insects, especially ants, and few of them obtrude themselves into public notice. One exception to this, however, is the Brahminy Blind-snake for which the alternative name of Flower-pot Snake has been suggested because of the frequency with which it is found amongst the roots of pot plants, a habit that has resulted in its being accidentally transported from its native land, between Arabia and Indonesia, and becoming established in places as far afield as Mexico, Hawaii and South Africa. A tiny creature, barely seven inches long at most, it is very abundant in cultivated soils, and is easily recognizable by its "directive mark" colour pattern; the general colour is a uniform grey to blackish-brown but the tip of the snout and the end of the tail are both picked out by a white spot, as if to confuse an enemy. It is only a shallow burrower, so that it is often washed out of its holes in very wet weather, and on one occasion many years ago, this led to no little consternation; large numbers were washed into the Calcutta water supply and emerged from domestic taps all over the city!

The Thread Snakes (family Leptotyphlopidae) are even smaller than the blind snakes (no more than six to ten inches) more slender and less numerous; some forty species are known, all referred to one genus (*Leptotyphlops*) which occurs in the Americas, from the United States to Argentina, in south-western Asia and in Africa, but not in Europe, eastern Asia, Australia or Madagascar. They inhabit the savannahs and rather arid regions, but not the true deserts, and their food consists largely of termites. In one of the very few instances where the feeding habits have been observed it was found that the contents of the termite's abdomen were sucked out and the remainder rejected (see Chapter V), but whether this is a general practice is unknown. Possibly it may be, for the dentition of the thread snakes has a basic similarity to that of the thirst snakes which habitually extract the soft parts of snails from their shells. In both groups the teeth of the upper jaw are reduced—to the limit in the thread snakes—whilst in the thirst snakes the lower jaw has more and larger teeth and in the thread snakes the only teeth. A Thirst Snake uses its upper jaw mainly as a fulcrum to provide resistance whilst the lower jaw, with its teeth hooked into the soft tissues, is pulled back and drags the snail out of its shell; perhaps the thread snakes use their rigidly immovable upper jaw in the same way as a point of resistance whilst the lower jaw is being drawn backwards with its teeth ripping open the termite's abdomen.

XI

Snakes and Man

Some of the many ways in which snakes are affected by mankind have been mentioned briefly in previous chapters. A few species may from time to time be able to profit from man's activities when increased food supplies arise: when rodents, birds, lizards and the like increase in numbers around farms and buildings: when water conservation and irrigation result in more frogs and fish: or when cultivation of the land produces more worms and insects. But, on balance, snakes are the losers, for man not only consistently over-exploits the wild-life resources of the world but is responsible for much incidental destruction in his progressive "development" of the earth's surface to satisfy his own needs.

The reciprocal effects, of snakes on mankind, are difficult to assess for their greatest impact has been in man's subjective thinking rather than in the biological and economic fields. Nevertheless snakes do play a considerable part in relation to man's welfare, both directly and indirectly. Their most obvious adverse effect arises from the deaths and injuries caused by snake-bite and the considerable efforts that have to be made to combat this menace. Reliable figures for deaths throughout the world do not exist, since, not only are there backward countries with inadequate registration, but it is also suspected that in some others the recorded figures are inflated by the inclusion of deaths from other causes—especially violence! Recent estimates place the figure at between thirty and forty thousand per annum, with the highest incidence in Burma, with a death rate of 15 per 100,000 of the population. Elsewhere mortality rates are much lower and they are also very variable, partly on account of differences in the abundance and nature of the snakes in different countries but even more because of the cus-

15 An Adder with its sloughed skin. (*Photo.* G. Kinns)

16(a)   The Boa Constrictor. (*Photo*. Hans Rosenberg)

16(b)   The Calabar Ground Python in defensive posture rolled up into a ball. (*Photo*. Hans Rosenberg)

toms and dress of the inhabitants. Thus, in Ceylon, India and Brazil, all tropical countries where clothing is naturally scanty and large numbers of the population either go barefoot or wear sandals, the death rate is between 4·1 and 5·4 per 100,000, whereas in Australia, where 77 per cent of the snakes are venomous, the rate is as low as six per ten million, and in the United States about two in ten million. Separate statistics for snake-bite in Europe are not available, but deaths from the stings or bites of all venomous animals combined do not exceed six per ten million and the figure for England is two. Deaths alone, however, represent but a small fraction of the total damage, and the numbers of persons who are bitten by venomous snakes and suffer some degree of temporary, or even permanent, disability must be very much greater. Once again exact figures cannot be given but before antivenins became available fatalities amounted to between 10 and 15 per cent of the persons bitten, at least in countries where the dangerous snakes are mainly vipers; these figures are based on independent estimates by observers in two such widely different places as the state of São Paulo in Brazil and the Japanese island of Okinawa. The higher estimate of annual deaths throughout the world (40,000) is based principally on old statistics so the total number of persons bitten each year must be of the order of 400,000, or even more. The expenditure of effort in combating a danger of this magnitude, though negligible in comparison with the resources man squanders in connexion with menaces of his own devising, is nevertheless not completely insignificant. Not only have the medical and sanitary services to be increased to deal with the casualties but the pharmaceutical industries and institutions must prepare and maintain stocks of perishable drugs and antivenins with considerable precautionary reserves above and beyond the actual consumption. The list of antivenins shown in the appendix gives some indication of the magnitude and ramifications of this effort which, fortunately, is achieving a considerable measure of success. For instance, in the United States in each of the ten years beginning in 1930, when antivenins had come on the market but had not reached a very high standard either of efficacy or distribution, the average number of deaths from all bites and stings exceeded 142. and snakes probably accounted for about ninety of these. In the decade 1943-1952, however, the comparable figure was thirty-four, which, since there were probably more bites owing to increases in the population and the spread of the rural holiday habit, implies at least a two thirds reduction of the fatality rate. In Australia, too, a similar reduction has taken place, the estimated death rate having fallen from twenty per 10,000,000 of the population in 1926 to six in 1952.

The efforts to combat the direct effects of snake-bite may be expected to be less successful in countries where communications are slower or where agricultural methods are more primitive, with tilling and harvesting largely done by hand. And there has probably been comparatively little reduction in the losses among domestic animals, though the extent of these are not known with any certainty. Estimates based on individual experience, even under similar conditions, vary widely, but it is nevertheless certain that losses are considerable, especially amongst the smaller types of farm stock and the younger animals. Naturally the frequency of snake-bite varies according to the type of grazing country and the density of the snake infestation but some comparative figures for mid-western and western North America are instructive. Pigs are everywhere relatively immune, not because of any special physiological immunity, but because their tough hides and the thick layer of fat beneath the skin form an effective armour. Sheep, however, suffer considerable losses in spite of the protection of a thick fleece; in Colorado it was estimated a few years ago that the incidence of snake-bite was at the rate of 300 per 100,000, with 60 per cent mortality amongst those bitten; and in South Dakota another estimate put the losses amongst lambs as high as fifteen per 1,000. These figures are only estimates, but more reliable information is available regarding cattle in California during the period 1936-1948, when human deaths were at the rate of about two per ten million inhabitants. On an experimental range of 4,600 acres, where the snake infestation was admittedly heavy, the deaths among cattle were more than eleven thousand times as numerous as the state average for human beings (2·2 per thousand head of cattle) and the numbers bitten at least six times greater still. The total damage was, therefore, serious, the more so since, although only 16 per cent of the bitten cattle died as a direct result of the bites, 10 per cent more were so seriously injured that they had to be culled and a further 25 per cent developed abscesses that needed veterinary treatment. In other animals the losses can be assumed to be at least equally serious; horses show a high recovery rate, at least from viperid poisoning, but losses of poultry from the combined effects of snake-bite and predation by non-poisonous snakes must be proportionally very much greater. In fish-ponds, too, the depredations of snakes cannot be ignored and this is a mounting menace since current trends are towards an increasing use of fish culture as a means of food production.

There is, however, a credit side to the ledger though no accurate profit and loss statement can be prepared. Probably the largest benefits that snakes confer are in the field of rodent destruction for, as noted several times in previous chapters, very many species take toll of rats, mice, voles and so forth, and these abundant and prolific animals are amongst man's greatest enemies; not only are many of them carriers of virulent diseases but their annual destruction of crops and stored foods is incalculable. With their ability to penetrate into the recesses of nests and burrows, snakes are probably a more effective control on the numbers of rodents than any other single natural agency. A recent study of the subject in Malaya provided evidence to suggest that snakes are responsible for about one quarter of all the deaths in the rat population which, when allowance is made for the rate at which the rats reproduce, means that in an area where the average rat population remains approximately constant at, say, 100, the snakes are destroying about seventy-six each year. The activities of the many burrowing snakes that prey on insects must also have beneficial effects in controlling the numbers of such destructive creatures, as, for instance, termites; but in the field of insect control this direct effect is probably more than offset indirectly by other snakes that prey on insect-eating birds, lizards, frogs and toads.

More direct benefits accrue to mankind from the use of snakes as food and as a source of raw materials. Reptile leathers are not only ornamental but durable, and snakes provide their quota towards a considerable though fluctuating market in this commodity. At the height of a boom period a few decades ago the stocks of snake-skins held by merchants and manufacturers ran into millions and the volume of the traffic may be gauged from the fact that 20—30,000 sea-snake skins were being exported annually to Japan from just one small area in the Philippine Islands. At that time it would have been difficult to find a woman in Britain who did not own at least one pair of snake-skin shoes, or a purse or handbag of the same material, and similar conditions existed throughout the world in places where western fashions prevailed; fortunately, such excessive demands have now waned to more reasonable dimensions. As an article of food, however, snakes have had little appeal in the western world but elsewhere, where living standards are lower and prejudices less irrational, they are highly appreciated. As mentioned in the previous chapter pythons are a welcome addition to the diet in some parts of Asia and Africa, and boas are equally acceptable to the indigenous peoples of tropical America. Other snakes, too, are relished but it would be rash to hazard even a guess at the contribution they make to the world's total food supply. At the time of the snake-skin boom the sea-snakes whose hides were being exported from the Philippines for leather were all sold as food and the flesh of these snakes is still a popular dish in Japan where thousands are sold every year, either fried or smoked, as eels are in other countries. In other places snakes may figure as a delicacy for special occasions. For example, in Hong Kong it is one of the customs of wealthy Chinese to hold an autumn feast, with snakes as one of the dishes, "to keep away the cold of winter," and Chinese shops normally maintain stocks of six species for culinary purposes—Hamadryad, cobra, Banded Krait, python, Asiatic Copperhead and Oriental Striped Racer. In the United States, too, rattlesnake is on the market and although it is now sold in cans as a rather high-priced novelty for social occasions, in earlier days it was fairly widely eaten and the consensus of opinion was that the meat was not merely wholesome but appetizing.

In recent years, with increasing knowledge of the composition of different venoms, there have been attempts to use some of them in pharmacology. These efforts do not appear to have had any general or spectacular successes, but with better techniques for the separation of complex mixtures of proteins now becoming available this field of investigation may still offer possibilities. Other derivatives of snakes, however, have been in use from time immemorial for it is one of the undying fallacies of the primitive mind that virtues such as strength, courage, wisdom, virility and so forth reside in certain organs and can be acquired by consuming the appropriate parts of the body or carrying them as amulets. So, snakes have always provided materials for witchcraft and curative or restorative preparations of many kinds. Pliny, for example, extols the virtues of snakes' blood and says "If you anoynt your lips with a little of it they will look passing red, and, if the face be annoynted therewith it will receive no spot or fleck. . ."; and the extraordinary brews of medieval medicine frequently called for materials derived from snakes. Even today the traditional Chinese pharmacopeia contains nostra utilizing parts or extracts of snakes; the gall-bladder, for instance, extracted from a live snake and swallowed is prized for its strength-giving properties. The suppleness and lissom movements of snakes have been associated in many minds with their large and oily fat-bodies so that adder-oil, or snake-oils of all kinds, became a recognized unguent for athletes and as the basis for liniments to be used in the treatment of stiffness or lameness, whether arising from bruises, sprains, arthritis or a host of other causes. Snakes' flesh, too, has been commonly used in the treatment of tuberculosis and there were widespread beliefs in an association of one kind or another between snakes and pregnancy. Thus, amongst some African tribes, if a snake enters a house and goes on to a woman's bed it may not be killed, for it is a messenger from an ancestral spirit come to tell her that her next child will be born safely; in North America a powder made from the dried skin of a rattlesnake, or from segments of the rattle, was taken to hasten parturition or to produce abortion; and in medieval Europe snake-skins were tied round the abdomen during the later stages of pregnancy to ease delivery.

To continue listing similar superstitions of the past would be beyond the scope of this book but some of the more persistent though misguided beliefs about the behaviour and habits of snakes need examination since a number of them contain a grain of truth overlaid by superstition and misinterpretation.

One very widely held belief is that a snake will not die until nightfall however severely injured it may be. As a generalization this is untrue, but snakes, like many of the lower vertebrates are tenacious of life and a great many of their movements are automatic and will continue in an unco-ordinated manner even though the brain may have been completely destroyed. So the heart continues to beat and the body to twitch for a long time; but when the temperature drops after sundown these movements, like those of an uninjured snake that is chilled, become progressively more and more sluggish until they cease. Another common misinterpretation of fact is found in the belief that snakes are born with two legs but that these are then hidden only to be used in times of stress; this legend may date back to Palaeolithic times for amongst rock engravings of that period there are representations of what appear to be snakes with a pair of short legs towards the hinder end of the body. These "legs" are, in fact, the male's paired penes that lie in an everted position during pre-natal development but which are retracted just before birth and not normally everted again except during copulation. Abnormal muscular contractions resulting from spinal injuries or intense pain may, however, sometimes force the organs out into view and then their position and paired nature would, not unnaturally, suggest a pair of short limbs. Less easily understood, though, is the even more widely held belief that female snakes, adders and rattlesnakes especially, in times of danger swallow their young for protection and regurgitate them when the peril is past. As Spenser wrote, more than three centuries ago (*Faerie Queene*):

"Soon as the uncouth light upon them shone, Into her mouth they crepte and suddaine all were gone." The subject is one that has raised innumerable controversies but, despite apparently well authenticated testimony in favour of the belief, few level-headed and scientific investigators are prepared to accept the stories. Perhaps an analysis of one of the earliest accounts, and a typical one, may show how facts may become confused by faulty observations and false deductions. The observer's account, published in Holinshed's Chronicle in 1577, states that an Adder was seen on a mole-hill and eleven young Adders "twelve or thirteen inches in length" came out of its mouth to play on the grass; when they noticed the observer they ran back "into the mouth of theyr damme whome I killed and then founde eache of them shrowded in a distinct celle or pannicle in hyr belly. . . ." Now, the young ones twelve to thirteen inches long must have been between two and three years old (see Chapter VII) whilst those found in the adder's belly each "shrowded" in its "celle" were clearly the unborn young of the year still surrounded by their egg-membrane. So, the ones seen "playing" were not those found inside the female and that she was "theyr damme" is an unwarrantable inference, for there is no evidence that young adders remain with their parent for two to three years. A more likely explanation of the observations is that all the individuals seen were issuing from, or returning to, the mole run but the pregnant female was too sluggish to escape.

Yet other beliefs with some factual basis concern "Glass-snakes" and, perhaps, "Crowing Crested Cobras." The former is very simple; there are, so it is said, snakes that break into pieces when struck, but reassemble themselves, none the worse, when their assailant has gone. This yarn is based on certain limbless lizards such as the European Scheltopusik and its close relatives in America, the Glass-lizards. In these animals, as in many other lizards, the tail is not only very fragile but can be voluntarily broken off; it is, moreover, very long, sometimes more than twice as long as the head and body. In consequence, when one of the lizards is molested and throws off its tail which breaks into several pieces it looks as if the whole animal has disintegrated; but that the pieces can come together again is, of course, nonsense, though a new tail is eventually grown. The Crowing Crested Cobra story is less straightforward. In various parts of Africa and in the West Indies, especially Sto. Domingo and Jamaica, there are persistent, though usually rather confused, accounts of the existence of a snake that has hitherto not been captured for examination but which has a comb and wattles and crows like a cock; it is highly dangerous and is almost always seen rather dimly in poor light. Two or three possible explanations of the phenomenon have been offered; a snake that was eating a live and still protesting rooster; or a snake that had had trouble in sloughing, leaving pieces of the old skin still adhering around the head; or, and more likely, that the objects seen were fabricated and connected with voodooism (originating in Africa but transported with the slaves to the Americas) in which both snakes and cocks have a ritualistic significance. However that may be, there are other even more incomprehensible beliefs that have no rational explanation and seem to be ogre-stories that have passed from generation to generation and been absorbed into folk-lore in the process. The Hoop-Snake, for instance, takes its tail in its mouth and, making itself into a circle bowls along at great speed until, having rolled violently against its selected victim it uncoils at the critical moment so that the horny tip of its tail inflicts a fatal stab. And the American Coachwhip Snake is equally nasty, for it binds its victim to a tree with coils of its body and then lashes him to death with its tail, the tip of which is plugged into his nostrils from time to time to ascertain whether he has lost consciousness! Oddly enough, however, there is a native African belief that a python plugs the nostrils of a victim with its claws to hasten suffocation and a Chinese legend asserts that if a python puts the tip of its tail in your arm-pit you are doomed!

Writers of sensational fiction have often used snakes in their stories either as guardians of secret places or, more frequently, as weapons of retribution or murder, and the idea is far from original. Two of the masterpieces of classical sculpture portray snakes in punitive or vindictive rôles. The famous group in the Vatican shows Laocoon and his two sons "with two hideous serpents clinging round his body gnawing it and injecting their poison," and the legend is that the snakes were sent by Apollo to exact vengeance; Laocoon was not only a priestly renegade from Apollo's service but had also traitorously attempted to warn the Trojans against admitting the Greeks' wooden horse into their city. And the equally famous statue of the infant Hercules strangling two snakes in his bare hands has a background of intrigue amongst the gods; the snakes were sent by Hera, consort of Zeus, to destroy the child who was her husband's bastard son. Doubtless the examples of the gods have had their counterparts in the actions of mortals through the centuries, and a mamba tethered by its tail on the track to the hut of a hated enemy is no novelty in Africa. A similar device is also sometimes used to secure meat for the pot, a venomous snake, usually a puff-adder, being tethered on a game trail; as many as ten buffaloes have been reported killed in a single day by this means. On the grander scale of indiscriminate slaughter in war snakes were employed in what is, perhaps, the first recorded instance of biological warfare. In about 186 B.C. Hannibal was a refugee at the court of the King of Bithynia who was at war with the King of Pergamum. He advised his host to have jars of live snakes thrown into the Pergamenian ships and this novel weapon brought victory. In medieval Europe the same method was sometimes used to reduce a beleaguered garrison and even the untutored Amerindians seem to have had the same notion. One of the earlier accounts of the West Indies, published in 1667, records a tradition amongst the Arawaks, a tribe from the mainland, that their ancestors had introduced a very venomous snake in basket-loads into Martinique to plague the native Caribs with whom they were at war. This tradition has an added interest, for the Fer-de-lance, a widespread species on the mainland of Central and South America, is found in the Antilles only on Martinique and Sta. Lucia.

The greatest impact that snakes have had on humanity seems, however, to have been in connexion with man's subjective speculations about himself and the universe. Realizing his own limitations and convinced of the existence of powers far transcending his own, he has always postulated the existence of supernatural worlds and visualized them in terms of his own preconceptions. Animals have their places in these visions and when they possess powers that man himself lacks they become symbols of, or incarnations from, the supernatural world. The death-dealing abilities of snakes and the other attributes in which they differ from mankind and the rest of the animal world set them aside as possessors of supernatural powers and knowledge, who are to be feared and must be propitiated. If the fear is accompanied by loathing they are the representatives of evil spirits to be cajoled, or exorcized to go elsewhere, but on no account to be antagonized; but if admiration combines with fear they are divine and must be adored and worshipped. Different human cultures have accepted one or the other of these alternatives and sometimes the one has been transmuted into the other, for the good spirits of an outmoded religious system become the execrated evil ones of its successor.

One of humanity's over-weening beliefs is that man has an

inherent right to immortality, and from this it is but a short step to the assumption that, since he is not immortal, an evil influence must have been at work to deny him his prerogative. Primitive and pastoral races, in closer contact with nature than more settled and civilized peoples, observed the periodic slough-ing of snakes, with apparent rejuvenation following each such event, and concluded that snakes, in addition to their other supernatural powers, had also acquired the secret of immortal-ity, presumably by theft. This belief in the immortality of snakes is very widespread, so that in many religions the arch-enemy of mankind, the evil one that robbed him of his greatest birthright, is symbolized by the serpent.

More civilized peoples, however, or at least those with a more developed aesthetic sense, have been impressed with the beauty of snakes and especially with their graceful movements re-sembling those of flowing water; even the very word serpent is derived from a Sanskrit root that means either a snake or run-ning water. It is not, therefore, surprising that in many cul-tures in which the image of an association with moving water prevailed, snakes symbolized a benign deity for, in the words of the Wisdom of Solomon "... all men by nature ... deemed either fire or wind or the circle of the stars or the violent water ... to be the gods which govern the world." In Greek mythology the serpent, representing wisdom and longevity, was a familiar of Athene, goddess of the arts, and was also one of the symbols of Agathodaemon, the "Good Deity," in whose honour a liba-tion was drunk at the end of every repast. In the earth's more arid regions, however, where the lives of men are beset with perpetual anxieties concerning water, snakes are intimately associated with the water-gods. They may be the tutelary deities of springs, lakes and rivers and are even more frequently as-sociated with religious ceremonies invoking rain. Cults in which a snake-god must be propitiated in times of drought have been recorded in various African tribes and the Hopi Snake Dance, now almost a national institution in the United States, is basic-ally a prayer for rain. It is a long and elaborate ceremony, or series of ceremonies, lasting nine days and is usually held in late August. Four of the nine days are devoted to hunting wild snakes with due ceremony and ritual and the catch, consisting of both rattlesnakes and harmless species, is confined in jars in a sacred, underground vault; the number of snakes varies with the number of participants in the festival and may range from less than twenty to more than sixty. After they have been collected, a series of other ceremonies takes place in which snakes play no part, but in which rain, thunder, lightning and growing crops are symbolized. On the ninth day the snakes are ceremonially washed and allowed a period of liberty in their vault until night-fall when the snake-dance proper begins. The snakes are then passed one by one to the snake priests, who put them in their mouths, holding them by the neck with lips and teeth, and carry them in this fashion whilst they circle in a dance to the accompaniment of chants and incantations. Finally the snakes are piled together in one squirming heap and the priests rush in, seizing them by handfuls, before running away to north, south, east, and west to release them at appointed places, near holes and crannies. The snakes are then supposed to carry the prayers and supplications they have heard during the dance to the god who gives rain to the world.

Important as ceremonies such as this may have seemed to primitive peoples, snakes were probably most venerated amongst the ancient Egyptians whose whole economy hinged on the Nile. In their mythology the Primeval Serpent came into being in the midst of the dark waters of the Abyss:

"I am the outflow of the Primeval Flood,
he who emerged from the waters.
I am the 'Provider of Attributes' serpent with its many coils.
I am the Scribe of the Divine Book
which says what has been and causes what is yet to be."

(Pyramid Texts, para. 1146).

And the Book of the Dead (Chapter CLXXV) prophesied that when the world reverted to a state of undifferentiated chaos the "Provider of Attributes" serpent would remain supreme. God the Serpent existed at both ends of time, when the world emerged from the waters and when, at the end of the present dispensation, it was engulfed in them once more. In the ordered world between, serpents stood for many things. The serpent-god Sito encircled the world in his coils and snakes symbolized the guardians of the Under-world. Apopis was a cosmic enemy and personified the darkness of the night whilst the Corn God, Nehet-

Kau, was a fertility spirit. The Water God living in the caverns from which the Nile floods came was a serpent, and snakes were a distinguishing mark of the non-human and incomprehensible. The cobra-divinity Ejo was goddess of the ancient capital of Lower Egypt and tutelary deity of its sovereigns so that her symbol worn as a head-dress, the Royal Uraeus, became the emblem of supreme power.

APPENDIX

List of Antivenins

Notes (1) Antivenins should, if possible, be administered under medical supervision on account of the possibility of allergic and shock reactions.

(2) If a choice of antivenins is available when an accident occurs and the identity of the snake is certainly known, it is preferable to use serum with the lowest appropriate valency. A serum specific to the snake that caused the accident is best but, failing that, a serum prepared for use against snakes of the same group is better than a polyvalent serum covering many groups. Antivenins of the latter kind are intended for use when the identity of the snake is uncertain or in places where only limited stocks can be maintained.

SNAKES	MAKERS	NAME OF SERUM
Europe		
(1) Adder and Asp-viper	Institut Pasteur, Paris	Serum Antiviperin E.R.
(2) Asp-viper and Sand Viper	Institut Pasteur, Paris	Serum Antiviperin E.O.
(3) Kufi	Institut Pasteur, Paris	Serum Antiviperin Lebetina
(4) All European Vipers	Instituto Sieroterapico, Milan	Siero Antivipera per l'Europa
(5) Adder and Sand Viper	Centr. Inst. Hygiene, Zagreb	Serum Antiviperinum
(6) All European Vipers	Serotherapeutisches Inst., Vienna	Schlangenbiss Serum
(7) Adder, Asp-viper, Sand Viper and Kufi	Behringwerke Aktiensgesellschaft, Marburg-Lahn	Schlangenbiss Serum (Antiammodytes serum)

SNAKES	MAKERS	NAME OF SERUM
Africa		
(1) All African Venomous Snakes	FitzSimons Snake Park Laboratory, Durban	FitzSimons Antivenomous Serum
(2) All African species of *Naja* (Cobras) and *Bitis* except the Gaboon Viper	South African Institute for Medical Research, Johannesberg	Antivenom, Polyvalent
(3) All African species of *Naja* and *Bitis*, including the Gaboon Viper	South African Institute for Medical Research, Johannesberg	Antivenom, Tropical
(4) Commoner species of Mamba	South African Institute for Medical Research, Johannesberg	Trivalent Mamba Antivenin
(5) Saw-scaled Viper	South African Institute for Medical Research, Johannesberg	Monovalent *Echis carinatus* Antivenom
(6) Asps	Institut Pasteur d'Algérie	Serum Antivenimeux *Cerastes*
(7) Saw-scaled Vipers	Institut Pasteur Paris	Serum Antivenimeux *Echis*
(8) Puff-adder and Gaboon Viper	Institut Pasteur Paris	Serum Antivenimeux *Bitis*
(9) Egyptian and Black-necked Cobras	Institut Pasteur Paris	Serum Antivenimeux *Naja*
(10) Green Mamba	Institut Pasteur Paris	Serum Antivenimeux *Dendraspis*
(11) Puff-adder, Gaboon Viper and Saw-scaled Vipers	Institut Pasteur Paris	Serum Antivenimeux *Bitis-Echis*
(12) Puff-adder, Gaboon Viper, Egyptian and Black-necked Cobras	Institut Pasteur Paris	Serum Antivenimeux *Bitis-Naja*
(13) Egyptian and Black-necked Cobras, Saw-scaled Vipers	Institut Pasteur Paris	Serum Antivenimeux *Echis-Naja*
(14) Puff-adder, Gaboon Viper, Saw-scaled Vipers	Institut Pasteur Paris	Serum Antivenimeux *Bitis-Echis-Naja*
(15) Egyptian Cobra, Cape Cobra and Ringhals	Behringwerke Aktiengesellschaft	Schlangenbiss Serum (Anti-Kobra Serum)
(16) Puff-adder	Behringwerke Aktiengesellschaft	Schlangenbiss Serum (Puff-Otter Serum)
(17) Saw-scaled Viper	Behringwerke Aktiengesellschaft	Schlangenbiss Serum (*Echis carinatus* Anti-serum)

1111

SNAKES	MAKERS	NAME OF SERUM
Asia		
(1) Indian Cobra, Indian Krait, Daboia and Saw-scaled Viper	Haffkine Institute, Bombay	Polyvalent Anti-snake-venom Serum
(2) Cobras of Egypt, India and Indo-China	Institut Pasteur, Paris	Serum Antivenimeux Cobra
(3) Malayan Pit-viper	Institut Pasteur, Paris	Serum Antivenimeux Ancistrodon
(4) Indian Cobra, Daboia, Saw-scaled Viper	Central Research Institute, Kasauli	Concentrated Anti-venom
(5) Daboia	Behringwerke Aktiengesellschaft	Schlangenbiss Serum (*Vipera russelli* Anti-serum)
(6) Saw-scaled Viper	Behringwerke Aktiengesellschaft	Schlangenbiss Serum (*Echis carinatus* Anti-serum)
(7) Bamboo Pit-viper and Pit-vipers of Formosa	Taiwan Serum Vaccine Laboratory, Taiwan	Polyvalent Haemorrhagic Antivenin
(8) Pallas Pit-viper and Habu	Institute for Infectious Diseases, University of Tokyo	Polyvalent Antivenom Serum
(9) Cobras, Vipers and Pit-vipers of Siam	Queen Saovabha Memorial Inst., Bangkok	Polyvalent Antivenin
(10) Indian Cobra and Hamadryad (Siamese races)	Queen Saovabha Memorial Inst., Bangkok	Cobra Antivenin
(11) Daboia (Siamese race)	Queen Saovabha Memorial Inst., Bangkok	Viper Antivenin
(12) Malayan Pit-viper	Queen Saovabha Memorial Inst., Bangkok	*Ancistrodon rhodostoma* Anti-venin
(13) Malayan Pit-viper, Malayan Krait and Indian Cobra	Pasteur Institute, Bandoeng	Polyvalent Antivenin
(14) Cobras of the Philippine Islands	Serum and Vaccine Laboratory, Manila	Philippine Cobra Antivenin

SNAKES	MAKERS	NAME OF SERUM
Australia		
(1) Australian Tiger Snakes, Copperheads, Brown-snakes and Black-snakes, Taipan, Death Adder	Commonwealth Serum Laboratories, Dept. of Health, Melbourne	Tiger-snake Antivenin
North America		
(1) All American rattlesnakes and other pit-vipers	Wyeth Laboratories, Philadelphia	Antivenin Crotalidae: Polyvalent
Central and South America		
(1) South American Rattlesnake	Behringwerke Aktiengesellschaft	Schlangenbiss-Serum (Crotalus terrificus Antivenin)
(2) South American Rattlesnake	Instituto Pinheiros, São Paulo Instituto Butantan, São Paulo Instituto Vital Brazil, Nichtheroy	Soro Anti-crotalico
(3) South American Rattlesnake and Fer-de-lance	Instituto Pinheiros Instituto Vital Brazil Instituto Butantan	Soro Anti-Ofidico (Polyvalent)
(4) Fer-de-lance, Jarraraca, Jararacussu and other species of Bothrops	Instituto Pinheiros Instituto Vital Brazil Instituto Butantan	Soro Anti-Botropico
(5) Fer-de-lance	Behringwerke Aktiengesellschaft	Bothrops atrox Antivenin
(6) Bushmaster	Instituto Butantan	Soro Anti-Laquetico
(7) American Coral-snakes	Instituto Butantan	Soro Anti-Elapidico

BIBLIOGRAPHY

A selection of well illustrated books which contain information about the habits, behaviour and occurrence of snakes.

Bellairs, A. d'A., 1957, *Reptiles*. Hutchinson.

Kinghorn, J. R., 1956, *The Snakes of Australia*. (2nd ed.) Angus & Robertson.

Klauber, L. M., 1956, *Rattlesnakes* (2 Vols). University of California Press.

Mertens, R., 1960, *The World of Amphibians and Reptiles*. George G. Harrap & Co.

Oliver, James A., 1955, *The Natural History of North American Amphibians and Reptiles*. D. Van Nestrand Co.

Pitman, C. R. S., 1938, *A Guide to the Snakes of Uganda*. Uganda Society, Kampala.

Pope, C. H., 1937, *Snakes Alive and How They Live*. Viking Press.

Pope, C. H., 1956, *The Reptile World*. Routledge & Kegan Paul.

Pope, C. H., 1961, *The Giant Snakes*. Alfred Knopf.

Rose, Walter, 1955, *Snakes—Mainly South African*. Maskew Miller Ltd.

Schmidt, K. P. & Inger, R. F., 1957, *Living Reptiles of the World*. Hamish Hamilton.

Smith, M. A., 1951, *The British Amphibians and Reptiles*. Collins.

INDEX OF POPULAR AND
SCIENTIFIC NAMES

A. Popular—Scientific

POPULAR NAME	SCIENTIFIC NAME	FAMILY OR SUB-FAMILY
Cobras	*Naja* spp.	Elapidae
Cobra, Banded Water	*Boulengerina annulata*	Elapidae
Cobra, Black-necked	*Naja nigricollis*	Elapidae
Cobra, Black & White	*N. melanoleuca*	Elapidae
Cobra, Cape	*N. nivea*	Elapidae
Cobra, Egyptian	*N. haje*	Elapidae
Cobra, Indian	*N. naja*	Elapidae
Cobras, Tree	*Pseudohaje*	Elapidae
Cobras, Water	*Boulengerina* spp.	Elapidae
Copperhead, American	*Ancistrodon contortrix*	Crotalinae
Copperhead, Asiatic	*Elaphe radiata*	Colubrinae
Copperhead, Australian	*Denisonia superba*	Elapidae
Coral-snakes (African)	*Elapsoidea: Elaps* spp.	Elapidae
Coral-snakes (American)	*Micrurus* spp.	Elapidae
Coral-snakes (Australian)	*Brachyurophis*: *Rhinelaps*	Elapidae
Coral-snakes, False	*Erythrolamprus* spp.	Boiginae
Coral-snake, Malayan Banded	*Maticora intestinalis*	Elapidae
Coral-snakes (Oriental)	*Callophis* spp.	Elapidae
Coral-snake, Sonora	*Micruroides euryxanthus*	Elapidae
Coral, Water	*Hydrops triangularis*	Colubrinae
Corn-snake	*Elaphe guttata*	Colubrinae
Cottonmouth	*Ancistrodon piscivorus*	Crotalinae
Daboia	*Vipera russelli*	Viperinae
Death-adder	*Acantophis antarcticus*	Elapidae
Egg-eating Snakes	—	Dasypeltinae
Egg-eater, African	*Dasypeltis* spp.	Dasypeltinae
Egg-eater, Indian	*Elachistodon westermanni*	Dasypeltinae
Elephant's Trunk Snake	*Acrochordus javanicus*	Acrochordinae
Fer-de-lance	*Bothrops atrox*	Crotalinae
Fiddle-string Snake	*Sibon nebulatus*	Dipsadinae
File-snakes (African)	*Mehelya* spp.	Colubrinae
File-snake (Asiatic)	*Acrochordus granulatus*	Acrochordinae
Fishing Snake	*Herpeton tentaculatum*	Homalopsinae
Flying Snake	*Chrysopelea ornata*	Boiginae
Fox-snake	*Elaphe vulpina*	Colubrinae
Gaboon Viper	*Bitis gabonicus*	Viperinae
Garter-snakes (American)	*Thamnophis* spp.	Colubrinae
Garter-snake, Common	*T. sirtalis*	Colubrinae
Gopher Snake	*Pituophis catenifer*	Colubrinae
Grass-snakes	*Natrix* spp.	Colubrinae
Grass-snake, The	*N. natrix*	Colubrinae
Habu	*Trimeresurus flavoviridis*	Crotalinae
Hamadryad	*Naja hannah*	Elapidae

POPULAR NAME	SCIENTIFIC NAME	FAMILY OR SUB-FAMILY
Hog-nosed Snakes	*Heterodon* spp.	Colubrinae
Hook-nosed Snake (African)	*Scaphiophis albopunctatus*	Colubrinae
Hook-nosed Snake (American)	*Ficimia cana*	Colubrinae
Indigo Snake	*Drymarchon corais*	Colubrinae
Jararaca	*Bothrops jararaca*	Crotalinae
Jararacussu	*B. jararacussu*	Crotalinae
Karung	*Acrochordus javanicus*	Acrochordinae
Keel-backs	*Macropisthodon, Natrix* etc.	Colubrinae
Keel-back, Chequered	*Natrix piscator*	Colubrinae
Keel-back, Olivaceous	*Atretium schistosum*	Colubrinae
King-snakes	*Lampropeltis* spp.	Colubrinae
King-snake, Scarlet	*L. doliata*	Colubrinae
Kraits	*Bungarus* spp.	Elapidae
Krait, Indian	*B. caeruleus*	Elapidae
Krait, Malayan	*B. candidus*	Elapidae
Kufi	*Vipera lebetina*	Viperinae
Leaf-nosed Snakes	*Phyllorhynchus* spp.	Colubrinae
Leopard Snake	*Elaphe situla*	Colubrinae
Long-nosed Snake	*Rhinocheilus lecontei*	Colubrinae
Mambas	*Dendroaspis* spp.	Elapidae
Mamba, Black	*D. polylepis*	Elapidae
Mamba, Common Green	*D. angusticeps*	Elapidae
Mapepire, Water	*Helicops angulatus*	Colubrinae
Milk Snake	*Lampropeltis doliata*	Colubrinae
Montpellier Snake	*Malpolon monspessulana*	Boiginae
Mud Snake	*Farancia abacura*	Colubrinae
Mussurana	*Clelia clelia*	Boiginae
Night Adders	*Causus* spp.	Viperinae
Night Adder, The	*C. rhombeatus*	Viperinae
Pine Snakes	*Pituophis* spp.	Colubrinae
Pipe-snakes	—	Aniliidae
Pipe-snake, Ceylon	*Cylindrophis maculatus*	Aniliidae
Pipe-snake, Malayan	*C. rufus*	Aniliidae
Pit-vipers	—	Crotalinae
Pit-viper, Himalayan	*Ancistrodon himalayanus*	Crotalinae
Pit-viper, Malayan	*A. rhodostoma*	Crotalinae
Pit-viper, Pallas'	*A. halys*	Crotalinae
Puff-adders	*Bitis* spp.	Viperinae
Puff-adder, The	*B. arietans*	Viperinae

POPULAR NAME	SCIENTIFIC NAME	FAMILY OR SUB-FAMILY
Puff-adder, Horned	*B. cornutus*	Viperinae
Pythons	—	Pythoninae
Python, African Rock	*Python sebae*	Pythoninae
Python, Asiatic Rock	*P. molurus*	Pythoninae
Pythons, Australian Rock	*Liasis* spp.	Pythoninae
Python, Calabar Ground	*Calabaria reinhardti*	Pythoninae
Python, N. Queensland Rock	*L. amethystinus*	Pythoninae
Python, Reticulate	*Python reticulatus*	Pythoninae
Racers (American)	*Coluber* spp.	Colubrinae
Racers (Asiatic)	*Coluber* spp. *Elaphe* spp.	Colubrinae
Racer, Black	*C. constrictor*	Colubrinae
Racer, Oriental Striped	*Elaphe taeniura*	Colubrinae
Rat-snakes (American)	*Elaphe* spp.	Colubrinae
Rat-snakes (Asiatic)	*Ptyas* spp. *Zaocys* spp.	Colubrinae
Rat-snake (Indian)	*P. mucosus*	Colubrinae
Rat-snake, Keeled	*Zaocys carinatus*	Colubrinae
Rattlesnake, Dusky Mexican	*Crotalus pusillus*	Crotalinae
Rattlesnake, Eastern Diamond	*C. adamateus*	Crotalinae
Rattlesnake, Great Basin	*C. viridis lutosus*	Crotalinae
Rattlesnake, Horned	*C. cerastes*	Crotalinae
Rattlesnake, Northern Pacific	*C. viridis oreganus*	Crotalinae
Rattlesnake, Prairie	*C. viridis viridis*	Crotalinae
Rattlesnake, Red Diamond	*C. ruber*	Crotalinae
Rattlesnake, South American	*C. durissus*	Crotalinae
Rattlesnake, Southern Pacific	*C. viridis helleri*	Crotalinae
Rattlesnake, Timber	*C. horridus*	Crotalinae
Rattlesnake, West Coast	*C. basiliscus*	Crotalinae
Rattlesnake, Western Diamond	*C. atrox*	Crotalinae
Ringhals	*Hemachatus hemachatus*	Elapidae
River Jack	*Bitis nasicornis*	Viperinae
Scarlet Snake	*Cemophora coccinea*	Colubrinae
Sea-snakes	—	Hydrophidae
Sea-snake, Yellow-bellied	*Pelamis platurus*	Hydrophidae
Shield-Tails	—	Uropeltidae
Shovel-nosed Snakes	*Chionactis* spp.	Colubrinae
Shovel-nosed Snake, Sonora	*C. palarostris*	Colubrinae
Sidewinder	*Crotalus cerastes*	Crotalinae
Smooth-snake, The	*Coronella austriaca*	Colubrinae
Sunbeam Snake	*Xenopeltis unicolor*	Xenopeltidae
Sunbeam Snakes	—	Xenopeltidae

POPULAR NAME	SCIENTIFIC NAME	FAMILY OR SUB-FAMILY
Taipan	*Oxyuranus scutellatus*	Elapidae
Temple Viper	*Trimeresurus wagleri*	Crotalinae
Thirst Snakes	—	Dipsadinae
Thread Snakes	—	Leptotyphlopidae
Tiger Snake (Australian)	*Notechis scutatus*	Elapidae
Tree-boa, Amazonian	*Corallus caninus*	Boinae
Tree-python, Papuan	*Chondropython viridis*	Pythoninae
Tree-vipers, African	*Atheris* spp.	Viperinae
Twig-snake, African	*Thelotornis kirtlandii*	Boiginae
Viper, Dwarf	*Bitis peringueyi*	Viperinae
Viper, Gaboon	*B. gabonicus*	Viperinae
Viper, Hump-nosed	*Ancistrodon hypnale*	Crotalinae
Vipers, Mole	*Atractaspis* spp.	Viperinae
Viper, Russell's	*Vipera russelli*	Viperinae
Viper, Sand	*V. ammodytes*	Viperinae
Viper, Saw-scaled	*Echis carinatus*	Viperinae
Wart Snakes	*Acrochordus* spp.	Acrochordinae
Water-snake, Macleay's	*Enhydris polylepis*	Homalopsinae
Water-snake, Tessellated	*Natrix tessellatus*	Colubrinae
Water-snake, Viperine	*N. maura*	Colubrinae
Water-snake, White-bellied	*Fordonia leucobalia*	Homalopsinae
Whip-snakes (American)	*Masticophis* spp.	Colubrinae
Whip-snakes (Asiatic)	*Ahaetulla* spp.	Boiginae
Whip-snakes (European)	*Coluber* spp.	Colubrinae
Whip-snake, Oriental	*Ahaetulla prasina*	Boiginae
White Snake	*Elaphe taeniura*	Colubrinae
Wolf-snakes (African)	*Lycophidion* spp.	Colubrinae
Wolf-snakes (Oriental)	*Lycodon* spp.	Colubrinae
Wood Snakes	*Trophidophis*	Boinae
Yellow-lipped Snake	*Rhadinaea flavillata*	Colubrinae

B. Scientific—Popular

SCIENTIFIC NAME	POPULAR NAME	FAMILY OR SUB-FAMILY
Acantophis antarcticus	Death Adder	Elapidae
Acrochordus spp.	Wart Snakes	Acrochordinae
A. granulatus	File Snake (Asiatic)	Acrochordinae
A. javanicus	Elephant's Trunk Snake: Karung	Acrochordinae
Ahaetulla spp.	Whip-snakes (Asiatic)	Boiginae
A. prasina	Oriental Whip-snake	Boiginae
Ancistrodon contortrix	American Copperhead	Crotalinae
A. halys	Pallas Pit-viper	Crotalinae
A. himalayanus	Himalayan Pit-viper	Crotalinae
A. hypnale	Hump-nosed Viper	Crotalinae
A. piscivorus	Cottonmouth	Crotalinae
A. rhodostoma	Malayan Pit-viper	Crotalinae

POPULAR NAME	SCIENTIFIC NAME	FAMILY OR SUB-FAMILY
Atheris spp.	African Tree-vipers	Viperinae
Atractaspis spp.	Mole Vipers	Viperinae
Atretium schistosum	Olivaceous Keel-back	Colubrinae
Bitis spp.	Puff-adders	Viperinae
B. *arietans*	Puff-adder, The	Viperinae
B. *cornutus*	Horned Puff-adder	Viperinae
B. *gabonicus*	Gaboon Viper	Viperinae
B. *nasicornis*	**River Jack**	Viperinae
B. *peringueyi*	Dwarf Viper	Viperinae
Boa constrictor	Boa Constrictor	Boinae
Bothrops ammodytoides		Crotalinae
B. *atrox*	Fer-de-lance	Crotalinae
B. *jararaca*	Jararaca	Crotalinae
B. *jararacussu*	Jararacussu	Crotalinae
Boulengerina spp.	Water Cobra	Elapidae
B. *annulata*	Banded Water Cobra	Elapidae
Brachyurophis spp.	Coral-snake (Australian)	Elapidae
Bungarus spp.	Kraits	Elapidae
B. *caeruleus*	Indian Krait	Elapidae
B. *candidus*	Malayan Krait	Elapidae
Calabaria reinhardti	Calabar Ground Python	Pythoninae
Callophis spp.	Coral-snakes (Oriental)	Elapidae
Causus spp.	Night Adders	Viperinae
C. *rhombeatus*	Night Adder, The	Viperinae
Cemophora coccinea	Scarlet Snake	Colubrinae
Cerastes cerastes	Horned Asp	Viperinae
C. *vipera*	Asp	Viperinae
Cerberus australis	Bockadam	Homalopsinae
Charina bottae	Rubber Boa	Boinae
Chionactis spp.	Shovel-nosed Snakes	Colubrinae
C. *palarostris*	Sonora Shovel-nosed Snake	Colubrinae
Chondropython viridis	Papuan Tree-python	Pythoninae
Clelia clelia	Mussurana	Boiginae
Coluber spp.	Racers (American and Asiatic)	Colubrinae
C. *constrictor*	Black Racer	Colubrinae
Corallus caninus	Amazonian Tree-boa	Boinae
C. *enydris*	Cook's Boa	Boinae
Coronella austriaca	Smooth-snake, The	Colubrinae
Crotalus adamanteus	Eastern Diamond Rattlesnake	Crotalinae
C. *atrox*	Western Diamond Rattlesnake	Crotalinae
C. *basiliscus*	West Coast Rattlesnake	Crotalinae
C. *cerastes*	Horned Rattlesnake: Sidewinder	Crotalinae
C. *durissus*	S. American Rattlesnake: Cascabel	Crotalinae
C. *horridus*	Timber Rattlesnake	Crotalinae

SCIENTIFIC NAME	POPULAR NAME	FAMILY OR SUB-FAMILY
C. pusillus	Mexican Dusky Rattlesnake	Crotalinae
C. ruber	Red Diamond Rattlesnake	Crotalinae
C. viridis helleri	Southern Pacific Rattlesnake	Crotalinae
C. viridis lutosus	Great Basin Rattlesnake	Crotalinae
C. viridis oreganus	Northern Pacific Rattlesnake	Crotalinae
C. viridis viridis	Prairie Rattlesnake	Crotalinae
Cylindrophis maculatus	Ceylon Pipe-snake	Aniliidae
C. rufus	Malayan Pipe-snake	Aniliidae
Dasypeltis spp.	African Egg-eating Snakes	Dasypeltinae
Demansia textilis	Australian Brown-snake	Elapidae
Dendrelaphis formosus	Malayan Bronze-back	Colubrinae
Dendroaspis spp.	Mambas	Elapidae
D. angusticeps	Green Mamba	Elapidae
D. polylepis	Black Mamba	Elapidae
Denisonia superba	Australian Copperhead	Elapidae
Dipsadinae	Thirst Snakes	Dipsadinae
Dispholidus typus	Boomslang	Boiginae
Drymarchon corais	Indigo Snake	Colubrinae
Echis carinatus	Saw-scaled Viper	Viperinae
Elachistodon westermanni	Indian Egg-eating Snake	Dasypeltinae
Elaphe spp.	Racers	Colubrinae
E. guttata	Corn-snake	Colubrinae
E. longissima	Aesculapian Snake	Colubrinae
E. radiata	Asiatic Copperhead	Colubrinae
E. situla	Leopard Snake	Colubrinae
E. taeniura	Oriental Striped Racer: White Snake	Colubrinae
E. vulpina	Fox-snake	Colubrinae
Elapsoidea spp.	Coral-snakes (African)	Elapidae
Enhydris polylepis	Macleay's Water-snake	Homalopsinae
Epicrates angulifer	Cuban Boa	Boinae
E. cenchris	Rainbow Boa	Boinae
Eryx spp.	Sand-boas	Boinae
Eunectes murinus	Anaconda	Boinae
Farancia abacura	Mud Snake	Colubrinae
Ficimia cana	Hook-nosed Snake (American)	Colubrinae
Fordonia leucobalia	White-bellied Water-snake	Homalopsinae
Helicops angulatus	Water Mapepire	Colubrinae
Hemachatus hemachatus	Ringhals	Elapidae
Herpeton tentaculatum	Fishing Snake	Homalopsinae

SCIENTIFIC NAME	POPULAR NAME	FAMILY OR SUB-FAMILY
Heterodon spp.	Hog-nosed Snakes	Colubrinae
Hydrops triangularis	Water Coral	Colubrinae
Lachesis mutus	Bushmaster	Crotalinae
Lampropeltis spp.	King-snakes	Colubrinae
L. *doliata*	Scarlet King-snake: Milk Snake	Colubrinae
Leptodeira annulata	Cat-eyed Snake (American)	Boiginae
Leptotyphlops spp.	Thread Snakes	Leptotyphlopidae
Liasis spp.	Australian Rock Pythons	Pythoninae
L. *amethystinus*	N. Queensland Rock Python	Pythoninae
Lichanura roseofusca	Rosy Boa	Boinae
Lycodon spp.	Wolf-snakes (Oriental)	Colubrinae
Lycophidion spp.	Wolf-snakes (African)	Colubrinae
Macropisthodon spp.	Keel-backs	Colubrinae
Malpolon monspessulana	Montpellier Snake	Boiginae
Masticophis spp.	Whip-snakes (American)	Colubrinae
M. *flagellum*	Coachwhip Snake (American)	Colubrinae
Maticora intestinalis	Malayan Banded Coral-snake	Elapidae
Mehelya spp.	File-snakes (African)	Colubrinae
Micruroides euryxanthus	Sonora Coral-snake	Elapidae
Micrurus spp.	Coral-snakes (American)	Elapidae
Morelia argus	Carpet Snake	Pythoninae
Naja spp.	Cobras	Elapidae
N. *haje*	Egyptian Cobra	Elapidae
N. *hannah*	Hamadryad	Elapidae
N. *naja*	Indian Cobra	Elapidae
N. *melanoleuca*	Black and White Cobra	Elapidae
N. *nigricollis*	Black-necked Cobra	Elapidae
N. *nivea*	Cape Cobra	Elapidae
Natrix spp.	Grass-snakes: Water Snakes	Colubrinae
N. *maura*	Viperine Water-snake	Colubrinae
N. *natrix*	Grass-snake, The	Colubrinae
N. *piscator*	Chequered Keel-back	Colubrinae
N. *tessellatus*	Tessellated Water-snake	Colubrinae
Notechis scutatus	Tiger Snake (Australian)	Elapidae
Oxyuranus scutellatus	Taipan	Elapidae
Pelamis platurus	Yellow-bellied Sea-snake	Hydrophidae
Phyllorhynchus spp.	Leaf-nosed Snakes	Colubrinae
Pituophis spp.	Bull Snakes: Pine Snakes	Colubrinae
P. *catenifer*	Gopher Snake	Colubrinae
Pseudechis porphyriacus	Australian Black-snake	Elapidae
Pseudohaje	Tree Cobras	Elapidae

SCIENTIFIC NAME	POPULAR NAME	FAMILY OR SUB-FAMILY
Ptyas spp.	Rat-snakes (Asiatic)	Colubrinae
P. mucosus	Indian Rat-snake	Colubrinae
Python molurus	Asiatic Rock Python	Pythoninae
P. reticulatus	Reticulate Python	Pythoninae
P. sebae	African Rock Python	Pythoninae
Rhadinaea flavillata	Yellow-lipped Snake	Colubrinae
Rhinelaps spp.	Coral-snakes (Australian)	Elapidae
Rhinocheilus lecontei	Long-nosed Snake	Colubrinae
Scaphiophis albopunctatus	Hook-nosed Snake (African)	Colubrinae
Sibon nebulatus	Fiddle-string Snake	Dipsadinae
Spilotes pullatus	Guiana Chicken-snake	Colubrinae
Thamnophis spp.	Garter Snakes (American)	Colubrinae
T. sirtalis	Common Garter Snake	Colubrinae
Thelotornis kirtlandii	African Twig-snake	Boiginae
Trimeresurus flavoviridis	Habu	Crotalinae
T. wagleri	Temple Viper	Crotalinae
Tropidophis	Wood Snakes	Boinae
Typhlopidae	Blind Snakes	Typhlopidae
Typhlops acutus	Beaked Blind-snake	Typhlopidae
T. braminus	Brahminy Blind-snake	Typhlopidae
T. congestus	Blotched Blind-snake	Typhlopidae
T. punctatus	Spotted Blind-snake	Typhlopidae
Uropeltidae	Shield-tails	Uropeltidae
Vermicella annulata	Bandy-bandy	Elapidae
Vipera ammodytes	Sand-viper	Viperidae
V. aspis	Asp-viper	Viperidae
V. berus	Adder	Viperidae
V. lebetina	Kufi	Viperidae
V. russelli	Russell's Viper: Daboia	Viperidae
Xenopeltidae	Sunbeam Snakes	Xenopeltidae
Xenopeltis unicolor	Sunbeam Snake, The	Xenopeltidae
Zaocys spp.	Rat-snakes (Asiatic)	Colubrinae
Z. carinatus	Keeled Rat-snake	Colubrinae

GENERAL INDEX

A CATALOGUE OF SELECTED DOVER BOOKS
IN ALL FIELDS OF INTEREST

A CATALOGUE OF SELECTED DOVER BOOKS
IN ALL FIELDS OF INTEREST

THE DEVIL'S DICTIONARY, Ambrose Bierce. Barbed, bitter, brilliant witticisms in the form of a dictionary. Best, most ferocious satire America has produced. 145pp.   20487-1 Pa. $1.50

ABSOLUTELY MAD INVENTIONS, A.E. Brown, H.A. Jeffcott. Hilarious, useless, or merely absurd inventions all granted patents by the U.S. Patent Office. Edible tie pin, mechanical hat tipper, etc. 57 illustrations. 125pp.   22596-8 Pa. $1.50

AMERICAN WILD FLOWERS COLORING BOOK, Paul Kennedy. Planned coverage of 48 most important wildflowers, from Rickett's collection; instructive as well as entertaining. Color versions on covers. 48pp. 8¼ x 11.   20095-7 Pa. $1.35

BIRDS OF AMERICA COLORING BOOK, John James Audubon. Rendered for coloring by Paul Kennedy. 46 of Audubon's noted illustrations: red-winged blackbird, cardinal, purple finch, towhee, etc. Original plates reproduced in full color on the covers. 48pp. 8¼ x 11.   23049-X Pa. $1.35

NORTH AMERICAN INDIAN DESIGN COLORING BOOK, Paul Kennedy. The finest examples from Indian masks, beadwork, pottery, etc. — selected and redrawn for coloring (with identifications) by well-known illustrator Paul Kennedy. 48pp. 8¼ x 11.   21125-8 Pa. $1.35

UNIFORMS OF THE AMERICAN REVOLUTION COLORING BOOK, Peter Copeland. 31 lively drawings reproduce whole panorama of military attire; each uniform has complete instructions for accurate coloring. (Not in the Pictorial Archives Series). 64pp. 8¼ x 11.   21850-3 Pa. $1.50

THE WONDERFUL WIZARD OF OZ COLORING BOOK, L. Frank Baum. Color the Yellow Brick Road and much more in 61 drawings adapted from W.W. Denslow's originals, accompanied by abridged version of text. Dorothy, Toto, Oz and the Emerald City. 61 illustrations. 64pp. 8¼ x 11.   20452-9 Pa. $1.50

CUT AND COLOR PAPER MASKS, Michael Grater. Clowns, animals, funny faces . . . simply color them in, cut them out, and put them together, and you have 9 paper masks to play with and enjoy. Complete instructions. Assembled masks shown in full color on the covers. 32pp. 8¼ x 11.   23171-2 Pa. $1.50

STAINED GLASS CHRISTMAS ORNAMENT COLORING BOOK, Carol Belanger Grafton. Brighten your Christmas season with over 100 Christmas ornaments done in a stained glass effect on translucent paper. Color them in and then hang at windows, from lights, anywhere. 32pp. 8¼ x 11.   20707-2 Pa. $1.75

DRIED FLOWERS, Sarah Whitlock and Martha Rankin. Concise, clear, practical guide to dehydration, glycerinizing, pressing plant material, and more. Covers use of silica gel. 12 drawings. Originally titled "New Techniques with Dried Flowers." 32pp. 21802-3 Pa. $1.00

ABC OF POULTRY RAISING, J.H. Florea. Poultry expert, editor tells how to raise chickens on home or small business basis. Breeds, feeding, housing, laying, etc. Very concrete, practical. 50 illustrations. 256pp. 23201-8 Pa. $3.00

HOW INDIANS USE WILD PLANTS FOR FOOD, MEDICINE & CRAFTS, Frances Densmore. Smithsonian, Bureau of American Ethnology report presents wealth of material on nearly 200 plants used by Chippewas of Minnesota and Wisconsin. 33 plates plus 122pp. of text. 6⅛ x 9¼. 23019-8 Pa. $2.50

THE HERBAL OR GENERAL HISTORY OF PLANTS, John Gerard. The 1633 edition revised and enlarged by Thomas Johnson. Containing almost 2850 plant descriptions and 2705 superb illustrations, Gerard's Herbal is a monumental work, the book all modern English herbals are derived from, and the one herbal every serious enthusiast should have in its entirety. Original editions are worth perhaps $750. 1678pp. 8½ x 12¼. 23147-X Clothbd. $50.00

A MODERN HERBAL, Margaret Grieve. Much the fullest, most exact, most useful compilation of herbal material. Gigantic alphabetical encyclopedia, from aconite to zedoary, gives botanical information, medical properties, folklore, economic uses, and much else. Indispensable to serious reader. 161 illustrations. 888pp. 6½ x 9¼. USO 22798-7, 22799-5 Pa., Two vol. set $10.00

HOW TO KNOW THE FERNS, Frances T. Parsons. Delightful classic. Identification, fern lore, for Eastern and Central U.S.A. Has introduced thousands to interesting life form. 99 illustrations. 215pp. 20740-4 Pa. $2.50

THE MUSHROOM HANDBOOK, Louis C.C. Krieger. Still the best popular handbook. Full descriptions of 259 species, extremely thorough text, habitats, luminescence, poisons, folklore, etc. 32 color plates; 126 other illustrations. 560pp. 21861-9 Pa. $4.50

HOW TO KNOW THE WILD FRUITS, Maude G. Peterson. Classic guide covers nearly 200 trees, shrubs, smaller plants of the U.S. arranged by color of fruit and then by family. Full text provides names, descriptions, edibility, uses. 80 illustrations. 400pp. 22943-2 Pa. $3.00

COMMON WEEDS OF THE UNITED STATES, U.S. Department of Agriculture. Covers 220 important weeds with illustration, maps, botanical information, plant lore for each. Over 225 illustrations. 463pp. 6⅛ x 9¼. 20504-5 Pa. $4.50

HOW TO KNOW THE WILD FLOWERS, Mrs. William S. Dana. Still best popular book for East and Central USA. Over 500 plants easily identified, with plant lore; arranged according to color and flowering time. 174 plates. 459pp. 20332-8 Pa. $3.50

MANUAL OF THE TREES OF NORTH AMERICA, Charles S. Sargent. The basic survey of every native tree and tree-like shrub, 717 species in all. Extremely full descriptions, information on habitat, growth, locales, economics, etc. Necessary to every serious tree lover. Over 100 finding keys. 783 illustrations. Total of 986pp.
20277-1, 20278-X Pa., Two vol. set $8.00

BIRDS OF THE NEW YORK AREA, John Bull. Indispensable guide to more than 400 species within a hundred-mile radius of Manhattan. Information on range, status, breeding, migration, distribution trends, etc. Foreword by Roger Tory Peterson. 17 drawings; maps. 540pp.
23222-0 Pa. $6.00

THE SEA-BEACH AT EBB-TIDE, Augusta Foote Arnold. Identify hundreds of marine plants and animals: algae, seaweeds, squids, crabs, corals, etc. Descriptions cover food, life cycle, size, shape, habitat. Over 600 drawings. 490pp.
21949-6 Pa. $4.00

THE MOTH BOOK, William J. Holland. Identify more than 2,000 moths of North America. General information, precise species descriptions. 623 illustrations plus 48 color plates show almost all species, full size. 1968 edition. Still the basic book. Total of 551pp. 6½ x 9¼.
21948-8 Pa. $6.00

AN INTRODUCTION TO THE REPTILES AND AMPHIBIANS OF THE UNITED STATES, Percy A. Morris. All lizards, crocodiles, turtles, snakes, toads, frogs; life history, identification, habits, suitability as pets, etc. Non-technical, but sound and broad. 130 photos. 253pp.
22982-3 Pa. $3.00

OLD NEW YORK IN EARLY PHOTOGRAPHS, edited by Mary Black. Your only chance to see New York City as it was 1853-1906, through 196 wonderful photographs from N.Y. Historical Society. Great Blizzard, Lincoln's funeral procession, great buildings. 228pp. 9 x 12.
22907-6 Pa. $6.00

THE AMERICAN REVOLUTION, A PICTURE SOURCEBOOK, John Grafton. Wonderful Bicentennial picture source, with 411 illustrations (contemporary and 19th century) showing battles, personalities, maps, events, flags, posters, soldier's life, ships, etc. all captioned and explained. A wonderful browsing book, supplement to other historical reading. 160pp. 9 x 12.
23226-3 Pa. $4.00

PERSONAL NARRATIVE OF A PILGRIMAGE TO AL-MADINAH AND MECCAH, Richard Burton. Great travel classic by remarkably colorful personality. Burton, disguised as a Moroccan, visited sacred shrines of Islam, narrowly escaping death. Wonderful observations of Islamic life, customs, personalities. 47 illustrations. Total of 959pp.
21217-3, 21218-1 Pa., Two vol. set $7.00

INCIDENTS OF TRAVEL IN CENTRAL AMERICA, CHIAPAS, AND YUCATAN, John L. Stephens. Almost single-handed discovery of Maya culture; exploration of ruined cities, monuments, temples; customs of Indians. 115 drawings. 892pp.
22404-X, 22405-8 Pa., Two vol. set $8.00

HOW TO SOLVE CHESS PROBLEMS, Kenneth S. Howard. Practical suggestions on problem solving for very beginners. 58 two-move problems, 46 3-movers, 8 4-movers for practice, plus hints. 171pp. 20748-X Pa. $2.00

A GUIDE TO FAIRY CHESS, Anthony Dickins. 3-D chess, 4-D chess, chess on a cylindrical board, reflecting pieces that bounce off edges, cooperative chess, retrograde chess, maximummers, much more. Most based on work of great Dawson. Full handbook, 100 problems. 66pp. 7⅞ x 10¾. 22687-5 Pa. $2.00

WIN AT BACKGAMMON, Millard Hopper. Best opening moves, running game, blocking game, back game, tables of odds, etc. Hopper makes the game clear enough for anyone to play, and win. 43 diagrams. 111pp. 22894-0 Pa. $1.50

BIDDING A BRIDGE HAND, Terence Reese. Master player "thinks out loud" the bidding of 75 hands that defy point count systems. Organized by bidding problem—no-fit situations, overbidding, underbidding, cueing your defense, etc. 254pp. EBE 22830-4 Pa. $2.50

THE PRECISION BIDDING SYSTEM IN BRIDGE, C.C. Wei, edited by Alan Truscott. Inventor of precision bidding presents average hands and hands from actual play, including games from 1969 Bermuda Bowl where system emerged. 114 exercises. 116pp. 21171-1 Pa. $1.75

LEARN MAGIC, Henry Hay. 20 simple, easy-to-follow lessons on magic for the new magician: illusions, card tricks, silks, sleights of hand, coin manipulations, escapes, and more —all with a minimum amount of equipment. Final chapter explains the great stage illusions. 92 illustrations. 285pp. 21238-6 Pa. $2.95

THE NEW MAGICIAN'S MANUAL, Walter B. Gibson. Step-by-step instructions and clear illustrations guide the novice in mastering 36 tricks; much equipment supplied on 16 pages of cut-out materials. 36 additional tricks. 64 illustrations. 159pp. 6⅝ x 10. 23113-5 Pa. $3.00

PROFESSIONAL MAGIC FOR AMATEURS, Walter B. Gibson. 50 easy, effective tricks used by professionals —cards, string, tumblers, handkerchiefs, mental magic, etc. 63 illustrations. 223pp. 23012-0 Pa. $2.50

CARD MANIPULATIONS, Jean Hugard. Very rich collection of manipulations; has taught thousands of fine magicians tricks that are really workable, eye-catching. Easily followed, serious work. Over 200 illustrations. 163pp. 20539-8 Pa. $2.00

ABBOTT'S ENCYCLOPEDIA OF ROPE TRICKS FOR MAGICIANS, Stewart James. Complete reference book for amateur and professional magicians containing more than 150 tricks involving knots, penetrations, cut and restored rope, etc. 510 illustrations. Reprint of 3rd edition. 400pp. 23206-9 Pa. $3.50

THE SECRETS OF HOUDINI, J.C. Cannell. Classic study of Houdini's incredible magic, exposing closely-kept professional secrets and revealing, in general terms, the whole art of stage magic. 67 illustrations. 279pp. 22913-0 Pa. $2.50

THE FITZWILLIAM VIRGINAL BOOK, edited by J. Fuller Maitland, W.B. Squire. Famous early 17th century collection of keyboard music, 300 works by Morley, Byrd, Bull, Gibbons, etc. Modern notation. Total of 938pp. 8⅜ x 11.
ECE 21068-5, 21069-3 Pa., Two vol. set $12.00

COMPLETE STRING QUARTETS, Wolfgang A. Mozart. Breitkopf and Härtel edition. All 23 string quartets plus alternate slow movement to K156. Study score. 277pp. 9⅜ x 12¼.
22372-8 Pa. $6.00

COMPLETE SONG CYCLES, Franz Schubert. Complete piano, vocal music of Die Schöne Müllerin, Die Winterreise, Schwanengesang. Also Drinker English singing translations. Breitkopf and Härtel edition. 217pp. 9⅜ x 12¼.
22649-2 Pa. $4.00

THE COMPLETE PRELUDES AND ETUDES FOR PIANOFORTE SOLO, Alexander Scriabin. All the preludes and etudes including many perfectly spun miniatures. Edited by K.N. Igumnov and Y.I. Mil'shteyn. 250pp. 9 x 12.
22919-X Pa. $5.00

TRISTAN UND ISOLDE, Richard Wagner. Full orchestral score with complete instrumentation. Do not confuse with piano reduction. Commentary by Felix Mottl, great Wagnerian conductor and scholar. Study score. 655pp. 8⅛ x 11.
22915-7 Pa. $10.00

FAVORITE SONGS OF THE NINETIES, ed. Robert Fremont. Full reproduction, including covers, of 88 favorites: Ta-Ra-Ra-Boom-De-Aye, The Band Played On, Bird in a Gilded Cage, Under the Bamboo Tree, After the Ball, etc. 401pp. 9 x 12.
EBE 21536-9 Pa. $6.95

SOUSA'S GREAT MARCHES IN PIANO TRANSCRIPTION: ORIGINAL SHEET MUSIC OF 23 WORKS, John Philip Sousa. Selected by Lester S. Levy. Playing edition includes: The Stars and Stripes Forever, The Thunderer, The Gladiator, King Cotton, Washington Post, much more. 24 illustrations. 111pp. 9 x 12.
USO 23132-1 Pa. $3.50

CLASSIC PIANO RAGS, selected with an introduction by Rudi Blesh. Best ragtime music (1897-1922) by Scott Joplin, James Scott, Joseph F. Lamb, Tom Turpin, 9 others. Printed from best original sheet music, plus covers. 364pp. 9 x 12.
EBE 20469-3 Pa. $6.95

ANALYSIS OF CHINESE CHARACTERS, C.D. Wilder, J.H. Ingram. 1000 most important characters analyzed according to primitives, phonetics, historical development. Traditional method offers mnemonic aid to beginner, intermediate student of Chinese, Japanese. 365pp.
23045-7 Pa. $4.00

MODERN CHINESE: A BASIC COURSE, Faculty of Peking University. Self study, classroom course in modern Mandarin. Records contain phonetics, vocabulary, sentences, lessons. 249 page book contains all recorded text, translations, grammar, vocabulary, exercises. Best course on market. 3 12" 33⅓ monaural records, book, album.
98832-5 Set $12.50

EARLY NEW ENGLAND GRAVESTONE RUBBINGS, Edmund V. Gillon, Jr. 43 photographs, 226 rubbings show heavily symbolic, macabre, sometimes humorous primitive American art. Up to early 19th century. 207pp. 8⅜ x 11¼.
21380-3 Pa. $4.00

L.J.M. DAGUERRE: THE HISTORY OF THE DIORAMA AND THE DAGUERREOTYPE, Helmut and Alison Gernsheim. Definitive account. Early history, life and work of Daguerre; discovery of daguerreotype process; diffusion abroad; other early photography. 124 illustrations. 226pp. 6⅙ x 9¼.
22290-X Pa. $4.00

PHOTOGRAPHY AND THE AMERICAN SCENE, Robert Taft. The basic book on American photography as art, recording form, 1839-1889. Development, influence on society, great photographers, types (portraits, war, frontier, etc.), whatever else needed. Inexhaustible. Illustrated with 322 early photos, daguerreotypes, tintypes, stereo slides, etc. 546pp. 6⅛ x 9¼.
21201-7 Pa. $5.00

PHOTOGRAPHIC SKETCHBOOK OF THE CIVIL WAR, Alexander Gardner. Reproduction of 1866 volume with 100 on-the-field photographs: Manassas, Lincoln on battlefield, slave pens, etc. Introduction by E.F. Bleiler. 224pp. 10¾ x 9.
22731-6 Pa. $4.50

THE MOVIES: A PICTURE QUIZ BOOK, Stanley Appelbaum & Hayward Cirker. Match stars with their movies, name actors and actresses, test your movie skill with 241 stills from 236 great movies, 1902-1959. Indexes of performers and films. 128pp. 8⅜ x 9¼.
20222-4 Pa. $2.50

THE TALKIES, Richard Griffith. Anthology of features, articles from Photoplay, 1928-1940, reproduced complete. Stars, famous movies, technical features, fabulous ads, etc.; Garbo, Chaplin, King Kong, Lubitsch, etc. 4 color plates, scores of illustrations. 327pp. 8⅜ x 11¼.
22762-6 Pa. $5.95

THE MOVIE MUSICAL FROM VITAPHONE TO "42ND STREET," edited by Miles Kreuger. Relive the rise of the movie musical as reported in the pages of Photoplay magazine (1926-1933): every movie review, cast list, ad, and record review; every significant feature article, production still, biography, forecast, and gossip story. Profusely illustrated. 367pp. 8⅜ x 11¼.
23154-2 Pa. $6.95

JOHANN SEBASTIAN BACH, Philipp Spitta. Great classic of biography, musical commentary, with hundreds of pieces analyzed. Also good for Bach's contemporaries. 450 musical examples. Total of 1799pp.
EUK 22278-0, 22279-9 Clothbd., Two vol. set $25.00

BEETHOVEN AND HIS NINE SYMPHONIES, Sir George Grove. Thorough history, analysis, commentary on symphonies and some related pieces. For either beginner or advanced student. 436 musical passages. 407pp.
20334-4 Pa. $4.00

MOZART AND HIS PIANO CONCERTOS, Cuthbert Girdlestone. The only full-length study. Detailed analyses of all 21 concertos, sources; 417 musical examples. 509pp.
21271-8 Pa. $4.50

HOUDINI ON MAGIC, Harold Houdini. Edited by Walter Gibson, Morris N. Young. How he escaped; exposés of fake spiritualists; instructions for eye-catching tricks; other fascinating material by and about greatest magician. 155 illustrations. 280pp. 20384-0 Pa. $2.50

HANDBOOK OF THE NUTRITIONAL CONTENTS OF FOOD, U.S. Dept. of Agriculture. Largest, most detailed source of food nutrition information ever prepared. Two mammoth tables: one measuring nutrients in 100 grams of edible portion; the other, in edible portion of 1 pound as purchased. Originally titled Composition of Foods. 190pp. 9 x 12. 21342-0 Pa. $4.00

COMPLETE GUIDE TO HOME CANNING, PRESERVING AND FREEZING, U.S. Dept. of Agriculture. Seven basic manuals with full instructions for jams and jellies; pickles and relishes; canning fruits, vegetables, meat; freezing anything. Really good recipes, exact instructions for optimal results. Save a fortune in food. 156 illustrations. 214pp. 6⅛ x 9¼. 22911-4 Pa. $2.50

THE BREAD TRAY, Louis P. De Gouy. Nearly every bread the cook could buy or make: bread sticks of Italy, fruit breads of Greece, glazed rolls of Vienna, everything from corn pone to croissants. Over 500 recipes altogether. including buns, rolls, muffins, scones, and more. 463pp. 23000-7 Pa. $3.50

CREATIVE HAMBURGER COOKERY, Louis P. De Gouy. 182 unusual recipes for casseroles, meat loaves and hamburgers that turn inexpensive ground meat into memorable main dishes: Arizona chili burgers, burger tamale pie, burger stew, burger corn loaf, burger wine loaf, and more. 120pp. 23001-5 Pa. $1.75

LONG ISLAND SEAFOOD COOKBOOK, J. George Frederick and Jean Joyce. Probably the best American seafood cookbook. Hundreds of recipes. 40 gourmet sauces, 123 recipes using oysters alone! All varieties of fish and seafood amply represented. 324pp. 22677-8 Pa. $3.00

THE EPICUREAN: A COMPLETE TREATISE OF ANALYTICAL AND PRACTICAL STUDIES IN THE CULINARY ART, Charles Ranhofer. Great modern classic. 3,500 recipes from master chef of Delmonico's, turn-of-the-century America's best restaurant. Also explained, many techniques known only to professional chefs. 775 illustrations. 1183pp. 6⅝ x 10. 22680-8 Clothbd. $17.50

THE AMERICAN WINE COOK BOOK, Ted Hatch. Over 700 recipes: old favorites livened up with wine plus many more: Czech fish soup, quince soup, sauce Perigueux, shrimp shortcake, filets Stroganoff, cordon bleu goulash, jambonneau, wine fruit cake, more. 314pp. 22796-0 Pa. $2.50

DELICIOUS VEGETARIAN COOKING, Ivan Baker. Close to 500 delicious and varied recipes: soups, main course dishes (pea, bean, lentil, cheese, vegetable, pasta, and egg dishes), savories, stews, whole-wheat breads and cakes, more. 168pp. USO 22834-7 Pa. $1.75

CONSTRUCTION OF AMERICAN FURNITURE TREASURES, Lester Margon. 344 detail drawings, complete text on constructing exact reproductions of 38 early American masterpieces: Hepplewhite sideboard, Duncan Phyfe drop-leaf table, mantel clock, gate-leg dining table, Pa. German cupboard, more. 38 plates. 54 photographs. 168pp. 8⅜ x 11¼. 23056-2 Pa. $4.00

JEWELRY MAKING AND DESIGN, Augustus F. Rose, Antonio Cirino. Professional secrets revealed in thorough, practical guide: tools, materials, processes; rings, brooches, chains, cast pieces, enamelling, setting stones, etc. Do not confuse with skimpy introductions: beginner can use, professional can learn from it. Over 200 illustrations. 306pp. 21750-7 Pa. $3.00

METALWORK AND ENAMELLING, Herbert Maryon. Generally coneeded best all-around book. Countless trade secrets: materials, tools, soldering, filigree, setting, inlay, niello, repoussé, casting, polishing, etc. For beginner or expert. Author was foremost British expert. 330 illustrations. 335pp. 22702-2 Pa. $3.50

WEAVING WITH FOOT-POWER LOOMS, Edward F. Worst. Setting up a loom, beginning to weave, constructing equipment, using dyes, more, plus over 285 drafts of traditional patterns including Colonial and Swedish weaves. More than 200 other figures. For beginning and advanced. 275pp. 8¾ x 6⅜. 23064-3 Pa. $4.00

WEAVING A NAVAJO BLANKET, Gladys A. Reichard. Foremost anthropologist studied under Navajo women, reveals every step in process from wool, dyeing, spinning, setting up loom, designing, weaving. Much history, symbolism. With this book you could make one yourself. 97 illustrations. 222pp. 22992-0 Pa. $3.00

NATURAL DYES AND HOME DYEING, Rita J. Adrosko. Use natural ingredients: bark, flowers, leaves, lichens, insects etc. Over 135 specific recipes from historical sources for cotton, wool, other fabrics. Genuine premodern handicrafts. 12 illustrations. 160pp. 22688-3 Pa. $2.00

THE HAND DECORATION OF FABRICS, Francis J. Kafka. Outstanding, profusely illustrated guide to stenciling, batik, block printing, tie dyeing, freehand painting, silk screen printing, and novelty decoration. 356 illustrations. 198pp. 6 x 9. 21401-X Pa. $3.00

THOMAS NAST: CARTOONS AND ILLUSTRATIONS, with text by Thomas Nast St. Hill. Father of American political cartooning. Cartoons that destroyed Tweed Ring; inflation, free love, church and state; original Republican elephant and Democratic donkey; Santa Claus; more. 117 illustrations. 146pp. 9 x 12.
22983-1 Pa. $4.00
23067-8 Clothbd. $8.50

FREDERIC REMINGTON: 173 DRAWINGS AND ILLUSTRATIONS. Most famous of the Western artists, most responsible for our myths about the American West in its untamed days. Complete reprinting of *Drawings of Frederic Remington* (1897), plus other selections. 4 additional drawings in color on covers. 140pp. 9 x 12.
20714-5 Pa. $3.95

THE MAGIC MOVING PICTURE BOOK, Bliss, Sands & Co. The pictures in this book move! Volcanoes erupt, a house burns, a serpentine dancer wiggles her way through a number. By using a specially ruled acetate screen provided, you can obtain these and 15 other startling effects. Originally "The Motograph Moving Picture Book." 32pp. 8¼ x 11. 23224-7 Pa. $1.75

STRING FIGURES AND HOW TO MAKE THEM, Caroline F. Jayne. Fullest, clearest instructions on string figures from around world: Eskimo, Navajo, Lapp, Europe, more. Cats cradle, moving spear, lightning, stars. Introduction by A.C. Haddon. 950 illustrations. 407pp. 20152-X Pa. $3.00

PAPER FOLDING FOR BEGINNERS, William D. Murray and Francis J. Rigney. Clearest book on market for making origami sail boats, roosters, frogs that move legs, cups, bonbon boxes. 40 projects. More than 275 illustrations. Photographs. 94pp. 20713-7 Pa. $1.25

INDIAN SIGN LANGUAGE, William Tomkins. Over 525 signs developed by Sioux, Blackfoot, Cheyenne, Arapahoe and other tribes. Written instructions and diagrams: how to make words, construct sentences. Also 290 pictographs of Sioux and Ojibway tribes. 111pp. 6⅛ x 9¼. 22029-X Pa. $1.50

BOOMERANGS: HOW TO MAKE AND THROW THEM, Bernard S. Mason. Easy to make and throw, dozens of designs: cross-stick, pinwheel, boomabird, tumblestick, Australian curved stick boomerang. Complete throwing instructions. All safe. 99pp. 23028-7 Pa. $1.50

25 KITES THAT FLY, Leslie Hunt. Full, easy to follow instructions for kites made from inexpensive materials. Many novelties. Reeling, raising, designing your own. 70 illustrations. 110pp. 22550-X Pa. $1.25

TRICKS AND GAMES ON THE POOL TABLE, Fred Herrmann. 79 tricks and games, some solitaires, some for 2 or more players, some competitive; mystifying shots and throws, unusual carom, tricks involving cork, coins, a hat, more. 77 figures. 95pp. 21814-7 Pa. $1.25

WOODCRAFT AND CAMPING, Bernard S. Mason. How to make a quick emergency shelter, select woods that will burn immediately, make do with limited supplies, etc. Also making many things out of wood, rawhide, bark, at camp. Formerly titled Woodcraft. 295 illustrations. 580pp. 21951-8 Pa. $4.00

AN INTRODUCTION TO CHESS MOVES AND TACTICS SIMPLY EXPLAINED, Leonard Barden. Informal intermediate introduction: reasons for moves, tactics, openings, traps, positional play, endgame. Isolates patterns. 102pp. USO 21210-6 Pa. $1.35

LASKER'S MANUAL OF CHESS, Dr. Emanuel Lasker. Great world champion offers very thorough coverage of all aspects of chess. Combinations, position play, openings, endgame, aesthetics of chess, philosophy of struggle, much more. Filled with analyzed games. 390pp. 20640-8 Pa. $3.50

MODERN CHESS STRATEGY, Ludek Pachman. The use of the queen, the active king, exchanges, pawn play, the center, weak squares, etc. Section on rook alone worth price of the book. Stress on the moderns. Often considered the most important book on strategy. 314pp. 20290-9 Pa. $3.00

CHESS STRATEGY, Edward Lasker. One of half-dozen great theoretical works in chess, shows principles of action above and beyond moves. Acclaimed by Capablanca, Keres, etc. 282pp. USO 20528-2 Pa. $2.50

CHESS PRAXIS, THE PRAXIS OF MY SYSTEM, Aron Nimzovich. Founder of hypermodern chess explains his profound, influential theories that have dominated much of 20th century chess. 109 illustrative games. 369pp. 20296-8 Pa. $3.50

HOW TO PLAY THE CHESS OPENINGS, Eugene Znosko-Borovsky. Clear, profound examinations of just what each opening is intended to do and how opponent can counter. Many sample games, questions and answers. 147pp. 22795-2 Pa. $2.00

THE ART OF CHESS COMBINATION, Eugene Znosko-Borovsky. Modern explanation of principles, varieties, techniques and ideas behind them, illustrated with many examples from great players. 212pp. 20583-5 Pa. $2.00

COMBINATIONS: THE HEART OF CHESS, Irving Chernev. Step-by-step explanation of intricacies of combinative play. 356 combinations by Tarrasch, Botvinnik, Keres, Steinitz, Anderssen, Morphy, Marshall, Capablanca, others, all annotated. 245 pp. 21744-2 Pa. $2.50

HOW TO PLAY CHESS ENDINGS, Eugene Znosko-Borovsky. Thorough instruction manual by fine teacher analyzes each piece individually; many common endgame situations. Examines games by Steinitz, Alekhine, Lasker, others. Emphasis on understanding. 288pp. 21170-3 Pa. $2.75

MORPHY'S GAMES OF CHESS, Philip W. Sergeant. Romantic history, 54 games of greatest player of all time against Anderssen, Bird, Paulsen, Harrwitz; 52 games at odds; 52 blindfold; 100 consultation, informal, other games. Analyses by Anderssen, Steinitz, Morphy himself. 352pp. 20386-7 Pa. $2.75

500 MASTER GAMES OF CHESS, S. Tartakower, J. du Mont. Vast collection of great chess games from 1798-1938, with much material nowhere else readily available. Fully annotated, arranged by opening for easier study. 665pp. 23208-5 Pa. $6.00

THE SOVIET SCHOOL OF CHESS, Alexander Kotov and M. Yudovich. Authoritative work on modern Russian chess. History, conceptual background. 128 fully annotated games (most unavailable elsewhere) by Botvinnik, Keres, Smyslov, Tal, Petrosian, Spassky, more. 390pp. 20026-4 Pa. $3.95

WONDERS AND CURIOSITIES OF CHESS, Irving Chernev. A lifetime's accumulation of such wonders and curiosities as the longest won game, shortest game, chess problem with mate in 1220 moves, and much more unusual material — 356 items in all, over 160 complete games. 146 diagrams. 203pp. 23007-4 Pa. $3.50

VICTORIAN HOUSES: A TREASURY OF LESSER-KNOWN EXAMPLES, Edmund Gillon and Clay Lancaster. 116 photographs, excellent commentary illustrate distinct characteristics, many borrowings of local Victorian architecture. Octagonal houses, Americanized chalets, grand country estates, small cottages, etc. Rich heritage often overlooked. 116 plates. 11³/₈ x 10.   22966-1 Pa. $4.00

STICKS AND STONES, Lewis Mumford. Great classic of American cultural history; architecture from medieval-inspired earliest forms to 20th century; evolution of structure and style, influence of environment. 21 illustrations. 113pp.
20202-X Pa. $2.00

ON THE LAWS OF JAPANESE PAINTING, Henry P. Bowie. Best substitute for training with genius Oriental master, based on years of study in Kano school. Philosophy, brushes, inks, style, etc. 66 illustrations. 117pp. 6¹/₈ x 9¼.   20030-2 Pa. $4.00

A HANDBOOK OF ANATOMY FOR ART STUDENTS, Arthur Thomson. Virtually exhaustive. Skeletal structure, muscles, heads, special features. Full text, anatomical figures, undraped photos. Male and female. 337 illustrations. 459pp.
21163-0 Pa. $5.00

AN ATLAS OF ANATOMY FOR ARTISTS, Fritz Schider. Finest text, working book. Full text, plus anatomical illustrations; plates by great artists showing anatomy. 593 illustrations. 192pp. 7⁷/₈ x 10¾.   20241-0 Clothbd. $6.95

THE HUMAN FIGURE IN MOTION, Eadweard Muybridge. More than 4500 stopped-action photos, in action series, showing undraped men, women, children jumping, lying down, throwing, sitting, wrestling, carrying, etc. "Unparalleled dictionary for artists," American Artist. Taken by great 19th century photographer. 390pp. 7⁷/₈ x 10⁵/₈.   20204-6 Clothbd. $12.50

AN ATLAS OF ANIMAL ANATOMY FOR ARTISTS, W. Ellenberger et al. Horses, dogs, cats, lions, cattle, deer, etc. Muscles, skeleton, surface features. The basic work. Enlarged edition. 288 illustrations. 151pp. 9³/₈ x 12¼.   20082-5 Pa. $4.00

LETTER FORMS: 110 COMPLETE ALPHABETS, Frederick Lambert. 110 sets of capital letters; 16 lower case alphabets; 70 sets of numbers and other symbols. Edited and expanded by Theodore Menten. 110pp. 8¹/₈ x 11.   22872-X Pa. $2.50

THE METHODS OF CONSTRUCTION OF CELTIC ART, George Bain. Simple geometric techniques for making wonderful Celtic interlacements, spirals, Kells-type initials, animals, humans, etc. Unique for artists, craftsmen. Over 500 illustrations. 160pp. 9 x 12.   USO 22923-8 Pa. $4.00

SCULPTURE, PRINCIPLES AND PRACTICE, Louis Slobodkin. Step by step approach to clay, plaster, metals, stone; classical and modern. 253 drawings, photos. 255pp. 8¹/₈ x 11.   22960-2 Pa. $4.50

THE ART OF ETCHING, E.S. Lumsden. Clear, detailed instructions for etching, drypoint, softground, aquatint; from 1st sketch to print. Very detailed, thorough. 200 illustrations. 376pp.   20049-3 Pa. $3.50

EGYPTIAN MAGIC, E.A. Wallis Budge. Foremost Egyptologist, curator at British Museum, on charms, curses, amulets, doll magic, transformations, control of demons, deific appearances, feats of great magicians. Many texts cited. 19 illustrations. 234pp. USO 22681-6 Pa. $2.50

THE LEYDEN PAPYRUS: AN EGYPTIAN MAGICAL BOOK, edited by F. Ll. Griffith, Herbert Thompson. Egyptian sorcerer's manual contains scores of spells: sex magic of various sorts, occult information, evoking visions, removing evil magic, etc. Transliteration faces translation. 207pp. 22994-7 Pa. $2.50

THE MALLEUS MALEFICARUM OF KRAMER AND SPRENGER, translated, edited by Montague Summers. Full text of most important witchhunter's "Bible," used by both Catholics and Protestants. Theory of witches, manifestations, remedies, etc. Indispensable to serious student. 278pp. 6⅝ x 10. USO 22802-9 Pa. $3.95

LOST CONTINENTS, L. Sprague de Camp. Great science-fiction author, finest, fullest study: Atlantis, Lemuria, Mu, Hyperborea, etc. Lost Tribes, Irish in pre-Columbian America, root races; in history, literature, art, occultism. Necessary to everyone concerned with theme. 17 illustrations. 348pp. 22668-9 Pa. $3.50

THE COMPLETE BOOKS OF CHARLES FORT, Charles Fort. Book of the Damned, Lo!, Wild Talents, New Lands. Greatest compilation of data: celestial appearances, flying saucers, falls of frogs, strange disappearances, inexplicable data not recognized by science. Inexhaustible, painstakingly documented. Do not confuse with modern charlatanry. Introduction by Damon Knight. Total of 1126pp.
23094-5 Clothbd. $15.00

FADS AND FALLACIES IN THE NAME OF SCIENCE, Martin Gardner. Fair, witty appraisal of cranks and quacks of science: Atlantis, Lemuria, flat earth, Velikovsky, orgone energy, Bridey Murphy, medical fads, etc. 373pp. 20394-8 Pa. $3.00

HOAXES, Curtis D. MacDougall. Unbelievably rich account of great hoaxes: Locke's moon hoax, Shakespearean forgeries, Loch Ness monster, Disumbrationist school of art, dozens more; also psychology of hoaxing. 54 illustrations. 338pp. 20465-0 Pa. $3.50

THE GENTLE ART OF MAKING ENEMIES, James A.M. Whistler. Greatest wit of his day deflates Wilde, Ruskin, Swinburne; strikes back at inane critics, exhibitions. Highly readable classic of impressionist revolution by great painter. Introduction by Alfred Werner. 334pp. 21875-9 Pa. $4.00

THE BOOK OF TEA, Kakuzo Okakura. Minor classic of the Orient: entertaining, charming explanation, interpretation of traditional Japanese culture in terms of tea ceremony. Edited by E.F. Bleiler. Total of 94pp. 20070-1 Pa. $1.25

Prices subject to change without notice.
Available at your book dealer or write for free catalogue to Dept. GI, Dover Publications, Inc., 180 Varick St., N.Y., N.Y. 10014. Dover publishes more than 150 books each year on science, elementary and advanced mathematics, biology, music, art, literary history, social sciences and other areas.